500 RECIPES FOR PUDDINGS AND DESSERTS

MONICA MAWSON

HAMLYN PAPERBACKS

500 RECIPES FOR PUDDINGS AND DESSERTS
ISBN 0 600 37228 6

First published in Great Britain 1979
by Hamlyn Paperbacks
Copyright © 1979 by The Hamlyn Publishing
Group Limited

Hamlyn Paperbacks are published by
The Hamlyn Publishing Group Ltd,
Astronaut House,
Feltham,
Middlesex, England

Phototypeset in Great Britain by
Filmtype Services Limited, Scarborough

Printed by G. A. Pindar & Son Ltd,
Scarborough, England

Cover photograph by Paul Williams shows Blackberry and apple
zebras, Grape flan, Pashka and Apricot pancake cake.

Contents

INTRODUCTION

The weight conscious often have a feeling almost of guilt when a pudding or dessert is offered or even mentioned, but some carbohydrates are good for all of us for they have a useful bodily purpose. It is only when people *over-eat* that weight becomes a problem.

Children, for example, need warming and filling puddings during their growing years; and those adults expending energy upon their work should have energy-giving carbohydrates. Both categories would suffer from lack of energy if too much carbohydrate were denied them.

Apart from health, there are times also when a sweet of some kind is imperative to balance a meal and round it off. I have a chapter on sweets for special occasions because what party or buffet would be complete without at least one gorgeous sweet to look forward to? I know the male sex particularly appreciate, and often demand 'a pud', which to them appears to cover everything from a simple steamed pudding to a sophisticated Baked Alaska!

Monica Mawson

Useful Facts and Figures

Notes on metrication

In this book quantities are given in metric and Imperial measures. Exact conversion from Imperial to metric measures does not usually give very convenient working quantities and so the metric measures have been rounded off into units of 25 grams. The table below shows the recommended equivalents.

Ounces	Approx. grams to nearest whole figure	Recommended conversion to nearest unit of 25
1	28	25
2	57	50
3	85	75
4	113	100
5	142	150
6	170	175
7	198	200
8	227	225
9	255	250
10	283	275
11	312	300
12	340	350
13	368	375
14	396	400
15	425	425
16 (1 lb)	454	450
17	482	475
18	510	500
19	539	550
20 (1¼ lb)	567	575

Note: When converting quantities over 20 oz first add the appropriate figures in the centre column, then adjust to the nearest unit of 25. As a general guide, 1 kg (1000 g) equals 2·2 lb or about 2 lb 3 oz. This method of conversion gives good results in nearly all cases, although in certain pastry and cake recipes a more accurate conversion is necessary to produce a balanced recipe.

Liquid measures: The millilitre has been used in this book and the following table gives a few examples.

Imperial	Approx. ml to nearest whole figure	Recommended millilitres
¼ pint	142	150
½ pint	283	300
¾ pint	425	450
1 pint	567	600
1½ pints	851	900
1¾ pints	992	1000 (1 litre)

Spoon measures: All spoon measures given in this book are level unless otherwise stated.

Can sizes: At present, cans are marked with the exact (usually to the nearest whole number) metric equivalent of the Imperial weight of the contents, so we have followed this practice when giving can sizes.

Oven temperatures

The table below gives recommended equivalents.

	°C	°F	Gas Mark
Very cool	110	225	¼
	120	250	½
Cool	140	275	1
	150	300	2
Moderate	160	325	3
	180	350	4
Moderately hot	190	375	5
	200	400	6
Hot	220	425	7
	230	450	8
Very hot	240	475	9

Notes for American and Australian users

In America the 8-oz measuring cup is used. In Australia metric measures are now used in conjunction with the standard 250-ml measuring cup. The Imperial pint, used in Britain and Australia, is 20 fl oz, while the American pint is 16 fl oz. It is important to remember that the Australian tablespoon differs from both the British and American tablespoons; the table below gives a comparison. The British standard tablespoon, which has been used throughout this book, holds 17·7 ml, the American 14·2 ml, and the Australian 20 ml. A teaspoon holds approximately 5 ml in all three countries.

British	American	Australian
1 teaspoon	1 teaspoon	1 teaspoon
1 tablespoon	1 tablespoon	1 tablespoon
2 tablespoons	3 tablespoons	2 tablespoons
3½ tablespoons	4 tablespoons	3 tablespoons
4 tablespoons	5 tablespoons	3½ tablespoons

An Imperial/American guide to solid and liquid measures

Solid measures:

IMPERIAL	AMERICAN
1 lb butter or margarine	2 cups
1 lb flour	4 cups
1 lb granulated or castor sugar	2 cups
1 lb icing sugar	3 cups
8 oz rice	1 cup

Liquid measures:

IMPERIAL	AMERICAN
¼ pint liquid	⅔ cup liquid
½ pint	1¼ cups
¾ pint	2 cups
1 pint	2½ cups
1½ pints	3¾ cups
2 pints	5 cups (2½ pints)

Note:
When making any of the recipes in this book, only follow one set of measures as they are not interchangeable.

Cooks' Tips

Here are a few notes to clarify what may seem incongruities in some of the recipes; and also a few hints which I consider important to make cooking easier.

1 The quantities given in grammes and ounces – particularly for 4 oz – will vary in different recipes where the completely accurate amount is not necessary.

2 Where I have given a choice of butter or margarine in the ingredients, either can be used without loss of flavour. Where butter alone is stated, the flavour of the dish will be improved if butter can be used, but for brevity in the instructions I have used only butter.

3 A 'wire whisk' is a small pear shaped whisk, either rounded or flat at the end, made simply of wire.

4 For rubbing ingredients through a sieve, it is infinitely easier to do so with a heavy china or glass pestle, rather than the normal wooden spoon or roller.

5 In some of the recipes I have suggested adding a few drops of colouring to a dish to enhance its appearance. In former times the addition of artificial colouring to any food was considered almost a crime, but these days no harmful colouring is allowed to be sold, and some world famous Chefs have told me that as the first requirement for the enjoyment of a dish is the attraction of its appearance, it is occasionally essential to add colouring judiciously.

6 Where whipped cream has been given as the decoration or ingredient for sweets, in many cases Dream Topping (from a packet) can be used instead.

7 Weighing golden syrup or black treacle can be a problem. The easiest way is to place the lidless tin on the scales, then deduct the weight of syrup needed. As a rough guide, 1 tablespoon = 25 g/1 oz.
To make the syrup easier to manipulate if it is too thick, stand the tin in very hot water until it becomes thinner.

Freezing and frying
It is a boon to store some sweets in a freezer for emergencies or when time is short, so here are a few points which may be of help.
Jellies will not freeze on their own, but if mixed with cream, evaporated milk, fruit purées and so on, are perfectly satisfactory.
For freezing a soufflé or mousse in the dish in which it is to be served, make the collar of foil, or cover the greaseproof paper with foil and secure firmly with string and freezer tape. Open freeze first, then overwrap with a polythene bag. When required for use, remove the overwrapping and allow to thaw, then

take off the collar in the usual way (see page 45) and decorate as desired. Cheesecakes freeze well and are a splendid standby for entertaining. For freezing, line the tin first (preferably loose-bottomed) with foil and when the cheesecake has set in a refrigerator, place it in the freezer and open freeze. When hard, pull out of the tin and overwrap. Remove the wrapping before thawing.

Meringues freeze satisfactorily, but as they will keep for weeks, and if dry for months, in a cake box or tin, it seems an unnecessary waste of freezer space.

Sweets made from cream cheese are useful to store, particularly party sweets such as Paskha, Easter flower pot pudding, Coeur à la crème (see page 72, 73 and 74), and so on.

It is not recommended that sweets should be stored for more than 2–3 months, although I find that the cream cheese party sweets mentioned above will last considerably longer than any containing gelatine. Leave all decorating until the sweet is removed and thawed.

If there is space in a freezer, it is a useful time-saver to steam two or three puddings at one time (for storage preferably in a foil bowl) and then one can be consumed immediately and the others frozen. Use from frozen by simply boiling or steaming again for 1–1½ hours.

Pastry, both cooked and uncooked, freezes extremely well. Baked lasts about 6 months, but uncooked is better used within 3 months.

Store cooked flan cases for quick use, but these are fragile so are best stored in a box if possible. Alternatively, cut pieces of dough to fit a flan tin or ring, or tartlet cases, or as a cover for a pie dish, and place film or greaseproof paper between each, then overwrap and freeze flat until hard.

To cook: leave unbaked pastry to thaw at room temperature until soft enough to bend to the shape required; cooked pastry should always be refreshed by being placed in a hot oven (220°C, 425°F, Gas Mark 7) for 10–12 minutes, depending upon size and type of pastry.

Frying
The old maxim for frying, 'wait until a blue smoke rises', is utterly wrong for the modern variety of fats. Vegetable oil, for example (which I consider the best for deep drying), has a much higher smoking temperature (225°–232°C/440°–450°F) than animal fats (180°–205°C/356°–400°F), although after the first usage the smoking temperature drops considerably. But vegetable oil is still the highest.

Butter, margarine, tub fats, or unrefined oils should NOT be used for deep frying.

An all-purpose Brannan thermometer for frying and jam and sweet making, is to my mind almost a necessity to take all the worry out of deep frying, etc. But if no thermometer is available, the following are good guide lines: A 2·5-cm/1-inch cube of brown bread will take 40 seconds to reach 187°–195°C/369°–383°F and white bread 60 seconds to reach 180°–187°C/356°–369°F.

Hot Puddings

Britain probably can boast of a larger variety of hot puddings than any other country in the world.

Our steamed and baked puddings have for generations offered solace to innumerable families all over the country, but especially in the Midlands and the North, which suffer considerably colder and damper weather than that experienced in the South. And what could be more comforting than a hearty warming pudding to round off a meal? Or for the cook, the satisfying feeling of producing to acclaim a fluffy soufflé or tasty pancake?

For deep frying please see Cook's Tips (page 5–6).

Mother's rice pudding

you will need for 4–5 servings:

METRIC/IMPERIAL
63 g/2½ oz short-grain rice
50 g/2 oz granulated sugar
600 ml/1 pint milk
150 ml/¼ pint evaporated milk
150 ml/¼ pint water
25 g/1 oz (approx) butter or margarine

1 Wash the rice and put into a generous 1-litre/2-pint pie dish, greased round the top. Add the sugar and liquids and stir well. Leave to soak for several hours.

2 Stir again and float slivers of butter all over the top. Bake in a moderate oven (180°C, 350°F, Gas Mark 4) for about 1 hour or until the pudding is rising in large bubbles all over, then lower the heat to a cool oven (140°C, 275°F, Gas Mark 1) and continue cooking for a further 1¾–2 hours.

Variation:
Mother's tapioca pudding Use 50 g/2 oz flake tapioca and 75 g/3 oz sugar and proceed as above.

My rice pudding

you will need for 4–5 servings:

METRIC/IMPERIAL
1 large can sweetened condensed milk
water
75 g/3 oz short-grain rice

1 Dilute the canned milk with water to make up to 900 ml/1½ pints.

2 Put the rice into a generous 1-litre/2-pint pie dish, greased round the top, and add the milk. Stir well. Bake in a cool oven (150°C, 300°F, Gas Mark 2) for about 2½ hours until creamy, stirring occasionally.

Variations: Use 65 g/2½ oz flaked rice or tapioca.

Baked custard

you will need for 4 servings:

METRIC/IMPERIAL

3 eggs
1 tablespoon castor sugar
600 ml/1 pint milk
grated nutmeg

1 Beat the eggs and sugar together.
2 Warm the milk, without allowing it to boil, and pour it over the eggs whilst stirring.
3 Strain into a generous 1-litre/2-pint pie dish, greased round the top, and sprinkle grated nutmeg over the top.
4 Stand the dish in a tin containing 2·5 cm/1 inch warm water (bain-marie) and bake in a moderate oven (160°C, 325°F, Gas Mark 3) for 55–60 minutes.
Note:
The custard must not be allowed to bubble or small holes will form throughout and the custard may separate and become watery.

Bread and butter pudding

you will need for 4 servings:

METRIC/IMPERIAL

10 slices (preferably thin) white bread from a sandwich loaf
butter or margarine
50 g/2 oz sultanas or seedless raisins
1–2 tablespoons castor sugar
450 ml/¾ pint milk
2 eggs, beaten
grated nutmeg (optional)

1 Spread the bread with butter, cut off crusts, and cut each slice into two or three pieces.
2 Lay slices, buttered side up, to cover the base of a generous 1-litre/2-pint ovenproof dish, greased round the sides. Sprinkle over a little of the fruit and sugar. Repeat layers, ending with bread.
3 Pour the warm milk onto the eggs and whisk well. Pour the milk and eggs over the bread almost to cover, adding a little more milk if necessary.
4 Sprinkle the top with nutmeg or more sugar and bake in a moderate oven (180°C, 350°F, Gas Mark 4) for 35–40 minutes, until set and nicely browned.

Variation:

Marmalade bread and butter pudding Use white or brown bread, buttered and spread with marmalade. Omit the fruit and sugar.

Bread pudding

you will need for 6 servings:

METRIC/IMPERIAL

225 g/8 oz bread with crusts
150 g/5 oz sultanas, or seedless raisins and currants, mixed
50 g/2 oz brown sugar
50 g/2 oz shredded suet
½ teaspoon mixed cake spice
2 eggs
150 ml/¼ pint milk
castor sugar

1 Break the bread into pieces and soak in cold water for ½–1 hour. Turn into a colander and squeeze out as much of the water as possible, then break up finely with a fork.
2 Mix in all the dry ingredients.
3 Beat the eggs and milk together and stir into the pudding.
4 Turn into a well-greased 25·5-cm/10-inch by 20-cm/8-inch (across the top) roasting tin and bake in a moderate oven (180°C, 350°F, Gas Mark 4) for 1¼ hours. Serve sprinkled with castor sugar.

Alice's banana bread pudding

you will need for 8 servings:

METRIC/IMPERIAL

200 g/7 oz slices from a white sandwich loaf
100 g/4 oz plain flour
½ teaspoon ground cinnamon
½ teaspoon grated nutmeg
1½ teaspoons baking powder
175 g/6 oz seedless raisins
125 g/4½ oz brown sugar
large can evaporated milk
¼ teaspoon vanilla essence
50 g/2 oz margarine, melted
3 ripe or overripe bananas, mashed

1 Pull the bread, including the crusts, into small pieces.
2 Sieve the flour, spices, and baking powder together.
3 Mix all the ingredients together thoroughly.
4 Turn into a greased 25·5 by 20-cm/10 by 8-inches (across the top) roasting tin, and bake in a moderate oven (180°C, 350°F, Gas Mark 4) for 1¼–1½ hours. Best served hot but can also be served cold.

Simple Sue or golden delight

you will need for 4 servings:

METRIC/IMPERIAL

4 slices from a white sandwich loaf
milk
vanilla essence
75 g/3 oz butter or margarine
2 tablespoons golden syrup

1 Remove crusts from the bread and cut each slice into four.
2 Flavour a little milk with vanilla essence and dip the bread quickly into it on both sides.
3 Melt the butter and golden syrup in a frying pan and fry the bread very slowly for about 30 minutes, until golden on both sides. These need to be moved around occasionally, and turned over once. Best served hot but can also be served cold, with lightly whipped cream.

Dutch wentelteefjes (cinnamon bread triangles)

you will need for 4 servings:

METRIC/IMPERIAL

4 slices bread from a white sandwich loaf
1 small egg
pinch of salt
25 g/1 oz castor sugar
½ teaspoon ground cinnamon
150 ml/¼ pint milk
butter or margarine

7

1 Remove crusts and cut the bread into neat triangles or squares.
2 Beat the egg and mix in the salt, half the sugar, and most of the cinnamon. Stir in the milk.
3 Soak the bread in the milk mixture for a few minutes, then fry gently in butter to a golden brown each side.
4 Mix the remaining sugar and cinnamon together and sprinkle over the bread to serve.

Baked coconut sponge

you will need for 4 servings:

METRIC/IMPERIAL

100 g/4 oz self-raising flour	2 eggs
1 teaspoon baking powder	2 tablespoons golden syrup
75 g/3 oz margarine	75 g/3 oz desiccated coconut
50 g/2 oz granulated sugar	

1 Sift the flour and baking powder together.
2 Cream the margarine and sugar until light and fluffy. Beat in the eggs and syrup gradually. Stir in the flour.
3 Keep aside a little of the coconut to scatter over the top and stir the rest into the sponge mixture.
4 Turn into a generous 1-litre/2-pint pie dish, greased round the sides, and scatter the reserved coconut over the top.
5 Bake in a moderately hot oven (190°C, 375°F, Gas Mark 5) for 35–40 minutes, until golden brown. Serve with diluted warm golden syrup or honey.

Baked almond pudding

you will need for 3–4 servings:

METRIC/IMPERIAL

50 g/2 oz soft breadcrumbs	50 g/2 oz butter or margarine
50 g/2 oz ground almonds	50 g/2 oz granulated sugar
½ teaspoon baking powder	1 egg
40–50 g/1½–2 oz chopped mixed peel	4 tablespoons milk few drops almond essence

1 Mix together the breadcrumbs, ground almonds, baking powder and mixed peel.
2 Cream the butter and sugar together until light and beat in the egg.
3 Stir in the dry ingredients alternately with the milk and almond essence.
4 Turn into a 900-ml/1½-pint pie dish, greased round the sides, and bake in a moderately hot oven (190°C, 375°F, Gas Mark 5) for 30–35 minutes until firm and lightly browned on top. Serve with Syrup sauce (see page 90), diluted golden syrup, or almond-flavoured custard.

Cake crumb special

you will need for 3 servings:

METRIC/IMPERIAL

150 g/5 oz stale plain cake	3 tablespoons lemon curd, honey, or jam
3 tablespoons desiccated coconut	1 large egg white
	50 g/2 oz castor sugar

1 Crumble the cake roughly into crumbs. Reserve about ½ tablespoon of the coconut and mix the rest with the cake crumbs.
2 Stir the lemon curd, honey or jam into the cake crumbs until well mixed and turn into a 600-ml/1-pint pie dish.
3 Whip the egg white stiffly with some of the sugar and fold in the rest. Cover the cake crumbs with the meringue to touch the pie dish all round and bake in a moderate oven (180°C, 350°F, Gas Mark 4) for 15–20 minutes, until the meringue is lightly browned.

Amberley inspiration

you will need for 4 servings:

METRIC/IMPERIAL

100 g/4 oz granulated sugar	4 trifle sponge cakes
150 ml/¼ pint water	50 g/2 oz butter
40 g/1½ oz currants	8 teaspoons brandy (optional)
40 g/1½ oz sultanas	150 ml/¼ pint
411 g/14½-oz can apricot halves	whipping or double cream (optional)

1 In a small saucepan dissolve the sugar in the water over a low heat, throw in the currants and sultanas, bring to the boil and boil for 4 minutes. Remove from the heat and stir in 3 tablespoons of the apricot syrup.
2 Cut the sponge cakes in halves lengthways.
3 Heat the butter over a low heat and fry the sponge halves gently to a light brown on both sides. Transfer to a shallow heatproof dish.
4 Place 3 apricot halves on each piece and when required heat through in a low oven.
5 Heat the dried fruit and syrup, spoon them over the apricots and finish with a teaspoon of brandy (if used). Serve with whipped cream swirled over the tops.

Fried Christmas or plum pudding

METRIC/IMPERIAL

1–2-cm/½–¾-inch thick slices of pudding	butter or margarine castor sugar

1 Melt the butter in a frying pan (allowing 25 g/1 oz per 4 slices of pudding).
2 Press both sides of each slice of pudding into castor sugar and fry over a low heat until lightly caramelized. Serve sprinkled with sugar.

Plum pudding pie

you will need for 4 servings:

METRIC/IMPERIAL

3 tablespoons finely cut marmalade
275–350 g/10–12 oz left-over plum pudding or fruit cake
1 tablespoon custard powder
300 ml/½ pint diluted evaporated or fresh milk
rum, brandy, or sherry (optional)
flaked almonds, toasted

1 Spread the marmalade in the bottom of a 1-litre/1¾–2-pint pie dish.
2 Cover with pieces of the pudding broken up roughly.
3 Make a custard with the custard powder and milk and flavour with spirit. Pour the custard over the pudding almost to cover.
4 Sprinkle with toasted almonds and bake in a moderate oven (180°C, 350°F, Gas Mark 4) for 25–30 minutes.

Toorak queen of puddings

you will need for 4 servings:

METRIC/IMPERIAL

100–125 g/3½–4½ oz left-over Christmas pudding or rich fruit cake
50 g/2 oz sultanas
40 g/1½ oz (about 4) ginger biscuits
2 eggs, separated
300 ml/½ pint milk
¼ teaspoon ground allspice
2 teaspoons granulated sugar
411-g/14½-oz can apricots
100 g/4 oz castor sugar
¼ teaspoon ground cinnamon

1 Grease a generous 1-litre/2-pint pie dish round the sides.
2 Chop the pudding or cake and spread in the dish, sprinkling with first the sultanas and then the biscuits broken into small pieces.
3 Beat the egg yolks with the milk, allspice, and granulated sugar and pour into the pie dish.
4 Leave for at least 1 hour, then mix up with a fork. Bake in a moderate oven (180°C, 350°F, Gas Mark 4) for 40–45 minutes until just set.
5 Drain the apricots (reserving the juice) and place them evenly over the pudding.
6 Whip the egg whites stiffly with a little of the castor sugar and the cinnamon and fold in the rest of the sugar. Spread over the pudding to touch the edge of the dish all round and replace in the oven for 15–20 minutes until the meringue is lightly browned. Serve with the heated apricot syrup.

Pancakes

Basic batter
you will need for 10 pancakes (allow 2 per person):

METRIC/IMPERIAL

115 g/4 oz plain flour
pinch of salt
1 egg
150 ml/¼ pint milk
150 ml/¼ pint (approx) water
oil, lard, or white vegetable fat

1 Sieve the flour and salt into a basin.
2 Make a well in the centre and break the egg into it. Pour some of the milk onto the egg and with a wooden spoon or wire whisk gradually stir in the flour, drawing it in from the sides, adding the rest of the milk and some of the water until the batter has the consistency of thick cream. Beat until perfectly smooth and little bubbles rise to the surface.
3 Leave to rest for 30 minutes or more, then before cooking beat in sufficient water to give a consistency which will just coat the back of a spoon.
4 Use a 16–18-cm/6½–7-inch frying pan with straight sides if possible. Heat the pan a little, pour in only just sufficient oil or melted fat to grease the base all over (pour out any excess) and when really hot lift the pan and pour in about 2 tablespoons of the batter and quickly swirl around so that the batter runs over the whole surface. It should be very thin. If too thick, pour a little back into the jug (see note). Cook over moderate heat for a minute or two, loosening the edge with a spatula, until the underside is golden brown, then toss, or turn over with a spatula and cook the second side. Repeat for each pancake.
5 For immediate consumption, as each pancake is made, stack them neatly between two plates over a pan of simmering water, or between plates in a warm oven. Serve sprinkled with castor sugar and lemon juice, and with lemon quarters.
Note:
To facilitate pouring, it is best to have both the oil or the melted fat in one small jug, and the batter in another, so that the quantities for pouring may be judged more accurately.
Cooked pancakes can be kept stacked and wrapped in greaseproof paper or foil in a refrigerator for a week or so. Alternatively, so long as they have been fried in oil, they can be stacked one on top of the other, wrapped in foil and frozen.
To reheat, loosen the foil and heat through in a moderate oven (180°C, 350°F, Gas Mark 4) for 25–30 minutes; or place each pancake in turn in a lightly greased heated pan and allow about ½ minute each side.

Rich sweet batter

METRIC/IMPERIAL

115 g/4 oz plain flour
pinch of salt
2 or 3 eggs
250 ml/8 fl oz milk
water to give the correct consistency
2 teaspoons castor sugar
15 g/½ oz butter, melted (oil may be used instead)
oil, lard, or white fat

1 Mix and make the pancakes in exactly the same way as for the basic mixture, but whisk in the melted butter just before cooking.

Variations:
Pancakes with jam or marmalade Spread each pancake with jam or marmalade, roll up, arrange in a shallow heatproof dish, sprinkle with icing sugar and glaze under a grill. If the pancakes are cold, place high up in a hot oven (230°C, 450°F, Gas Mark 8) for 8–10 minutes.

Pancakes with fruit pie filling Use a 383-g/13½-oz can of any fruit pie filling. Spread each pancake with the filling, roll up, sprinkle with sugar, desiccated coconut, flaked almonds, or chopped walnuts and heat as above.

Pancakes with ice cream and chestnut sauce (see page 91) **or caramel sauce** (see page 90) Place slices of ice cream on half of each pancake (8 for 4 servings), fold it over and pour the warm sauce over the top.

Pancakes with cranberry sauce

you will need for 5 servings:

METRIC/IMPERIAL

grated rind and juice of 1 orange	1 apple
rich sweet (see page 9) or basic (see page 9) batter	382-g/13½-oz jar cranberry sauce icing or castor sugar

1 Stir the grated orange rind and juice into the batter and make 10 pancakes (see page 9).
2 Peel and core the apple and chop finely. Stir it into the cranberry sauce.
3 Spread each pancake with the sauce, roll up and place in a shallow heatproof dish. Cover with foil.
4 When required, heat through in a low to moderate oven and serve sprinkled with icing or castor sugar.

Apricot pancakes with orange almond sauce

you will need for 4 servings:

METRIC/IMPERIAL

1 large orange	8 pancakes of rich sweet (see page 9) or basic (see page 9) batter
1 teaspoon arrowroot or cornflour	
castor sugar	
40 g/1½ oz flaked almonds, toasted	397-g/14-oz can apricot pie filling

1 Grate the rind of the orange, squeeze the juice and make up to 250 ml/8 fl oz with bottled orange juice or water.
2 Make the arrowroot or cornflour into a smooth paste with a little of the liquid. Turn into a saucepan with the rest of the liquid, the grated orange rind, and 40 g/1½ oz castor sugar. Bring to the boil and boil for 1–2 minutes until clear. Remove from the heat and stir in the toasted almonds.
3 Heat the pie filling, spread it over each pancake and roll up. Spoon the heated sauce over the pancakes and serve at once.

Danish ice cream stuffed pancakes

you will need for 6 servings:

METRIC/IMPERIAL

rich sweet (see page 9) or basic (see page 9) batter	strawberry, raspberry or other jam
vanilla ice cream	liqueur (optional)

1 Make the batter (see page 9) a little thicker than usual and make 6 pancakes in a 20–21-cm/8–8½-inch (across the base) frying pan.
2 Place a thick slice of ice cream on one half of each pancake, cover it with strawberry, raspberry or other jam, fold the pancakes in two and pour over any liqueur.
Note:
These pancakes can be made ahead. To reheat, fold each in half, stack on a heatproof dish, cover with foil and heat through in a low oven. Then fill them and serve at once.

Monsieur Lacourt's chocolate and nut pancakes

you will need for 4 servings:

METRIC/IMPERIAL

175 g/6 oz mixed nuts (walnuts, almonds, hazelnuts)	1 tablespoon lemon juice
25 g/1 oz plain chocolate, grated	8 pancakes of rich sweet batter (see page 9)
4 tablespoons honey	castor sugar

1 Put the nuts through a 'parsmint' or fine mincer and mix with the chocolate, honey and lemon juice.
2 Fill the pancakes with the mixture and roll up.
3 Arrange on a shallow heatproof dish, sprinkle with castor sugar and place under a hot grill until the sugar begins to melt.

Pannequet soufflé flambé Lasserre

you will need for 4 servings:

METRIC/IMPERIAL

4 tablespoons extra thick Crème pâtissière (see page 89)	Grand Marnier
	4 egg whites
1 egg yolk	8 pancakes from rich sweet batter (see page 9)
1 small egg	
1 tablespoon castor sugar	icing sugar
	brandy

1 Warm the Crème pâtissière in a saucepan, remove from the heat and beat in the egg yolk, small egg, castor sugar, and 1 tablespoon Grand Marnier.
2 Whip the egg whites stiffly and fold into the Crème pâtissière mixture.
3 Spread out the pancakes, place equal quantities of the filling across the full width of each and roll up.
4 Place in a buttered shallow heatproof dish and bake in a moderately hot oven (190°C, 375°F, Gas Mark 5) for 6–7 minutes.
5 Sprinkle well with icing sugar and at table pour Grand Marnier over them to taste and then flambé with warm brandy.

Surprise apple pancakes

you will need for 4 servings:

METRIC/IMPERIAL

50 g/2 oz sultanas	4 tablespoons honey
½ teaspoon ground cinnamon	150 ml/¼ pint soured cream
½ teaspoon Angostura bitters	8 pancakes rich sweet (see page 9) or
0·75 kg/1½ lb apple purée	basic (see page 9) batter

1 To plump the sultanas, bring to the boil in water to cover, remove from the heat and leave for 10–15 minutes, then drain and pat dry.
2 Mix the sultanas, cinnamon, and Angostura into the apple purée.
3 Place equal quantities across the whole width of each pancake, roll up and place in a shallow heatproof dish.
4 Mix the honey with the soured cream until thoroughly blended, pour over the pancakes and heat through in a low oven.

Spicy cream pancakes

you will need for 4 servings:

METRIC/IMPERIAL

50 g/2 oz sultanas	ground cinnamon
2 tablespoons cream	½ teaspoon (approx)
2 tablespoons castor sugar	grated nutmeg
225 g/8 oz curd cheese	8 pancakes from basic batter (see page 9)
½ teaspoon (approx)	icing sugar

1 To plump the sultanas, bring to the boil in water to cover, remove from the heat and leave for 10–15 minutes, then drain and pat dry.
2 Mix the cream and sugar into the cheese. Stir in cinnamon and nutmeg to give a spicy flavour. Add the sultanas.
3 Place equal quantities across each pancake and roll up. Place in a shallow heatproof dish, cover with foil and heat through in a low oven. Sprinkle with icing sugar to serve.

Apricot pancake cake

you will need for 4 servings:

METRIC/IMPERIAL

350 g/12 oz dried apricots	6 pancakes from rich sweet (see page 9) or basic (see page 9) batter made a little thicker than usual in an 18-cm/7-inch pan
600 ml/1 pint water	
100 g/4 oz granulated sugar	
grated rind and juice of ½ lemon	
25 g/1 oz flaked almonds, toasted	icing sugar

1 Soak the apricots in the water overnight. Put in a saucepan with the sugar and lemon juice and stew until soft.
2 Keep 5 or 6 halves aside for decoration. Purée the rest in a blender or rub through a sieve. Stir in the grated lemon rind.
3 Place one pancake on a dish, cover with some of the apricot pureé and repeat layers, ending with a pancake.
4 Place reserved apricots on the top with the almonds mounded in the centre and sprinkle with sifted icing sugar.

Panequeque de monzana banana

you will need for 4 servings:

METRIC/IMPERIAL

1 150–175 g/5–6 oz cooking apple	50 g/2 oz butter
1 large banana	4 tablespoons castor sugar
rich sweet batter (see page 9) made thicker than normal	2 tablespoons rum

1 Peel and core the apple and cut into quarters. Slice each quarter across fairly thinly. Peel and slice the banana.
2 For each pancake (4) heat 15 g/½ oz butter in an 18-cm/7-inch (across the base) frying pan, spoon in sufficient batter to cover the base. Spread a quarter of the apple and banana slices over it and press in lightly.
3 Fry over medium heat until a light golden brown on both sides. As soon as the second side is brown, sprinkle over ½ tablespoon sugar, flip over immediately and cook until caramelized. Repeat for the second side.
4 Keep each one warm, and to serve pour over the warmed rum and flame it.

Crêpes Suzette

you will need for 4 servings:

METRIC/IMPERIAL

12 extra thin pancakes made from rich sweet batter (see page 9) in a 15-cm/6-inch frying pan	1 orange
	castor sugar
	Grand Marnier, Orange Curaçao, Cointreau
75 g/3 oz butter	brandy
finely grated rind and juice of 1 lemon and	

1 Fold each cold pancake in four and then prepare 6 at a time.
2 In a large frying pan over a spirit stove (if possible) or over low heat, melt half the butter, stir in half the grated rind and juice of the lemon and orange and 1–2 tablespoons castor sugar and stir until melted.
3 Place 6 folded pancakes in the pan and gently heat through. Pour in 2–3 tablespoons of the liqueurs and move the pancakes around in the sauce.
4 Pour in about 1 tablespoon of brandy, tip the pan to set the alcohol alight (or set alight with a match if on an electric hotplate) and as soon as the flames have subsided, place 3 pancakes on each of two hot plates.
5 Repeat the process with the rest of the pancakes, and then pour the remaining sauce over all four plates.

Blinchiki (Russian pancakes)

1 Make the batter (rich sweet, see page 9).
2 Cook on one side only.
3 Place filling (curd cheese alone, or mixed with apple, strawberries, or any fruit in season, or stewed prunes) on the cooked side and fold up like an envelope.
4 Fry in butter on both sides until golden, scatter with sugar and serve with a bowl of Smatana (soured cream or natural yogurt can be used instead).
Note:
When filled with jam or plain fruit, they are served scattered liberally with icing sugar and with melted butter poured over instead of Smatana.

French pancakes

you will need for 4 servings:
METRIC/IMPERIAL

50 g/2 oz butter or margarine	50 g/2 oz self-raising flour
50 g/2 oz castor sugar	1–2 tablespoons milk
2 eggs, separated	jam

1 Cream the butter and sugar together until fluffy. Beat in the egg yolks and then the flour and milk alternately.
2 Whip the egg whites stiffly and fold in.
3 Divide the mixture equally into 4 greased saucers or 10-cm/4-inch patty pans and bake in a moderately hot oven (190°C, 375°F, Gas Mark 5) for 30–35 minutes.
4 Remove from the saucers and serve with a spoonful of jam in the centre of each.

Apple fritters

you will need for 4 servings:
METRIC/IMPERIAL

115 g/4 oz plain flour	
¼ teaspoon salt	
4 teaspoons vegetable oil	1 large or 2 small egg whites
8 tablespoons (approx) tepid water	3 medium to large cooking apples

1 Make the batter. Sieve the flour and salt into a basin, and with a wire whisk gradually beat in the oil and water to give a smooth batter of coating consistency. Leave to rest for 30 minutes or more.
2 Peel and core the apples and cut into 0·5–1-cm/¼–½-inch thick rings.
3 Whip the egg white stiffly and whisk into the batter.
4 Dip each apple ring into the batter and drop into moderately hot (180°–190°C, 350°–375°F) deep fat and fry until golden brown all over.
5 Drain on kitchen paper and toss in castor sugar. Serve immediately.

Variations:
Banana fritters Use 8 small or 4 large bananas. Cut large ones in halves.
Pineapple fritters Use whole slices or small or half slices of large fresh pineapples, or drained slices of canned pineapples.

Baked apples

you will need for 4 servings:
METRIC/IMPERIAL

4 large (225 g/8 oz each) cooking apples	butter or margarine
	4 tablespoons water
demerara or soft brown sugar	

1 Wash the apples and run the point of a knife just through the skin all round the centre of each.
2 Core the apples and stand them in a heatproof dish. Fill the cavities with the sugar, pressing down well, and place a knob of butter on top.
3 Pour the water into the dish and bake in a moderately hot oven (200°C, 400°F, Gas Mark 6) for 45–60 minutes until the apples are soft.

Variations for stuffings:

1 Stuff with 125 g/4½ oz mincemeat.
2 Stuff with mixed dried fruit and honey.
3 Stuff with chopped dates and chopped nuts, and place a knob of butter on top.

Apple Charlotte

you will need for 4 servings:
METRIC/IMPERIAL

1 kg/2 lb cooking apples	3 slices from a sandwich loaf
1 tablespoon lemon juice	50 g/2 oz soft breadcrumbs
butter or margarine	brown sugar
100 g/4 oz granulated sugar	

1 Peel and core the apples and chop into small pieces. Stew with the lemon juice, 25 g/1 oz butter and the granulated sugar until soft.
2 Butter the bread slices, remove crusts, and cut each slice in half. Line a generous 1-litre/2-pint pie or other heatproof dish, greased round the sides, with the bread, buttered side against the dish.
3 Put the apple into the dish. Cover with the breadcrumbs, sprinkle thickly with brown sugar, dot with flakes of butter and bake, above centre, in a moderately hot oven (200°C, 400°F, Gas Mark 6) for 40–50 minutes until crisp and golden brown.

Variation:
Add 1 tablespoon sultanas, 3 cloves, and ½ teaspoon ground cinnamon to the apple before stewing.

Apple amber

you will need for 4 servings:
METRIC/IMPERIAL

0·75 kg/1½ lb cooking apples	1 small lemon
	25 g/1 oz butter
100 g/4 oz granulated sugar	2 eggs, separated
	100 g/4 oz castor sugar

1 Peel, core, and slice the apples. Stew with the granulated sugar, grated rind and juice of the lemon and the butter until the apple is soft.

2 Remove from the heat, beat with a fork and stir in the egg yolks.

3 Turn into a generous 1-litre/2-pint pie dish, greased round the sides.

4 Whip the egg whites stiffly with a little of the castor sugar and fold in the rest. Spread over the apple to touch the dish all round and bake in a moderate oven (180°C, 350°F, Gas Mark 4) for 15–20 minutes until the meringue is lightly browned.

Apple and date cracknel

you will need for 4 servings:

METRIC/IMPERIAL

225 g/8 oz stoned dates	75 g/3 oz self-raising flour
150 ml/¼ pint water	25 g/1 oz margarine
450 g/1 lb cooking apples	15 g/½ oz lard (or all margarine)
50 g/2 oz granulated sugar	50 g/2 oz soft brown sugar

1 Chop the dates roughly and stew with the water until soft and mushy, about 5 minutes. Spread in the base of a generous 1-litre/2-pint pie or other heatproof dish, greased round the sides.

2 Peel and core the apples, slice thinly and arrange over the dates, sprinkling with the granulated sugar.

3 Rub the fats into the flour until the mixture resembles fine breadcrumbs. Stir in the brown sugar.

4 Sprinkle the mixture over the apple and bake in a moderately hot oven (200°C, 400°F, Gas Mark 6) for 40–45 minutes.

Cranberry-apple toffee crisp

you will need for 4 servings:

METRIC/IMPERIAL

450 g/1 lb cooking apples	50 g/2 oz butter or margarine
184-g/6½-oz jar cranberry sauce	75 g/3 oz soft brown sugar
1 tablespoon granulated sugar	50 g/2 oz cornflakes
150 ml/¼ pint soured cream	

1 Peel and core the apples and slice thinly. Place in layers in a generous 1-litre/2-pint pie or other heat-proof dish.

2 Mix the cranberry sauce and granulated sugar with the soured cream and pour over the apples.

3 Cover the dish with greaseproof paper and bake in a moderately hot oven (190°C, 375°F, Gas Mark 5) for 45 minutes or until the apples are tender.

4 Heat the butter and brown sugar together over a low heat until well blended, remove from the heat and stir in the roughly crushed cornflakes. Spread over the apple.

5 When required for serving, place under a low grill to heat and crisp the topping without allowing it to burn.

Bramley Betty

you will need for 5–6 servings:

METRIC/IMPERIAL

75 g/3 oz margarine	4 tablespoons water
225 g/8 oz packaged muesli	0·75 kg/1½ lb Bramley or other cooking apples
125 g/4½ oz demerara sugar	

1 Melt the margarine in a large saucepan, remove from the heat and stir in the cereal and sugar.

2 Peel and core the apples and slice thinly.

3 Pour the water into a generous 1-litre/2-pint pie or other heatproof dish, greased round the sides, and arrange half the apple slices in it. Cover with half the cereal mixture, repeat layers and bake in a moderate oven (180°C, 350°F, Gas Mark 4) for 40–45 minutes.

Apple sponge

you will need for 4 servings:

METRIC/IMPERIAL

0·75 kg/1½ lb cooking apples	50 g/2 oz castor sugar
3 tablespoons golden syrup	1 large egg
juice of ½ lemon	125 g/4½ oz self-raising flour
50 g/2 oz butter or margarine	1 tablespoon boiling water

1 Peel, core and chop the apples. Stew with the golden syrup and lemon juice until the apple is mushy.

2 Put into a generous 1-litre/2-pint pie dish, greased round the sides, and allow to cool.

3 Cream the butter and sugar together until fluffy, beat in the egg and a little of the flour, then fold in the rest.

4 Stir in the boiling water, spread evenly over the apple and bake in a moderately hot oven (190°, 375°F, Gas Mark 5) for 30–35 minutes until risen and lightly browned on top.

Variation:

Rhubarb sponge Trim 0·5 kg/1¼ lb rhubarb and cut into 2·5-cm/1-inch lengths. Stew lightly with 100 g/4 oz granulated sugar and 1 tablespoon water. Proceed from stage 2.

Gooseberry sponge Top and tail 450 g/1 lb gooseberries. Stew lightly with 100 g/4 oz granulated sugar and 1 tablespoon water. Proceed from stage 2.

Fried bananas

you will need for 4 servings:

METRIC/IMPERIAL

4 large or 8 small bananas	75 g/3 oz castor sugar
25 g/1 oz butter	3 tablespoons water

1 Peel the bananas and if large cut in halves length-ways. Leave small ones whole.

2 In a large frying pan bring the butter, sugar and water to simmering point and allow to simmer until the syrup turns a golden brown.

3 Place the bananas in the caramel syrup and allow them to cook gently, turning them over once, until they are soft. Remove to a hot dish, or serve straight onto plates, and pour remaining syrup over them. Serve with cream or ice cream.

Banana ginger meringue

you will need for 4 servings:

METRIC/IMPERIAL

4–5 bananas
½ lemon
75 g/3 oz castor sugar
butter or margarine
150 g/5 oz cake crumbs
(any plain cake or
sponge)

1 egg white
1–2 pieces preserved
ginger

1 Peel and mash the bananas and mix with the grated rind and juice of the lemon and 25 g/1 oz of the sugar.
2 Grease a 900-ml/1½-pint pie dish round the sides with butter and sprinkle a layer of crumbs in the bottom.
3 Cover with a layer of banana. Repeat layers and end with crumbs.
4 Dot with slivers of butter, cover the dish with greaseproof paper and bake in a moderately hot oven (190°C, 375°F, Gas Mark 5) for 25 minutes.
5 Whip the egg white with a little of the remaining sugar until stiff, then fold in the rest. Cover the pudding with the meringue to touch the dish all round.
6 Cut enough thin slices of preserved ginger to decorate the top and replace in the oven for 10–15 minutes. Serve with hot ginger syrup, cream, or custard flavoured with ginger.

Jamaica spiced bananas

you will need for 4 servings:

METRIC/IMPERIAL

4 large firm bananas
2 teaspoons lime or 1.
tablespoon lemon
juice
25 g/1 oz butter
1 orange
4 tablespoons rum
175 g/6 oz soft brown
sugar
½ teaspoon ground
cinnamon

½ teaspoon grated
nutmeg
½ teaspoon ground
allspice
50 g/2 oz sweet biscuit
crumbs
2 tablespoons finely
chopped salted
peanuts

1 Cut the peeled bananas in halves across, and then cut each piece in two lengthways. Sprinkle with lime or lemon juice.
2 Fry gently in the hot butter to a light brown on each side and transfer to a shallow heatproof dish in one layer.
3 Grate the rind of the orange and mix with 4 tablespoons of the juice (or make up with water), and the rum, sugar, and spices. Pour this mixture over the bananas.
4 Mix the biscuit crumbs and chopped nuts together and sprinkle over the top.
5 Bake in a moderately hot oven (190°C, 375°F, Gas Mark 5) for 12–15 minutes. Serve with ice cream or lightly whipped cream.

Note:
An impressive way of serving this sweet for guests is to place 1 teaspoon of sugar in a ladle, fill it with warm rum, set alight and pour flaming over the bananas at table.

Crispy Barbados bananas

you will need for 4 servings:

METRIC/IMPERIAL

4 large bananas
2 tablespoons golden
syrup
127-g/4½-oz can
pineapple juice
½ teaspoon ground
cinnamon

1 tablespoon rum
(optional)
100 g/4 oz packaged
muesli
25 g/1 oz demerara
sugar
butter

1 Cut each peeled banana into three and cut the pieces in halves lengthways. Lay in one layer in a shallow heatproof dish.
2 Melt the syrup with the pineapple juice and cinnamon, remove from the heat and add the rum.
3 Stir in the muesli until well blended and spread this mixture over the bananas.
4 Sprinkle with the sugar, dot with flakes of butter and grill under medium heat until lightly browned and crisp. Serve with ice cream or cream.

Rakwana bananas

you will need for 4 servings:

METRIC/IMPERIAL

2½ tablespoons black
treacle
grated rind and juice
of ½ orange
grated rind and juice
of ½ lemon
4 large bananas

3 tablespoons grated
block creamed
coconut, or
desiccated coconut
mixed with 1
tablespoon castor
sugar

1 Mix together the treacle, orange and lemon rinds and juice.
2 Peel the bananas and place, whole, in a shallow heatproof dish, pour the treacle mixture over them and sprinkle with the coconut.
3 Bake in a moderate oven (180°C, 350°F, Gas Mark 4) for 15–20 minutes, basting occasionally, until the bananas are just soft. Serve with cream or ice cream.

Honey baked bananas

you will need for 3 servings:

METRIC/IMPERIAL

40 g/1½ oz butter
6 smallish bananas
40 g/1½ oz demerara
sugar

2 teaspoons lemon
juice
1 tablespoon clear
honey

1 Grease a shallow heatproof dish, just large enough to take the bananas side by side, with a little of the butter.
2 Lay the peeled bananas in the dish and pour over the rest of the butter, melted, to coat the bananas completely. Sprinkle with the sugar.

3 Mix the lemon juice with the honey and pour over the top. Bake in a moderately hot oven (190°C, 375°F, Gas Mark 5) for 15 minutes, then slip under a hot grill until lightly browned. Serve with ice cream or cream.

Baked banana pudding

you will need for 4 servings:

METRIC/IMPERIAL
40 g/1½ oz cornflakes 175 ml/6 fl oz milk
50 g/2 oz seedless 450 g/1 lb bananas
  raisins 25 g/1 oz brown sugar
1 egg, beaten

1 Put the cornflakes and raisins in a basin.
2 Mix the beaten egg with the milk, pour this mixture over the cornflakes and allow to stand for 30 minutes or so.
3 Mash the peeled bananas and stir into the mixture with the sugar.
4 Turn into a 900-ml/1½-pint pie dish, greased round the sides, and bake in a moderate oven (180°C, 350°F, Gas Mark 4) for 30 minutes, until set and lightly browned on top.

Banana sultana caramel

you will need for each serving:

METRIC/IMPERIAL
1 tablespoon sultanas 1 banana
1 teaspoon rum or soft brown sugar
  sweet sherry

1 Pour boiling water over the sultanas and leave for an hour or so to plump up. Drain, and pour the liquor over them.
2 Peel the banana, cut in half lengthways and place in the bottom of a grill pan, cut side up.
3 Cover thickly with soft brown sugar and place under a medium grill until the sugar bubbles and caramelizes, 3–4 minutes.
4 Transfer to a plate, sprinkle with the sultanas and serve at once with cream or ice cream.

Gooseberry upside-down pudding

you will need for 5–6 servings:

METRIC/IMPERIAL
50 g/2 oz butter ⅛ teaspoon salt
75 g/3 oz soft brown 100 g/4 oz margarine
  sugar 100 g/4 oz castor sugar
450 g/1 lb gooseberries 2 eggs
175 g/6 oz self-raising ¼ teaspoon almond
  flour   essence (optional)
½ teaspoon baking 1 tablespoon milk
  powder

1 Cream the butter and brown sugar together until fluffy and spread over the base of a 20-cm/8-inch greased cake tin.
2 Top, tail and wash the gooseberries. Dry and place in the creamed mixture to cover completely.
3 Sift together the flour, baking powder and salt.
4 Cream the margarine and castor sugar until fluffy and

beat in the eggs and almond essence. Stir in the flour alternately with the milk (adding a little more if the mixture is not sufficiently soft), and spread evenly over the gooseberries.
5 Bake in a moderate oven (180°C, 350°F, Gas Mark 4) for 50–55 minutes. leave in the tin for 5 minutes before turning out onto a warm dish.

Variation:
Plum or damson Halve and stone the fruit and place, cut sides down, on the creamed mixture.

Chocolate and walnut upside-down pudding

you will need for 6 servings:

METRIC/IMPERIAL
150 g/5 oz butter or 225 ml/8 fl oz milk
  margarine 175 g/6 oz plain flour
150 g/5 oz golden 2 teaspoons baking
  syrup   powder
50 g/2 oz walnuts, 1 teaspoon
  chopped   bicarbonate of soda
50 g/2 oz glacé 1 egg, beaten
  cherries, chopped vanilla essence
75 g/3 oz plain
  chocolate

1 In a small saucepan melt together 50 g/2 oz of the butter and 50 g/2 oz of the golden syrup.
2 Pour this mixture into a 21·5-cm/8½-inch non-stick sandwich tin and sprinkle the nuts and cherries all over it.
3 Put broken up chocolate, milk and the remaining butter and golden syrup into the saucepan and stir over gentle heat until the chocolate is completely melted. Cool for 5 minutes.
4 Sift flour, baking powder and bicarbonate into a basin. Stir in the chocolate mixture, the egg and a few drops of vanilla essence and beat until smooth.
5 Carefully pour into the tin and bake in a moderate oven (180°C, 350°F, Gas Mark 4) for 35–40 minutes, until risen and firm to the touch.
6 Turn out and serve hot, with or without Chocolate sauce (see page 91). If served cold, the sauce is an improvement.

Rhubarb upside-down pudding

you will need for 4–5 servings:

METRIC/IMPERIAL
65 g/2½ oz butter ⅛ teaspoon salt
100 g/3½ oz soft 125 g/4½ oz margarine
  brown sugar 125 g/4½ oz castor
1 teaspoon grated   sugar
  orange rind 2 eggs
450 g/1 lb rhubarb 1 tablespoon orange
175 g/6 oz self-raising   juice
  flour

1 Cream the butter, brown sugar and orange rind together until fluffy and spread over the base of a greased 15-cm/6-inch square cake tin.
2 Wash and trim the rhubarb and cut into equal 2·5-4-cm/1–1½-inch lengths. Arrange them over the creamed mixture in neat rows.

15

3 Sift together the flour, baking powder and salt.
4 Cream the margarine and castor sugar together and beat in the eggs. Stir in the flour alternately with the orange juice and spread evenly over the rhubarb.
5 Bake in a moderate oven (180°C, 350°F, Gas Mark 4) for 50–55 minutes. Leave in the tin for 5 minutes before turning out onto a warm dish.

Rhubarb Charlotte

you will need for 4 servings:

METRIC/IMPERIAL

25–40 g/1–1½ oz butter or margarine	0·75 kg/1½ lb rhubarb grated rind of ½ small
4 tablespoons sugar	orange or ¼ lemon
thin slices of bread with crusts removed	1 tablespoon orange or lemon juice
clear honey	

1 Butter a 1-kg/2-lb loaf tin generously, and sprinkle all over with 1 tablespoon of sugar.
2 Measure bread to line the tin. Spread each slice with honey and press the honey side against the sugar to cover the tin completely.
3 Wash and trim the rhubarb and cut into 2·5-cm/1-inch lengths. Fill the tin neatly, sprinkling each layer with a little of the grated rind and a tablespoon of the sugar. Pour in the juice.
4 Butter enough slices of bread to cover the top and place in position, buttered side upwards. Sprinkle with remaining sugar and bake in a moderately hot oven (190°C, 375°F, Gas Mark 5) for 35–40 minutes, until the bread is brown and crisp.
5 Turn out onto a hot dish and serve with cream or custard.

Rhubarb toffee crunch

you will need for 4 servings:

METRIC/IMPERIAL

0·75 kg/1½ lb rhubarb	50 g/2 oz butter or
175 g/6 oz granulated sugar	margarine
1 small orange or	75 g/3 oz soft brown sugar
lemon (optional)	50 g/2 oz cornflakes
2 bananas	

1 Wash and trim the rhubarb and cut into 2·5-cm/1-inch lengths. Put into a casserole.
2 In a saucepan over medium heat stir the granulated sugar, grated rind of half the orange or lemon and 2 tablespoons of the juice (or use 2 tablespoons water), until the sugar is dissolved. Pour this mixture over the rhubarb and cover.
3 Bake in a moderate oven (160°C, 325°F, Gas Mark 3) for 25–30 minutes. Stir around carefully and continue cooking for 10–15 minutes or until the rhubarb is just tender, but do not allow it to boil or the rhubarb will fall to pieces. Turn into a generous 1-litre/2-pint pie dish.
4 Peel and slice the bananas and arrange over the rhubarb.
5 Heat the butter and sugar together over a low heat until well blended, remove from the heat and stir in the roughly crushed cornflakes. Spread over the banana.
6 When required for serving, place under a low grill to heat and crisp the topping, without allowing it to burn.

Variations:

Australian apricot crunch I Drain an 822-g/1 lb 13-oz can apricots. Put the apricots in a pie dish with 3–4 tablespoons of the syrup and proceed from stage 4.

Apricot crunch II Soak 225 g/8 oz dried apricots in 250 ml/scant ½ pint water overnight, then stew with 75 g/3 oz sugar for 8–10 minutes. Put them in a pie dish and proceed from stage 4.

Date crunch Stew 225 g/8 oz stoned dates with 300 ml/½ pint water. Put them in a pie dish and proceed from stage 4.

Rhubarb whirligig

you will need for 4 servings:

METRIC/IMPERIAL

1 kg/2 lb rhubarb	½ teaspoon ground
175 g/6 oz self-raising flour	cinnamon
25 g/1 oz rolled oats	50 g/2 oz seedless raisins
25 g/1 oz castor sugar	2 tablespoons golden
100 g/4 oz margarine	syrup
milk	
75 g/3 oz demerara sugar	

1 Trim and stew the rhubarb (see page 44). Drain off most of the juice and put the fruit in a wide shallow casserole.
2 Mix together the flour, oats, and castor sugar, rub in 75 g/3 oz of the margarine and stir in sufficient milk to make a pliable dough.
3 Roll out on a floured board to a rectangle 28–30·5 cm/11–12 inches by about 20 cm/8 inches. Brush with the remaining margarine, melted, then sprinkle with two-thirds of the demerara sugar, the cinnamon, and the raisins.
4 Roll up from the long side and cut into 8 or 9 pieces. Arrange these on top of the rhubarb, spread them all over with the syrup and sprinkle with the rest of the sugar.
5 Bake in a moderately hot oven (200°C, 400°F, Gas Mark 6) for 30–35 minutes.

Fruit crumble or cracknel

you will need for 4 servings:

METRIC/IMPERIAL

0·75 kg/1½–1¾ lb raw fruit (apples, apples	castor sugar
& blackberries,	65 g/2½ oz margarine
gooseberries,	150 g/5 oz plain flour
plums, rhubarb,	75 g/3 oz demerara or
etc.)	castor sugar

1 Prepare the fruit as for stewing (see page 43–4), mix with castor sugar according to the fruit used and put

into a generous 1-litre/2-pint pie or other heatproof dish, greased round the sides.
2 Rub the margarine into the flour until the mixture resembles fine breadcrumbs. Stir in the demerara sugar.
3 Sprinkle the crumble mixture evenly all over the fruit and bake in a moderately hot oven (190°C, 375°F, Gas Mark 5) for 40–45 minutes.

Note:
Fruit crumble can also be made with stewed fruit, in which case bake for 25–30 minutes only, or until the crumble is sufficiently brown.

Variation:
When in season, a quince thinly sliced and mixed with apple produces a delightful tartness.

Crispy topping

25 g/1 oz margarine	scant ¼ teaspoon
50 g/2 oz granulated	almond essence
sugar	2 teaspoons ground
1 egg	almonds
2 tablespoons water	50 g/2 oz semolina

1 Cream the margarine and sugar together.
2 Beat the egg with the water and almond essence and stir into the creamed mixture with the ground almonds and semolina.
3 Spread over the fruit and bake as above.

Cider pears

you will need for 4 servings:
METRIC/IMPERIAL

150 ml/¼ pint medium	2 tablespoons
or sweet cider	(approx) demerara
50 g/2 oz sultanas	sugar
4 pears	butter or margarine

1 Bring the cider and sultanas to the boil (to plump the sultanas), remove from the heat and allow to cool.
2 Peel the pears, cut in halves and scoop out the cores. Place, cut side up, in a shallow heat-proof dish.
3 Pour the cider and sultanas over the pears, sprinkle liberally with demerara sugar and dot with flakes of butter.
4 Cover the dish with foil and bake in a moderate oven (180°C, 350°F, Gas Mark 4) for 30–35 minutes, according to the ripeness of the pears, or until tender. Serve with cream or ice cream or custard.

Butterscotch pears

you will need for 4 servings:
METRIC/IMPERIAL

300 ml/½ pint water	25 g/1 oz butter
100 g/4 oz granulated	100 g/4 oz soft dark
sugar	brown sugar
1 teaspoon lemon	125 ml/¼ pint
juice	whipping or double
4 pears (slightly	cream
underripe)	

1 Bring the water and granulated sugar to the boil, stirring until the sugar is dissolved. Boil for 2–3 minutes, remove from the heat and add the lemon juice.
2 Meanwhile peel two of the pears and cut in halves. Lower into the syrup and simmer gently, covered, for 5–15 minutes, depending upon the size and type of pears, until only just tender. Remove with a straining spoon. Repeat with the other two pears.
3 When cool enough to handle, carefully scoop out the cores with a teaspoon.
4 Lay all the halves, cut sides upwards, in a shallow heatproof dish, dot with flakes of the butter and cover thickly with the brown sugar.
5 Bake in a hot oven (220°C, 425°F, Gas Mark 7) for 20 minutes. Pour over the unwhipped cream and serve immediately.

Pear castle

you will need for 4 servings:
METRIC/IMPERIAL

4 large firm pears	5 tablespoons clear
2 tablespoons lemon	honey
juice	ground cinnamon
25 g/1 oz butter,	
melted	

1 Peel the pears but leave the stalks on. Stand upright in a heat-proof dish.
2 Spoon over the lemon juice, melted butter, and honey, in that order. Sprinkle lightly with cinnamon.
3 Bake in a moderate oven (180°C, 350°F, Gas Mark 4) for 20–30 minutes, until the pears are just tender. Serve hot with ice cream or cream.

Poires au vin rouge

you will need for 4 servings:
METRIC/IMPERIAL

0·5–0·75 kg/1¼–1½ lb	4 firm (Comice if
dessert apples	possible) pears
1 tablespoon water	10–12 almonds, sliced
15 g/½ oz butter	lengthways and
150 g/5 oz granulated	toasted
sugar	4 tablespoons rum
4 tablespoons	(optional)
raspberry jam	
300 ml/½ pint red	
wine	

1 Peel, core, and slice the apples.
2 Stew with the water, butter, and 1 tablespoon of the sugar until soft and mushy. Mash with a potato masher or fork.
3 Stir in the jam and spread evenly in a shallow heat-proof dish.
4 Dissolve the rest of the sugar with the wine over a low heat in a saucepan large enough to take the halved pears, or cook in two batches.
5 Peel the pears and cut in halves. Remove the cores with a sharp pointed teaspoon and place the halves in the gently simmering wine. Cover and simmer for 5 minutes, turn the halves over and continue simmering for a further 5–8 minutes until just tender.

6 Remove the pears with a straining spoon and place on the bed of apples. Keep warm in the oven.

7 Reduce the wine to about half by boiling fast, uncovered, and pour it over the pears. Scatter the almonds over them.

8 If liked, warm the rum, pour it over the pears and ignite.

Apricot sunshine

you will need for 4 servings:

METRIC/IMPERIAL	
450 g/1 lb fresh apricots	50 g/2 oz desiccated coconut
5 tablespoons water	75 g/3 oz demerara sugar
100 g/4 oz granulated sugar	50 g/2 oz cornflakes

1 Wash the apricots and cut into quarters, discarding the stones.

2 In a saucepan bring the water and granulated sugar to the boil, stirring. Drop in the apricots and simmer gently, covered, until they are tender, turning them over occasionally.

3 Mix together the coconut, demerara sugar, and lightly crushed cornflakes.

4 Place just under half the apricots in a generous 1-litre/2-pint pie or other heatproof dish, cover with half the cornflake mixture, repeat layers and bake in a moderately hot oven (190°C, 375°F, Gas Mark 5) for 20 minutes, or until lightly browned.

Variation:

Canned apricot sunshine Use an 822-g/1 lb 13-oz can of apricot halves, drained, and 1 lemon. Mix grated lemon rind with the cornflake mixture. Mix the lemon juice with 8 tablespoons of the apricot juice and pour this mixture over layers as above in a 900-ml/1½-pint pie dish. Bake as above.

Baked apricot fluff

you will need for 2 servings:

METRIC/IMPERIAL	
2 tablespoons apricot jam	2 egg whites

1 Sieve the jam.

2 Beat the egg whites stiffly and fold in the jam.

3 Turn into a 900-ml/1½-pint soufflé dish and bake in a cool oven (150°C, 300°F, Gas Mark 2) for 18–20 minutes, until well risen and lightly coloured on top. Serve immediately.

Apricot walnut Charlotte

you will need for 4 servings:

METRIC/IMPERIAL	
175 g/6 oz dried apricots	grated rind and juice of ½ lemon
4½ slices from a thin sandwich loaf	25 g/1 oz walnuts, chopped
butter or margarine	25 g/1 oz demerara sugar
75 g/3 oz soft brown sugar	

1 Cover the apricots with boiling water and leave to soak for several hours or overnight. Drain, but keep 150 ml/¼ pint of the liquid.

2 Remove crusts from the bread and spread the slices with butter.

3 Mix together the apricots, reserved juice, soft brown sugar, and grated rind and juice of the lemon.

4 Spread half in a generous 1-litre/2-pint pie dish, greased round the sides. Lay 2 slices of the bread on top and spread the rest of the apricots over them.

5 Cut the remaining bread into smaller pieces and lay, butter side up and slightly overlapping, all over the apricots.

6 Sprinkle with the nuts and demerara sugar and bake in a moderately hot oven (190°C, 375°F, Gas Mark 5) for 35–40 minutes, until the top is crisp and golden.

Stuffed peaches

you will need for 4 servings:

METRIC/IMPERIAL	
150 ml/¼ pint water	1 tablespoon castor sugar
125 g/4½ oz granulated sugar	1 egg white
4 large peaches (slightly underripe)	1 tablespoon Grand Marnier (optional)
50 g/2 oz ratafias	
25 g/1 oz ground almonds	

1 Bring the water and granulated sugar to the boil, stirring. Boil for 5 minutes without stirring.

2 Skin the peaches by dropping them into boiling water for 30–40 seconds. Remove and plunge into cold water. Cut the skinned peaches in halves and remove the stones.

3 Crush the ratafias and mix with the ground almonds and castor sugar. Bind with lightly beaten egg white and Grand Marnier, if used.

4 Fill the peach halves with the stuffing, mounding the tops. Place in a casserole, pour the syrup over them, cover the casserole and bake in a moderate oven (170°C, 325°, Gas Mark 3) for 25–30 minutes.

Note:

If a stronger flavour of Grand Marnier is desired, add 1–2 tablespoons to the syrup.

Baked mincemeat peaches

you will need for 4 servings:

METRIC/IMPERIAL	
822-g/1 lb 13-oz can cling peach halves	2 egg whites
mincemeat	100 g/4 oz castor sugar
brandy or sherry (optional)	

1 Drain the peaches and lay them in a heatproof dish, hollow side up. Fill and mound the centres with mincemeat, flavoured with brandy or sherry if liked.

2 Whip the egg whites stiffly with a little of the castor sugar and fold in the rest.

3 Pile on top of the peaches, covering the cut surfaces completely, and bake in a moderate oven (180°C,

350°F, Gas Mark 4) for 15–20 minutes, until the meringue is lightly browned.

Prickly peaches

you will need for 4 servings:
METRIC/IMPERIAL
4 ripe peaches
2 large egg whites
100 g/3½ oz castor
  sugar
8–10 blanched
  almonds

1 Drop the peaches into boiling water for 15–20 seconds, remove with a straining spoon, plunge into cold water and then skin. Stand them on a flat heatproof dish.
2 Whip the egg whites stiffly with a little of the sugar and fold in the rest. Cover the peaches completely with the meringue, leaving no holes.
3 Cut the almonds into long needles and stick 6–8 through the meringue into each peach.
4 Bake in a moderate oven (180°C, 350°F, Gas Mark 4) for 15–20 minutes until lightly browned.

Baked stuffed pineapple

you will need for 4 servings:
METRIC/IMPERIAL
1 large or 2 small
  pineapples
298-g/10½-oz can
  mandarin segments
  or red cherries
25 g/1 oz flaked
  almonds, toasted
2 tablespoons rum
  (optional)
castor sugar
butter

1 Cut the stalk end level so that the pineapple will stand upright. Trim the leaves and then cut off a slice from the top.
2 Scoop out the flesh, leaving the outside wall intact. Cut away the centre hard core and cut the rest of the flesh into 1-cm/½-inch pieces.
3 Drain the mandarin segments and cut each in half. Mix with the pineapple, almonds and rum, and sweeten to taste with sugar.
4 Fill the pineapple in layers, dotting each layer with butter. Replace the top and bake in a moderate oven (180°C, 350°F, Gas Mark 4) for 30 minutes.

Note:
A fresh peach, strawberries, or raspberries are also good in place of the mandarin.
For more spectacular serving, remove the top from the pineapple at table, pour in a little warm rum or brandy and set it alight.

Basic vanilla soufflé

Although it used to be traditional to tie a band of greased paper around a soufflé dish to project about 5 cm/2 inches above the rim, I much prefer to use a larger dish and dispense with the paper. However, it is important to use the correct size of soufflé dish for the quantity of ingredients.

you will need for 4 servings:
METRIC/IMPERIAL
40 g/1½ oz butter
40 g/1½ oz plain flour
scant 300 ml/9 fl oz
  milk
50 g/2 oz castor sugar
few drops vanilla
  essence
3 eggs, separated
1 extra egg white
  (optional)
pinch of salt
icing sugar

1 Prepare the dish first. Grease a generous 1-litre/2-pint (18-cm/7-inch) soufflé dish with melted butter and dust with castor sugar.
2 Melt the butter in a large saucepan. With a wooden spoon stir in the flour until well blended, gradually add the milk and bring to the boil, stirring continuously. Simmer for 1–2 minutes.
3 Remove from the heat and beat in the sugar and vanilla essence. Allow to cool a little, then beat in the egg yolks one at a time.
4 Whip the egg whites and salt until stiff and, with a metal spoon, gently but thoroughly fold them into the mixture. Be sure there are no lumps of egg white left or the soufflé will rise unevenly.
5 Turn into the prepared dish (it should be two-thirds full) and place in a moderately hot oven (200°C, 400°F, Gas Mark 6), then turn the heat down to moderate (190°C, 375°F, Gas Mark 5) and bake for 25–30 minutes, until well risen and nicely browned.
6 Dust with icing sugar and serve immediately.

Variations:
Chocolate soufflé Melt 50–75 g/2–3 oz plain chocolate in the milk before adding it to the panada. Add 2 tablespoons rum if liked.

Lemon or orange soufflé Omit vanilla essence and add the grated rind of 1 large or 2 small lemons or oranges with 75 g/3 oz sugar to the panada, and use the juice with the milk to make up to the correct quantity of liquid.

Coffee soufflé Use half milk and half strong black coffee. A teaspoon of coffee essence may also be added.

Soufflé au Grand Marnier

you will need for 4 servings:
METRIC/IMPERIAL
200 ml/7 fl oz milk
100 g/3½ oz vanilla
  sugar or castor
  sugar with ¼
  teaspoon vanilla
  essence
40 g/1½ oz butter
40 g/1½ oz plain flour
4 eggs, separated
1 extra egg yolk
2 tablespoons Grand
  Marnier (plus 4
  teaspoons for the
  plates if liked)

1 Prepare a scant 1·5-litre/2½-pint soufflé dish (see above).
2 Bring the milk and sugar almost to the boil, stirring. Remove from the heat and cool.
3 Melt 25 g/1 oz butter in a saucepan large enough to accommodate the beaten egg whites. Blend in the flour, pour in the milk and bring to the boil, stirring.
4 Remove from the heat and beat in the rest of the butter, the beaten egg yolks and the Grand Marnier.
5 Whip the egg whites stiffly and fold into the mixture.

6 Turn into the prepared soufflé dish and bake as stage 5 of the Basic vanilla soufflé (see page 19).
7 Pour a teaspoon of Grand Marnier onto each warm plate and quickly twist it around to cover the plate. Serve immediately.

Soufflé or fluffy omelette

you will need per person:

METRIC/IMPERIAL
2 eggs
2 teaspoons cold
  water
1 teaspoon castor
  sugar
15 g/½ oz butter
1–2 tablespoons jam,
  warmed

1 Separate the yolks and whites into two bowls.
2 Beat together the yolks, water and sugar with a wire whisk or wooden spoon until pale and creamy.
3 Place the butter in a small frying pan over a gentle heat and allow it to melt and become hot, then swivel the pan around to grease the sides as well.
4 Whip the egg whites stiffly, mix a tablespoonful into the yolks thoroughly and then fold in the rest. Turn into the pan and spread evenly.
5 Cook gently without stirring until the underside is a light golden brown, 4–5 minutes. Loosen the edge by running a spatula round the pan. If a very fluffy omelette is preferred, spread quickly with the jam, fold over, turn out onto a plate and serve immediately, sprinkled with castor sugar. If a lightly set and browned omelette is preferred, slip it under a moderate grill for a minute or two before adding the jam.

Variation:

Fluffy fruit omelette Add the grated rind of ½ an orange or lemon to the yolks, then spread the omelette with fruit purée in place of jam.

Lemon surprise pudding

you will need for 4 servings:

METRIC/IMPERIAL
50 g/2 oz butter or
  margarine
100 g/4 oz castor sugar
1 large lemon
2 eggs, separated
50 g/2 oz self-raising
  flour
250 ml/8 fl oz milk

1 Cream together the butter, sugar, and grated lemon rind.
2 Beat in the egg yolks, flour, lemon juice and milk.
3 Whip the egg whites stiffly and fold in.
4 Turn into a greased 900-ml/1½-pint pie or other heatproof dish.
5 Stand the dish in a roasting tin with hot water to come a quarter or half way up the dish (bain-marie) and bake in a moderately hot oven (190°C, 375°F, Gas Mark 5) for 40–45 minutes until risen and lightly browned on top. The pudding should have a spongy top with lemony custard sauce beneath.

Brandy oranges

you will need per person:

METRIC/IMPERIAL
1 orange
1–2 teaspoons castor
  sugar
2 teaspoons brandy
whipped cream

to decorate:
halved toasted
almonds

1 Remove all the skin and pith from the orange. Slice thinly, removing the pips.
2 Lay the slices in a heatproof dish. Sprinkle with the sugar and leave to marinate for 30 minutes.
3 Pour the brandy over them and heat through in the oven.
4 Place rough heaps of whipped cream on top, stick in the almonds and serve immediately.

Queen of puddings

you will need for 4 servings:

METRIC/IMPERIAL
450 ml/¾ pint milk
25 g/1 oz butter
finely grated rind of 1
  lemon
2 eggs, separated
75 g/3 oz soft
  breadcrumbs
100 g/4 oz castor sugar
3 tablespoons
  raspberry or
  strawberry jam

1 Warm the milk, butter, and lemon rind until the butter has melted.
2 Remove from the heat and beat in the egg yolks, breadcrumbs, and 25 g/1 oz of the sugar.
3 Pour into a greased generous 1-litre/2-pint ovenproof dish and leave to stand for 15–30 minutes.
4 Bake in a moderate oven (180°C, 350°F, Gas Mark 4) for 25–30 minutes until set.
5 Spread the jam over the pudding and if too thick warm it a little.
6 Whip the egg whites stiffly with a little of the remaining sugar and fold in the rest.
7 Pile the meringue on top of the jam and return to the oven for 15–20 minutes, until the meringue is lightly browned.

Jolly Johns

you will need for 4 servings:

METRIC/IMPERIAL
75 g/3 oz plain flour
1 teaspoon golden
  raising powder
50 g/2 oz castor sugar
25 g/1 oz desiccated
  coconut
65 g/2½ oz currants
40 g/1½ oz cut mixed
  peel
milk

1 Sieve the flour and raising powder into a basin.
2 Mix in the sugar, coconut, currants and mixed peel, and stir in enough milk to form a stiff batter.
3 Drop small balls of the batter into deep hot fat (180°C, 350°F) and fry until golden brown on both sides.
4 Drain on kitchen paper and serve sprinkled with castor sugar.

Butterscotch meringue pie

you will need for 4 servings:

METRIC/IMPERIAL
75 g/3 oz butter or margarine
65 g/2½ oz flour
568 ml/1 pint milk
175 g/6 oz granulated sugar
2 eggs, separated
75 g/3 oz castor sugar

1 Melt 50 g/2 oz of the butter, blend in the flour, add the milk and bring to the boil, stirring with a wire whisk. Boil for 2–3 minutes, remove from the heat and stir in 50 g/2 oz of the granulated sugar and the egg yolks.

2 In a small thick-bottomed saucepan melt the rest of the butter and granulated sugar together over a low heat and allow to bubble, stirring constantly, until a good dark brown. Remove immediately and stir into the sauce. Pour into a generous 1-litre/2-pint pie dish, greased round the sides.
3 Whip the egg whites stiffly with a little of the castor sugar and fold in the rest. Turn into the pie dish, making sure that the meringue touches the dish all round.
4 Bake in a moderate oven (180°C, 350°F, Gas Mark 4) for 15–20 minutes, until lightly browned.

Steamed and Boiled Puddings

These fall into two main categories: sponge or cake mixtures, and suet.

Those made by the creaming method as for cakes, with butter or margarine as the fat, are lighter and softer in texture than those made with suet. Those made with suet as the fat are usually made from commercially cleaned and packaged shredded suet. But if fresh butcher's suet is used, it must first be rendered down and cleaned thoroughly, then finely chopped.

To render: Cut the fat into small pieces, turn into a saucepan, cover with cold water and bring to the boil. Boil until nearly all the water has evaporated, then simmer more slowly, stirring occasionally, until clear and any pieces of skin are shrivelled and brown. Strain into a bowl through a strainer with a J-cloth on top. When cold, scrape off any impurities which may have formed at the bottom.

General rules for steamed or boiled puddings
1 Grease the pudding bowl thoroughly with margarine or white fat, or brush with oil, dust with flour and shake out surplus.
2 Fill the bowl not more than two-thirds full to allow the pudding to rise.
The exception is for rich plum or Christmas puddings which may be filled to within 2·5 cm/1 inch or less of the rim.
3 If the pudding is for immediate consumption, cover it with a double thickness of greased greaseproof paper or foil and tie down, or use a special aluminium basin with its own lid.
If a rich fruit pudding is to be kept, remove the covering, wipe the rim, and re-cover with first greaseproof paper and then foil, as the acid in the fruit will eat through the foil if it is allowed to come into contact with it.
4 Have the water boiling fast when the steamer containing the pudding is placed over it, then lower the heat but be sure that the water never goes off the boil during cooking or the pudding will sink and be heavy. Replenish with *boiling* water if necessary. If no steamer is available, place an upturned saucer or pastry cutter in a saucepan, place the bowl on it and see that the water comes one-third to half way up the sides of the bowl.
5 For boiled puddings, tie the roll in a floured cloth, allowing room for the pudding to swell, and tuck in the ends well.
6 Left-over pieces of pudding can be resteamed to their original lightness by simply replacing them in a bowl and steaming for 30–45 minutes. Or they can be cut into slices and fried (see page 8). This is particularly good for any kind of fruit pudding.

Steamed sponge (or Canary) pudding

you will need for 4 servings:

METRIC/IMPERIAL
175 g/6 oz self-raising flour
pinch of salt
100 g/4 oz butter or margarine
100 g/4 oz castor or granulated sugar
2 eggs
few drops vanilla essence
1–2 tablespoons milk

1 Sift the flour and salt together.
2 Cream the butter and sugar until light and fluffy, beat in the eggs and vanilla essence. Stir in the flour and add sufficient milk to give a soft consistency.
3 Turn into the prepared (see above) generous 1-litre/2-pint pudding bowl and level the top.
4 Cover (see above) and steam for 1½–1¾ hours. Turn out and serve with Jam sauce (see page 90).

Variations:
Jam cap sponge pudding Place 3-4 tablespoons of jam at the bottom of the prepared bowl, then proceed from stage 1. When turned out the jam will flow down the sides as well.
Ginger sponge pudding Sift 1-2 teaspoons ground ginger with the flour. 50-75 g/2-3 oz chopped preserved ginger may also be added if liked. Or 1-2 tablespoons 'Ginger-up' may be used in place of the milk. Proceed from stage 1. Serve with warm diluted golden syrup or custard flavoured with ginger.

Chocolate sponge pudding Substitute 25 g/1 oz cocoa powder for 25 g/1 oz of the flour and sift in ¼ teaspoon baking powder. Proceed from stage 1. Serve with Chocolate sauce (see page 89–90) or chocolate flavoured custard.

Marmalade sponge pudding Proceed to stage 2, then substitute 2 tablespoons chopped marmalade for the milk. Marmalade can also be placed in the bottom of the bowl as for Jam cap (see page 21).

Coconut sponge pudding Substitute 50-75 g/2-3 oz desiccated coconut for 50/2 oz of the flour and sift in ½ teaspoon baking powder. Proceed from stage 1.

Fruit sponge pudding Place a layer of stewed fruit or drained canned fruit at the bottom of the bowl. Proceed from stage 1.

Serve with the chosen fruit or canned fruit, chopped and thickened with arrowroot or cornflour (allow 1 tablespoon for 250 ml/8 fl oz liquid). Bring to the boil and boil for 2-3 minutes.

Dried fruit sponge pudding Add 75 g/3 oz mixed dried fruit to the flour. Proceed from stage 1 to 2, then substitute 1 tablespoon lemon juice for the milk. Serve with warm diluted golden syrup, or golden syrup and black treacle mixed.

Castle puddings Half fill 10 greased castle pudding moulds with the basic mixture (see page 21) and bake in a moderate oven (180°C, 350°F, Gas Mark 4) for 20-22 minutes until well risen and golden.

Apricot pudding

you will need for 4 servings:

METRIC/IMPERIAL

125 g/4½ oz dried apricots	100 g/4 oz butter or margarine
water	100 g/4 oz castor sugar
175 g/6 oz self-raising flour	2 eggs
pinch of salt	few drops vanilla essence

1 Soak the apricots in water to cover for several hours or overnight. Drain and keep the liquid. Reserve 4 apricots for the sauce (see below) and from the remainder leave one whole, cut 3 into halves, and chop the rest.
2 Sift the flour and salt together.
3 Cream the butter and sugar until light and fluffy, beat in the eggs and vanilla essence.
4 Stir in the flour and chopped apricots and sufficient of the apricot liquid to give a soft consistency.
5 Place the whole apricot in the centre of the base of the prepared (see page 21) generous 1-litre/2-pint bowl and arrange the 6 halves up the sides around it. Carefully pour in the sponge mixture.
6 Cover and tie down (see page 21) and steam for 1¾-2 hours.
7 Turn out and serve with the apricot sauce.

Apricot sauce

METRIC/IMPERIAL

4 (reserved) apricots	250 ml/8 fl oz apricot liquid
1 tablespoon arrowroot or cornflour	25 g/1 oz sugar

1 Chop the apricots finely and make the arrowroot into a smooth cream with a little of the liquid.
2 Put everything into a small saucepan, bring to the boil and boil for 2-3 minutes until clear.

Banana pudding

you will need for 4-5 servings:

METRIC/IMPERIAL

75 g/3 oz butter or margarine	3 small bananas
75 g/3 oz castor or granulated sugar	175 g/6 oz self-raising flour
1 egg	½ teaspoon baking powder
few drops vanilla essence	300 ml/½ pint custard

1 Cream the butter and sugar together until fluffy.
2 Beat in the egg and vanilla essence.
3 Mash 2 bananas well and stir into the mixture with the sieved flour and baking powder.
4 Turn into a prepared (see page 21) generous 1-litre/2-pint pudding bowl. Cover (see page 21) and steam for 2 hours.
5 Mash the third banana and rub through a sieve into the custard, or blend together in a liquidizer. Serve with the pudding.

Honey date pudding

you will need for 5-6 servings:

METRIC/IMPERIAL

175 g/6 oz self-raising flour	3 tablespoons (75 g/3 oz) honey
pinch of salt	2 eggs, beaten
75 g/3 oz butter or margarine	175 g/6 oz stoned dates, chopped
grated rind of ½ lemon	

1 Sift the flour and salt together.
2 Cream the butter and lemon rind until light, then beat in the honey.
3 Gradually stir in the eggs and flour alternately, stir in the dates and if too stiff to drop off the spoon easily, add a little milk or more lemon juice.
4 Put into a prepared (see page 21) generous 1-litre/2-pint pudding bowl and level the top. Cover (see page 21) and steam for 2 hours.
5 Turn out and serve with Honey-syrup sauce (see page 90).

Rainbow pudding

you will need for 4-5 servings:

METRIC/IMPERIAL

150 g/5 oz self-raising flour	1 tablespoon milk
pinch of salt	few drops green colouring
100 g/4 oz margarine	few drops red colouring
100 g/4 oz granulated sugar	2 teaspoons cocoa powder
2 eggs	
few drops vanilla essence	

1 Sift the flour and salt together.
2 Cream the margarine and sugar until light and fluffy, beat in the eggs and vanilla essence.
3 Stir in the flour and add the milk if necessary to give a soft consistency.
4 Divide the mixture into three. Add the green colouring to one part; the red colouring to another; and the cocoa to the last.
5 Put the green portion into a prepared (see page 21) generous 1-litre/2-pint bowl and level it. Spread the pink portion over it, and top with the chocolate portion.
6 Cover (see page 21) and steam for 1¾ hours.
7 Turn out and serve with Sherry sauce (see page 91) or sherry flavoured custard.

Orange foam pudding

you will need for 4 servings:

METRIC/IMPERIAL

75 g/3 oz butter or margarine	50 g/2 oz soft breadcrumbs
100 g/4 oz castor sugar	75 g/3 oz self-raising flour
2 egg yolks	pinch of salt
2 small oranges	

Apple meringue topping

1 dessert apple	50 g/2 oz castor sugar
1 egg white	

1 Cream the butter and sugar together until light.
2 Beat in the egg yolks and the grated rinds and juice of the oranges. Stir in the breadcrumbs and sifted flour and salt.
3 Put into a prepared (see page 21) 900-ml/1½-pint pudding bowl. Cover (see page 21) and steam for 1 hour.
4 To make the apple meringue, grate the apple and whip the egg white until stiff. Fold the apple and sugar into the egg white.
5 Turn out the pudding and serve topped with Apple meringue.

Steamed Suet Puddings

Basic mixture I
you will need for 4-5 servings:

METRIC/IMPERIAL

225 g/8 oz self-raising flour	75 g/3 oz castor sugar
⅛ teaspoon salt	150 ml/¼ pint (approx) milk
½ teaspoon baking powder	3-4 tablespoons golden syrup or jam
100 g/4 oz shredded suet	

Basic mixture 2

150 g/5 oz self-raising flour	75 g/3 oz castor sugar
⅛ teaspoon salt	100 g/4 oz shredded suet
½ teaspoon baking powder	150 ml/¼ pint (approx) milk
75 g/3 oz soft breadcrumbs	3-4 tablespoons golden syrup or jam

1 For basic mixture 1, sieve the flour, salt and baking powder together.
2 Stir in the suet and sugar and sufficient milk to give a soft dropping consistency.
3 For basic mixture 2, proceed as for basic pudding 1.
4 Place the golden syrup or jam in the base of a prepared (see page 21) generous 1-litre/2-pint pudding bowl, put in the pudding mixture and level the top.
5 Cover (see page 21) and steam for 2 hours.
OR
Make the dough a little drier, roll out on a floured board and spread with jam. (If using golden syrup mix with some soft breadcrumbs.) Roll up and wrap loosely in greased greaseproof paper and foil, sealing the ends well, and steam for 2 hours.

Spotted Dick or dog

you will need for 4-5 servings:

METRIC/IMPERIAL

100 g/3½ oz self-raising flour	75 g/3 oz castor sugar
pinch of salt	100 g/3½ oz shredded suet
100 g/3½ oz soft breadcrumbs	175 g/6 oz currants
	milk

1 Sift the flour and salt into a basin.
2 Stir in the breadcrumbs, sugar, suet and currants and then sufficient milk to give a fairly soft dough.
3 Turn onto a floured board and form into a roll.
4 Wrap loosely in greased greaseproof paper and boil, or in a greased and floured pudding cloth. Seal the ends securely and steam or boil for 2 hours. Serve with custard of sweetened white sauce flavoured with grated lemon rind, cinnamon, or nutmeg.

Mixed fruit pudding

you will need for 6 servings:

METRIC/IMPERIAL

150 g/5 oz self-raising flour	1 egg
⅛ teaspoon salt	1 tablespoon black treacle
½ teaspoon baking powder	milk
75 g/3 oz soft breadcrumbs	175 g/6 oz mixed dried fruit and chopped candied peel, mixed
50 g/2 oz castor sugar	
100 g/4 oz shredded suet	

1 Sift the flour, salt, and baking powder into a basin.
2 Mix in the breadcrumbs, sugar and suet.
3 Beat the egg with the black treacle and stir into the dry ingredients with sufficient milk to give a soft consistency.
4 Stir in the dried fruit and put into a prepared (see page 21) generous 1-litre/2-pint pudding bowl.
5 Cover (see page 21) and steam for 2¼-2½ hours.
6 Turn out and serve sprinkled with sugar and/or diluted golden syrup and black treacle mixed, or custard flavoured with cinnamon, nutmeg, or ginger.

Kruger's hat

you will need for 5-6 servings:

METRIC/IMPERIAL

200 g/7 oz self-raising
  flour
pinch of salt
75 g/3 oz soft
  breadcrumbs

125 g/4½ oz shredded
  suet
cold water
golden syrup

1 Sift the flour and salt into a basin.
2 Mix in the breadcrumbs, suet, and enough cold water to give a pliable dough.
3 Turn onto a floured board and knead lightly to remove cracks. Cut in half.
4 Roll out one half into a circle large enough to line a prepared (see page 21) generous 1-litre/2-pint pudding bowl, and place in the bowl. Cut out a quarter in a triangle from the centre outwards and add to the rest of the dough. Overlap the two cut edges in the bowl and seal together firmly with cold water.
5 Roll out the rest of the dough into circles from small to large to fit the lined bowl.
6 Place 1 tablespoon of golden syrup in the bottom of the bowl, cover with the smallest circle of pastry, add more syrup, and continue thus until the last circle of pastry is in position. Brush around the edge of the last circle with cold water, fold down the piece lining the bowl onto it and seal firmly.
7 Cover (see page 21) and steam for 2¼-2½ hours.
8 Turn out onto a dish deep enough to hold the syrup which will ooze out.

Delaware pudding

you will need for 4-5 servings:

METRIC/IMPERIAL

150 g/5 oz self-raising
  flour
pinch of salt
75 g/3 oz soft
  breadcrumbs

100 g/4 oz shredded
  suet
cold water

filling:

2 dessert apples
50 g/2 oz soft brown
  sugar
25 g/1 oz butter or
  margarine

½ lemon
25 g/1 oz chopped
  mixed peel
1 teaspoon mixed
  spice

1 Sift the flour and salt into a basin.
2 Mix in the breadcrumbs, suet, and sufficient cold water to give a pliable dough.
3 Turn onto a floured board and knead lightly to remove cracks. Roll out and cut into circles from small to large to fit a prepared (see page 21) generous 1-litre/2-pint pudding bowl.
4 To make the filling, peel and core the apples and chop finely. Cream the butter and sugar until light and beat in the grated rind and juice of the lemon. Stir in the rest of the ingredients.
5 Place the smallest circle at the bottom of the bowl, cover with a little of the filling and continue with alternate layers, ending with pastry.
6 Cover (see page 21) and steam for 2 hours. Serve with Ginger-up sauce or ginger flavoured custard.

Steamed fruit pudding

you will need for 5-6 servings:

METRIC/IMPERIAL

150 g/5 oz self-raising
  flour (or 225 g/8 oz
  flour and no
  breadcrumbs)
pinch of salt
75 g/3 oz soft
  breadcrumbs
100 g/4 oz shredded
  suet

cold water
prepared fruit (apples,
  rhubarb,
  blackcurrants,
  gooseberries,
  plums, etc.)

1 Sift the flour and salt into a basin.
2 Stir in the breadcrumbs, suet, and enough cold water to give a pliable dough.
3 Turn onto a floured board and knead lightly to remove cracks. Roll out to a scant 0.5 cm/¼ inch in thickness and cut into a circle slightly larger than sufficient to line a generous 1-litre/2-pint pudding bowl. Cut out a quarter in a triangle from the centre outwards and reserve.
4 With the large piece line a prepared (see page 21) bowl to stand just above the edge. Trim the top and add to the reserved piece. Overlap the two cut edges in the bowl and seal together firmly with cold water.
5 Fill the bowl with layers of the chosen fruit and sugar to taste.
6 Roll out the remaining pastry into a circle to fit the top. Place in position, brush the edge of the upstanding piece with cold water, bring it down onto the lid and press together to seal firmly.
7 Cover (see page 21) and steam for 2-2½ hours.
8 Turn out onto a dish deep enough to hold the juice when the pudding is cut.

Date pudding

you will need for 5-6 servings:

METRIC/IMPERIAL

225 g/8 oz stoneless
  dates
100 g/4 oz self-raising
  flour
75 g/3 oz soft
  breadcrumbs
75 g/3 oz shredded
  suet
50 g/2 oz soft brown
  sugar

⅛ teaspoon salt
¼ teaspoon ground
  cinnamon
½ teaspoon grated
  nutmeg
½ teaspoon baking
  powder
1 egg
150 ml/¼ pint (approx)
  milk

1 Cut the dates into fairly small pieces.
2 Mix all the dry ingredients together, including the dates.
3 Beat the egg with most of the milk and stir into the dry ingredients to give a soft consistency, adding a little more milk if necessary.
4 Turn into a prepared (see page 21) generous 1-litre/2-pint pudding bowl. Cover (see page 21) and steam for 2½ hours.
5 Turn out and serve with warm diluted golden syrup, custard, or any sweet sauce.

Winter pudding

you will need for 4 servings

METRIC/IMPERIAL
75 g/3 oz soft
 breadcrumbs
150 g/5 oz shredded
 suet
¾ teaspoon ground
 ginger

175 g/6 oz golden
 syrup
1 egg
1 teaspoon
 bicarbonate of soda
2 tablespoons milk

1 In a basin mix together the breadcrumbs, suet, and ginger.
2 Warm the syrup just enough to make it runny, and stir in the beaten egg and bicarbonate dissolved in the milk.
3 Mix into the dry ingredients thoroughly.
4 Put into a prepared (see page 21) 900-ml/1½-pint pudding bowl.
5 Cover (see page 21) and steam for 2 hours.
6 Turn out and serve with warmed golden syrup diluted with a little water and lemon juice, or with single cream.

Sussex pond pudding

you will need for 4 servings:

METRIC/IMPERIAL
225 g/8 oz butter or
 margarine
115 g/4 oz demerara
 sugar
175 g/6 oz self-raising
 flour
¼ teaspoon salt

40 g/1½ oz castor
 sugar
65 g/2½ oz shredded
 suet
40 g/1½ oz currants
cold water

1 Cream the butter and demerara sugar together, roll into a ball and leave in a refrigerator to harden.
2 Sift the flour and salt into a basin and stir in the castor sugar, suet, and currants. Make into a stiff dough with cold water.
3 Divide in half and roll the pieces out into approximately 15-cm/6-inch circles.
4 Place the butter ball in the centre of one piece and draw up the sides. Cover the top with the second piece and seal the join together firmly with cold water.
5 Wrap in greased foil, place in a pan of boiling water and boil for 2 hours, or steam for 2½ hours.
6 Turn out into a deep dish to accommodate the syrup which will run out into a pond.

Chester pudding

you will need for 5 servings:

METRIC/IMPERIAL
125 g/4½ oz
 self-raising flour
100 g/3½ oz soft
 breadcrumbs
100 g/3½ oz shredded
 suet

50 g/2 oz castor sugar
125 g/4½ oz
 blackcurrant jam
150 ml/¼ pint milk
1 teaspoon
 bicarbonate of soda

1 Mix the dry ingredients together in a basin.
2 Make a well in the centre and put in the jam.
3 Warm the milk and dissolve the bicarbonate in it, pour onto the jam and mix everything together thoroughly.
4 Put into a prepared (see page 21) generous 1-litre/2-pint pudding bowl.
5 Cover (see page 21) and steam for 1¾-2 hours.
6 Turn out and serve with hot diluted jam or custard flavoured with the jam.

Baroness pudding

you will need for 6 servings:

METRIC/IMPERIAL
150 g/5 oz self-raising
 flour
50 g/2 oz soft
 breadcrumbs
100 g/4 oz shredded
 suet
175 g/6 oz seedless
 raisins
50 g/2 oz currants

50 g/2 oz cut mixed
 peel
25 g/1 oz almonds,
 coarsely chopped
1½ teaspoons
 bicarbonate of soda
200 ml/7 fl oz (approx)
 milk

1 In a basin mix together the flour, breadcrumbs, suet, fruit and almonds.
2 Dissolve the bicarbonate in most of the milk and stir into the dry ingredients, adding a little more milk if necessary to give a soft consistency.
3 Turn into a prepared (see page 21) generous 1-litre/2-pint pudding bowl.
4 Cover (see page 21) and steam for 2¼-2½ hours.
5 Turn out and serve with almond flavoured custard or any sweet sauce.

Jamaica pudding

you will need for 4-5 servings:

METRIC/IMPERIAL
100 g/4 oz self-raising
 flour
100 g/4 oz semolina
50 g/2 oz soft dark
 brown sugar
50 g/2 oz shredded
 suet

½ teaspoon
 bicarbonate of soda
milk
1 tablespoon golden
 syrup
1 tablespoon rum

1 In a basin mix the flour, semolina, sugar and suet.
2 Dissolve the bicarbonate in a little milk, then stir in the golden syrup and rum.
3 Mix into the dry ingredients and if not soft enough to drop off a spoon easily, add a little more milk.
4 Put into a prepared (see page 21) generous 1-litre/2-pint pudding bowl.
5 Cover (see page 21) and steam for 2½ hours.
6 Turn out and serve with hot golden syrup flavoured with rum.

Speedy jam pudding

you will need for 5 servings:

METRIC/IMPERIAL

150 g/5 oz self-raising flour	4 tablespoons milk
75 g/3 oz shredded suet	1 teaspoon bicarbonate of soda
50 g/2 oz sugar	175 g/6 oz plum or other jam

1 In a basin mix the flour, suet, and sugar.
2 Warm the milk slightly and dissolve the bicarbonate in it.
3 Stir the milk and jam into the dry ingredients and put into a prepared (see page 21) generous 1-litre/2-pint pudding bowl.
4 Cover (see page 21) and steam for 2 hours.
5 Turn out and serve with diluted jam.

Rich Christmas puddings

you will need for 2 puddings of 5-6 servings each:

METRIC/IMPERIAL

100 g/4 oz each large stoned raisins, cut in halves, and seedless raisins (or use all seedless)	175 g/6 oz soft brown sugar
225 g/8 oz sultanas	225 g/8 oz shredded suet
225 g/8 oz currants	25 g/1 oz grated carrot
75 g/3 oz cut mixed peel	3 eggs
50 g/2 oz almonds, chopped	¾ tablespoon black treacle
75 g/3 oz self-raising flour	grated rind of ½ orange
¼ teaspoon salt	grated rind of ½ small lemon
1 teaspoon mixed cake spice	6 tablespoons Guinness or other stout
¼ teaspoon grated nutmeg	2½-3 tablespoons brandy or sherry
150 g/5 oz soft breadcrumbs	

1 Put the fruit and almonds in a large basin.
2 Sift together the flour, salt, and spices and mix into the fruit. Stir in the breadcrumbs, brown sugar, suet and carrot.
3 Beat the eggs with the black treacle, grated rinds and the stout, and mix into the dry ingredients thoroughly.
4 Leave overnight, then stir in the brandy or sherry and mix well.
5 Turn into 2 prepared (see page 21) 900-ml/1½-pint pudding bowls.
6 Cover (see page 21) and steam for 6 hours. If no steamer is available, place each bowl on an upturned saucer in separate saucepans, with the water to come one-third to half way up the sides of the bowls.
Note:
Remove the puddings from the pan and allow to cool, then remove the coverings and replace with clean ungreased greaseproof paper. If stored in a cool dry place these puddings will keep for a year.
To serve: Re-cover as before (see page 21) and steam for 2–3 hours. Serve with brandy or rum butter (see page 21) or custard flavoured with brandy, sherry, or rum.

Prune Christmas puddings

you will need for 2 puddings of 5-6 servings each:

METRIC/IMPERIAL

125 g/4½ oz prunes after stoning	1 teaspoon mixed cake spice
150 g/5 oz seedless and stoned halved raisins, mixed (or use all seedless)	175 g/6 oz shredded suet
200 g/7 oz sultanas	175 g/6 oz soft brown sugar
200 g/7 oz currants	150 g/5 oz soft breadcrumbs
100 g/4 oz cut mixed peel	2 eggs
25 g/1 oz nuts, chopped	6 tablespoons milk and water, mixed
50 g/2 oz self-raising flour	grated rind and juice of ½ lemon
½ teaspoon baking powder	2 tablespoons brandy or sherry
½ teaspoon salt	

1 Cut the prunes into small pieces.
2 Put all the fruit, peel, and nuts into a large basin.
3 Sift together the flour, baking powder, salt and spices, and add to the fruit. Stir in the suet, sugar and breadcrumbs.
4 Beat the eggs with the milk and water and grated rind and juice of the lemon, and mix into the pudding thoroughly.
5 Leave overnight, then stir in the brandy or sherry.
6 Turn into 2 prepared (see page 21) 900-ml/1½-pint pudding bowls.
7 Cover (see page 21) and steam for 6 hours.
Note:
Follow instructions for storing and serving Rich Christmas pudding (see above).

Australian Christmas pudding

you will need for 6-7 servings:

METRIC/IMPERIAL

225 g/8 oz large stoned raisins (or use seedless)	½ teaspoon ground nutmeg
75 g/3 oz glacé cherries	50 g/2 oz cut mixed peel
125 g/4½ oz soft breadcrumbs	2 large eggs
75 g/3 oz shredded suet	grated rind of 1 orange
75 g/3 oz soft dark brown sugar	2 tablespoons stout
½ teaspoon bicarbonate of soda	1 tablespoon brandy

1 If stoned raisins are used, cut into halves. Cut the cherries into halves or quarters.
2 Mix all the dry ingredients together well and stir in the fruit.
3 Beat the eggs with the grated orange rind, stout and brandy, and stir into the pudding.
4 Put into a prepared (see page 21) generous 1-litre/2-pint pudding bowl.
5 Cover (see page 21) and steam for 5 hours.
Note:
Follow note instructions for storing and serving Rich Christmas pudding (see above).

Time-saving plum pudding

you will need for 8 servings:

METRIC/IMPERIAL

0.75 kg/1½ lb fruit cake	1 tablespoon black
2 tablespoons dark	treacle
marmalade	½ teaspoon mixed
225-275 g/8-10 oz	cake spice
mincemeat	2 eggs
50 g/2 oz cut mixed	2-3 tablespoons stout
peel (optional)	or milk

1 Crumble the cake into a basin.
2 Cut the peel in the marmalade finely and stir into the cake crumbs with the mincemeat, mixed peel, treacle, mixed spice and well-beaten eggs.

3 Stir in enough stout to give a soft but not sloppy consistency.
4 Put into a prepared (see page 21) generous 1-litre/2-pint pudding bowl.
5 Cover (see page 21) and steam for 2½-3 hours.
Note:
It is best to make this pudding 2-3 weeks in advance, and then give it 1 hour's steaming before serving. Follow the note instructions for storing and serving Rich Christmas pudding (see page 26).

Cold Sweets

There is a limitless number of cold sweets throughout the world, each nation having its own favourites. Many are based upon the varieties of fruit grown in that particular country, or imported from other parts of the globe.

Cold desserts are a boon to hostesses and mothers because they can be prepared or made ahead. This also allows the textures and flavours to blend and mellow.

Many are set with gelatine which sometimes holds terror for the inexperienced. But this need not be so if a few simple points are understood and adhered to, the most important being to measure the quantity of gelatine very accurately or the finished dish may be completely spoilt.

The dissolved gelatine and mixture to which it is added should both be roughly at the same temperature.

Never pour hot dissolved gelatine into a cold liquid without stirring vigorously as you do so, or the gelatine will set immediately and so form lumps of 'ropes.'

To dissolve the modern powdered gelatine, there is no need to soak it first. The simplest way is to place the required quantity in a cup and pour over it the amount of boiling water or hot liquid stated in the recipe, then stir occasionally until it is completely dissolved and clear. The quantity of gelatine needed to set a jelly for turning out is normally 21 g/¾ oz (2 tablespoons) per 600 ml/1 pint liquid. But if the weather is warm and no refrigerator is available, increase the amount of gelatine by at least half. For a soufflé or mousse, which does not have to be turned out, it is better to use only 2 teaspoons (15 g/¼ oz) or the texture will be stiff and unpalatable instead of light and fluffy.

Jelly moulds should first be rinsed out with cold water before the liquid jelly is poured in. To unmould, run a knife blade around the inside edge to loosen it. Fill a large basin with hot water for a glass or china mould, or warm water for a metal one, and hold the mould in it up to the rim for a few moments. Have a serving dish ready wetted with cold water, to allow the jelly to

be moved slightly after turning out if it is not absolutely centred on the dish. Remove the mould from the water and quickly dry the base. Place the dish on top, turn right side up, and give a sharp jerk to loosen the jelly. If it does not turn out, repeat the process. If the mould is held in the hot water for too long, the jelly will begin to melt and be unsightly when unmoulded. There is often confusion over the difference between a soufflé and a mousse. In my opinion a soufflé has only egg whites to lighten it, whereas a mousse includes cream and is therefore a richer sweet, but there is no hard and fast rule. Soured cream is another item which seems to confuse. This is commercially sour*ed* cream with the same fat content as single cream, namely 18%. It is not the same in texture or flavour as *sour* cream, in other words fresh cream made sour by the addition of lemon juice or vinegar.

Junket

you will need for 4 servings:

METRIC/IMPERIAL
568 ml/1 pint milk
1 tablespoon sugar
1 teaspoon rennet (or
  as directed on the
  packet)

1 Heat the milk until just warm (38°-65°C/100°-150°F). If the milk is hotter than this the junket will not set.
2 Remove from the heat, add the sugar and stir until dissolved.
3 Pour into a serving dish and leave in a warm place to set.

Note:
Rennet does not enjoy a long shelf life and loses its setting power. If it does not set, warm again and add more rennet.

Variations:
1 Sprinkle the top with grated nutmeg.
2 Add vanilla or almond essence to the milk.

3 Spread lightly whipped whipping cream flavoured with rum, brandy or a liqueur over the top and sprinkle with grated nutmeg, or castor sugar and cinnamon mixed.

Old English syllabub

you will need for 4-5 servings:

METRIC/IMPERIAL

1 orange	3 tablespoons
150 ml/¼ pint white wine	marmalade (with the peel chopped)
25 g/1 oz castor sugar	to decorate:
300 ml/½ pint double cream	A twist of orange or decorative wafer

1 Grate the rind of the orange and squeeze out the juice.
2 Turn into a basin with the wine, sugar and cream.
3 Whisk all together with a rotary or electric beater until the mixture forms peaks when the whisk is lifted up.
4 Gently fold in the marmalade, spoon into sundae glasses and leave in a refrigerator or cold place for several hours.
5 Put a twist of orange or a decorative wafer on top of each.

Variation:

Simple English syllabub

300 ml/½ pint double cream	75 g/3 oz castor sugar finely grated rind and juice of 1 small lemon
150 ml/¼ pint brandy and sherry or Madeira mixed, or sweet white wine	

1 Turn everything into a bowl and whisk with a rotary or electric beater until thick.
2 Spoon into sundae glasses and leave in a cold place for several hours.
3 Serve with a brandy snap or ice cream wafer in each.

Caramel custard or crème caramel

you will need for 4 servings:

METRIC/IMPERIAL

100 g/4 oz granulated sugar	25 g/1 oz castor sugar few drops vanilla essence
water	
4 eggs (or 2 eggs plus 2 yolks)	600 ml/1 pint milk

1 First prepare the mould with caramel. Put the granulated sugar into a small saucepan and just cover with water. Bring to the boil, stirring until the sugar is completely dissolved. Boil without further stirring to a rich golden brown (watch carefully because if allowed to become too dark the caramel will be bitter).
2 Pour immediately into a 15-cm/6-inch ungreased cake tin, or into individual heatproof moulds, and turn around quickly so that the caramel coats the bottom and up the sides a little before it sets.
3 In a basin whisk the eggs with the castor sugar and a few drops of vanilla essence, then whisk in the milk.

4 Strain carefully over the cold caramel.
5 Place the tin or moulds, covered with foil or greaseproof paper, in a tin containing a generous 1 cm/½ inch of warm water (bain-marie) and bake in a moderate oven (170°C, 325°F, Gas Mark 3) for 40-60 minutes, depending upon the size of the moulds, until just set in the centre.
6 Leave until cold (preferably the following day), loosen the edge all round with a knife and turn out into a dish sufficiently deep to contain the caramel.

Swiss caramel cream

you will need for 4 servings:

METRIC/IMPERIAL

25 g/1 oz cornflour	2 tablespoon water
600 ml/1 pint evaporated milk diluted according to can instructions, or fresh milk	2 eggs, separated
	to decorate:
	chopped hazelnuts or walnuts
75 g/3 oz granulated sugar	

1 Make the cornflour into a smooth paste with a little of the milk, add the rest and bring to the boil, stirring. Boil for 1-2 minutes.
2 Meanwhile bring the sugar and water to the boil in a small saucepan, stirring only until the sugar is dissolved, then allow to boil without further stirring until the caramel turns a golden brown. Remove at once from the heat and whisk into the milk sauce.
3 Beat in the egg yolks one at a time and leave until cold.
4 Shortly before serving, stir in the stiffly beaten egg whites and pour into sundae glasses.
5 Decorate by sprinkling with chopped nuts.

Caramel mould

you will need for 4 servings:

METRIC/IMPERIAL

75 g/3 oz ground rice	1½ tablespoons golden syrup
500 ml/18 fl oz milk	
1 tablespoon black treacle	

1 Make the rice into a smooth paste with a little of the milk.
2 Put in a saucepan with the rest of the milk, treacle and golden syrup. Bring to the boil and boil for 5-6 minutes, stirring continuously.
3 Turn into a greased (with oil) 900-ml/1½-pint ring or other mould and allow to set.
4 Turn out and pour Caramel sauce (see page 90) over it.

Stone cream

you will need for 4 servings:

METRIC/IMPERIAL
150 ml/¼ pint double cream
150 ml/¼ pint milk
1 tablespoon sugar
few drops vanilla essence
2 tablespoons boiling water
2 teaspoons gelatine
jam or lemon curd
1 egg white
to decorate:
chopped nuts, glacé cherries, angelica, or decorative wafer biscuits

1 Whip the cream and gradually stir in the milk, sugar, and vanilla essence.
2 Pour the boiling water over the gelatine in a cup and stir occasionally until completely dissolved and smooth. Pour into the cream while stirring vigorously.
3 Cover the base of 4 sundae glasses with jam or lemon curd. Fold the whipped egg white into the cream and pour it over the jam. Leave to set in a refrigerator.
4 Decorate with chopped nuts, glacé cherries and angelica, or put a decorative wafer biscuit in each glass.

Norwegian cream

you will need for 4 servings:

METRIC/IMPERIAL
2-3 tablespoons apricot jam
3 eggs
1 tablespoon castor sugar
½ teaspoon vanilla essence
450 ml/¾ pint milk
150 ml/¼ pint double or whipping cream
25-50 g/1-2 oz chocolate

1 Spread jam over the bottom of a 900-ml/1½-pint soufflé dish.
2 Break 2 whole eggs and 1 egg yolk into a bowl and cream with the sugar and vanilla essence until light and fluffy.
3 Pour on the hot milk, stir well and strain into the soufflé dish. Cover with foil.
4 Stand the dish in a tin containing hot water to come half way up the dish (bain-marie) and bake in a moderate oven (180°C, 350°F, Gas Mark 4) for 50 minutes. Leave to get quite cold.
5 Whip the remaining egg white stiffly and fold in the lightly whipped cream.
6 Grate chocolate to cover the custard, pile cream on top and grate more chocolate coarsely over the cream.
Note:
The base can be cooked a day ahead and the cream added when required.

Melbourne nut cream

you will need for 6 servings:

METRIC/IMPERIAL
600 ml/1 pint water
4 teaspoons gelatine
large can sweetened condensed milk
50 g/2 oz desiccated coconut
50 g/2 oz mixed nuts, chopped
12 glacé cherries, chopped
⅛ teaspoon vanilla essence
to decorate:
halved glacé cherries and angelica 'leaves'

1 Bring less than half the water to the boil, remove from the heat, sprinkle the gelatine over it and stir occasionally until completely dissolved and smooth.
2 Pour into a large basin with the rest of the water and leave until just beginning to set around the edges, then whisk with a wire whisk and stir in the condensed milk, coconut, nuts, cherries, and vanilla essence.
3 Pour into a 900-ml/1½-pint ring or other mould rinsed out with cold water and leave to set.
4 Turn out and decorate with glacé cherries and angelica 'leaves'. If made in a ring mould, the centre may be filled with whipped cream.

Sagou (sago) a la Plaza

you will need for 4-5 servings:

METRIC/IMPERIAL
900 ml/1½ pints milk
1 vanilla pod or ¼ teaspoon vanilla essence
50 g/2 oz sago
50 g/2 oz granulated sugar
1 egg yolk
to decorate:
whipped cream and chopped glacé fruits or nuts

1 Bring the milk to the boil with the vanilla pod.
2 Stir in the sago and sugar and boil, stirring, until the sago is completely transparent, 15-20 minutes.
3 Remove from the heat, take out the vanilla pod (or add the essence) and beat in the egg yolk.
4 Stir occasionally while cooling, then pour into sundae glasses.
5 Decorate with whipped cream, piped or in spoonfuls, and scatter with glacé fruits and/or nuts. Serve well chilled.

Ginger curdy cream

you will need for 4 servings:

METRIC/IMPERIAL
2 tablespoons cream
1 tablespoon ginger syrup
75 g/3 oz soft brown sugar
450 g/1 lb curd or cottage cheese
75 g/3 oz glacé cherries
100 g/4 oz preserved ginger

1 Beat the cream, syrup, and sugar into the cheese until smooth (if cottage cheese is used, rub it through a sieve first).
2 Reserve 4 cherries and a few slices of ginger. Cut the rest of the cherries roughly into eighths and chop the ginger fairly finely.

3 Mix both into the cheese and turn into 4 sundae glasses.
4 Decorate with the reserved cherries and ginger.

Floating islands

you will need for 4-5 servings:

METRIC/IMPERIAL
600 ml/1 pint milk
1 vanilla pod or ¼ teaspoon vanilla essence
3 eggs, separated
100 g/3½ oz castor sugar

1 Bring the milk with the vanilla pod or essence just to simmering point.
2 Whip the egg whites stiffly with a little of the sugar and fold in the rest.
3 With 2 tablespoons form into egg shapes and drop one by one into the milk; do not let the milk boil. Poach gently for about 2 minutes each side, remove with a straining spoon and drain on a cloth.
4 Make a custard with the milk, egg yolks, etc. (see page 89). When cold pour into a shallow dish and float the 'islands' on top.
Note:
If the sweet is to be served quickly a simpler method is to omit the poaching of the egg whites.

Variation:
Turn the custard into a shallow heatproof dish, float the 'island' on top and place in a very hot oven (240°C, 475°F, Gas Mark 9) for 3 minutes or until the 'islands' are lightly browned.

Magic islands

100 g/4 oz granulated sugar
3 tablespoons water
1 recipe Floating islands

1 Bring the sugar and water to the boil in a small saucepan, stirring only until the sugar is dissolved, then allow to boil without further stirring until the caramel turns a light brown.
2 Remove from the heat, cool for a second or two and pour over the 'islands.'
Note:
The caramel should not be allowed to stand for more than an hour or two or it will begin to melt into the custard.

Peanut butterscotch

you will need for 4 servings:

METRIC/IMPERIAL
115 g/4 oz flake tapioca
generous pinch of salt
900 ml/1½ pints milk
50 g/2 oz butter or margarine
115 g/4 oz dark soft brown sugar
2 tablespoons desiccated coconut (optional)
to decorate:
coarsely chopped salted peanuts

1 Bring the tapioca, salt, and milk to the boil, stirring. Simmer for 15 minutes until thick and creamy, stirring occasionally and then continuously.
2 In a small saucepan melt the butter and sugar until thick and thoroughly blended, 4-5 minutes.
3 Stir in the tapioca and, when quite smooth, remove from the heat and add the coconut, if used.
4 Allow to cool a little, then pour into sundae glasses and chill.
5 Serve sprinkled with coarsely chopped peanuts.

Dzem z piana (Polish jam froth)

you will need for 4-5 servings:

METRIC/IMPERIAL
450 g/1 lb jam, or jelly type marmalade
2 tablespoons boiling water
2 teaspoons gelatine
3 egg whites
50 g/2 oz castor sugar
for decoration:
whipped cream and jam

1 Put the jam in a basin and beat with a fork or wire whisk (not a rotary beater or it will clog).
2 Pour the boiling water over the gelatine in a cup and stir occasionally until dissolved and completely smooth.
3 Whip the egg whites stiffly, adding the sugar gradually, then whip in the gelatine.
4 Whisk into the jam and spoon into individual sundae glasses. Leave to set.
5 Decorate with whipped cream with a spoonful of the jam used in the centre.

Birchermüsli

you will need for 4 servings:

METRIC/IMPERIAL
8 tablespoons porridge oats
6 tablespoons milk
4 tablespoons sweetened condensed milk or sweetened yogurt
1 tablespoon lemon juice
40-50 g/1½-2 oz sultanas
25 g/1 oz lightly toasted hazelnuts or almonds
450 g/1 lb dessert apples
brown sugar

1 Soak the oats in the milk for about 30 minutes.
2 Stir in the condensed milk or yogurt, lemon juice, sultanas, nuts, and grated unpeeled apples. Sweeten to taste with brown sugar.

Variation:
Any fruit may be used in place of the apple, or 225 g/8 oz dried fruit soaked overnight and chopped.

Fruit trifle

you will need for 5-6 servings:

METRIC/IMPERIAL

1 round of Victoria sandwich cake	450 ml/¾ pint evaporated milk diluted according to directions, or fresh milk
450 g/1 lb fresh or frozen fruit, stewed with less water than usual (keep a little aside for decoration)	25 g/1 oz castor sugar
25 g/1 oz custard powder	250 ml/8 fl oz whipping or double cream

1 Lay the sponge cake cut into pieces in a deep dish.
2 Pour the fruit over it.
3 Make the custard powder into a smooth paste with a little of the milk, add the rest and bring to the boil stirring. Simmer for a minute or two. Remove and stir in half the sugar. Leave until cold.
4 Whisk with a wire whisk and pour the custard over the fruit.
5 Whip the cream with the rest of the sugar and spread it over the custard.
6 Decorate with the reserved fruit.

Variations:

Jellied fruit trifle

6-7 trifle sponge cakes, or 1 round of Victoria sandwich cake	300 ml/½ pint custard (made as above)
425-g/15-oz can of fruit	to decorate:
½ packet jelly cubes	150 ml/¼ pint double cream

1 Cut the cakes or cake into pieces and lay over the base of a deep dish.
2 Drain the fruit, keeping the syrup. Reserve some of the fruit for decoration and if large cut the rest into halves. Spread over the sponge.
3 Make up the fruit syrup to 300 ml/½ pint and dissolve the jelly cubes in it. When cool enough, pour it over the fruit and allow to set.
4 Pour the custard over the jelly.
5 Whip the cream and decorate the top with the cream and reserved fruit.

Banana trifle

1 round Victoria sandwich cake	3 large or 4 small bananas
3 tablespoons custard powder	250 ml/8 fl oz whipping or double cream
600 ml/1 pint milk (diluted, evaporated or fresh)	lemon juice
50 g/2 oz castor sugar	to decorate: angelica 'leaves'

1 Cut the sponge cake in half horizontally and lay one half in a deep dish.
2 Make up the custard with most of the sugar as for Fruit trifle (see page 31), cool a little and then pour half of it over the sponge.
3 Keep half a banana aside for decoration and peel and slice the rest. Cover the custard with half the slices.
4 Place the second sponge half on top and cover with the rest of the banana slices.

5 Cover the banana with the rest of the custard and then the lightly whipped cream.
6 Shortly before serving, peel and slice the reserved half banana, brush the slices with lemon juice and decorate the trifle with them and with angelica 'leaves'.

Chocolate trifle

1 round of an 18-cm/7-inch chocolate cake	25 g/1 oz butter
35 g/1¼ oz cocoa powder	1 egg, separated
35 g/1¼ oz flour	rum or brandy (optional)
300 ml/½ pint milk	300 ml/½ pint whipping or double cream
100 g/4 oz granulated sugar	to decorate:
150 ml/¼ pint water	chocolate vermicelli or chocolate drops

1 Cut the cake in half horizontally and place one half in a deep serving dish.
2 Make the sauce. Mix the cocoa and flour into a smooth paste with a little of the milk and gradually stir in the rest.
3 Bring the sugar and water to the boil and boil for 1 minute. Add the milk mixture and return to the boil, stirring with a wire whisk. Boil for 2-3 minutes.
4 Remove from the heat and stir in the butter and egg yolk. Flavour with rum or brandy if liked and pour one-third over the sponge in the dish.
5 Cover with the second half of the cake.
6 Leave the rest of the sauce until cold, stir in the stiffly beaten egg white and pour over the cake.
7 Cover with the lightly whipped cream and rough up the top.
8 Decorate with chocolate vermicelli or chocolate drops.

Sherry trifle

6-7 trifle sponge cakes	300 ml/½ pint double cream
strawberry or raspberry jam	castor sugar
6-8 tablespoons sweet or medium sherry	to decorate:
100 g/4 oz ratafias or macaroons	toasted flaked almonds, glacé cherries, angelica, or as desired
450 ml/¾ pint custard (preferably egg custard, page 89, or see Fruit trifle, above)	

1 Split the sponge cakes in halves and spread with jam. Cut into pieces and place in the bottom of a deep glass dish.
2 Pour the sherry over the cake and allow to soak for 30 minutes.
3 Keep a few ratafias aside for decoration if liked and break up the rest roughly. Scatter them over the sponge cakes.
4 Pour the cold custard over the ratafias.
5 Whip the cream and flavour with sugar to taste. If liked, keep some aside for decorative piping and spread the rest all over the custard.

6 Decorate as desired.

Variation:

A 425-g/15-oz can of fruit (apricots, raspberries, black cherries) may be used in place of the ratafias. Use 3 tablespoons of the juice and 4-5 tablespoons of sherry.

Meringues

you will need for 4-6 servings:

METRIC/IMPERIAL
2 egg whites
50 g/2 oz granulated sugar
50 g/2 oz castor sugar
150-300 ml/¼-½ pint double cream

1 First prepare a baking tray. Line it with silicone paper (non-stick); rub a dab of oil on the underside of the paper at the four corners to stop it from sliding about on the tray. Alternatively, turn the tray upside-down, cover with greaseproof paper and brush *very* lightly with oil.
2 In a large bowl whisk the egg whites, slowly at first then increasing the speed, until they are stiff enough to stand up in a straight peak when the whisk is lifted out.
3 Add about half the granulated sugar and whisk again to the original stiffness; then with a metal spoon fold in the rest of the sugars.
4 With a large plain or star nozzle pipe the meringue onto the paper. Alternatively, shape with spoons: dip one into cold water and shake off surplus, fill with meringue mixture, smooth the sides and top with a knife and with the second wetted spoon gently ease the meringue onto the tin. Dredge with castor sugar if liked.
5 Bake in a very cool oven (110°C, 225°F, Gas Mark ¼) for 3-4 hours until the meringues are dry and crisp both on the top and underside. If they begin to brown, prop open the oven door slightly. If preferred tinged with brown, increase the heat.
6 Remove from the tray and leave until cold.
7 Sandwich together with whipped cream. This is best done with a forcing bag and piping nozzle.

Note:

Well dried unfilled meringues will keep in a tin for many weeks or months.

Variations:

1 Tint any colour with a few drops of colouring folded in with the sugar.
2 Add 2 teaspoons cocoa powder, or to taste.

Fillings:

1 Stir any liqueur into the cream.
2 Add chopped nuts and glacé cherries into the cream.
3 Stir 50 g/2 oz melted chocolate into the cream.
4 Stir any fresh fruit into the cream such as raspberries, strawberries, wild strawberries, loganberries, blackberries.

Eclairs

you will need for about 12 éclairs:

1 recipe Choux pastry (see page 52)
250 ml/8 fl oz double cream with 1 teaspoon icing or castor sugar, or thick Crème pâtissière (see page 89), or flavoured thick custard
chocolate or coffee glacé icing (made with 125 g/4½ oz icing sugar, etc.), or 75 g/3 oz melted chocolate

1 Put the choux paste in a forcing bag with a 1-cm/½-inch plain nozzle. Onto a greased baking tray, pipe even fingers, 9-10-cm/3½-4-inches in length, well spaced, cutting the paste off for each finger with a wet knife against the nozzle.
2 Bake above centre in a hot oven (220°C, 425°F, Gas Mark 7) for 20-25 minutes until risen and golden brown. Remove, cut a slit in the side of each to allow the steam to escape and return to the oven for 3-4 minutes to dry out. Cool on a wire cake rack.
3 When cold, use a piping bag to fill each éclair with whipped cream, Crème pâtissière, or thick custard.
4 Ice the top with the chosen glacé icing, or dip the tops into melted chocolate.

Cream puffs or buns

you will need for 8–9 puffs:

METRIC/IMPERIAL
1 recipe Choux pastry (see page 52)
250 ml/8 fl oz double cream, or Crème pâtissière (see page 89), or thick custard flavoured with vanilla
icing sugar or melted chocolate

1 Pipe or place scant tablespoons of the paste in 4–5-cm/1½-2-inch circles on an oiled baking tray, leaving plenty of room for spreading. Cover with an inverted roasting tin.
2 Bake in a moderately hot oven (200°C, 400°F, Gas Mark 6) for 40–50 minutes without moving the covering. Test by shaking the baking tray, and if the puffs move easily they are done.
3 Remove from the oven, make a slit in the side of each to allow the steam to escape and cool on a wire rack.
4 When cold, fill with whipped cream sweetened to taste with icing sugar, or Crème pâtissière, or thick custard flavoured with vanilla. Dust the tops with icing sugar or dip into melted chocolate.

Apple snow

you will need for 4 servings:

METRIC/IMPERIAL
450 g/1 lb cooking apples after peeling and coring
1 tablespoon water
1 tablespoon lemon juice
75-100 g/3-4 oz granulated sugar
2 large egg whites
to decorate:
halved grapes, pistachio nuts, glacé cherries, nuts

1 Chop the apples roughly and stew with the water and lemon juice until soft and mushy, stirring occasionally.
2 Remove from the heat, add sugar to taste and stir until thoroughly dissolved.
3 Pour into a liquidiser and blend to a purée or rub through a sieve.
4 When cold, whip the egg whites stiffly and fold into the apple.
5 Pour into sundae glasses and decorate with halved grapes, pistachio nuts, glacé cherries or nuts.

Variation:
Apple and quince snow Use 350 g/12 oz apples and 160-225 g/6-8 oz quinces. Stew and proceed as above (3 egg whites makes a lighter snow).

Apple yogurt snow

you will need for 2 servings:
METRIC/IMPERIAL
225 g/8 oz cooking apple after peeling and coring
25 g/1 oz sugar
grated rind and juice of ½ lemon
1 piece preserved stem ginger
2 teaspoons ginger syrup
150 ml/¼ pint natural yogurt
1 egg white

1 Cut the apple into small pieces and put into a saucepan with the sugar, lemon rind and juice.
2 Bring to the boil, stirring, and boil until mushy. Mash well with a potato masher.
3 When cool, stir in the finely chopped ginger, ginger syrup and yogurt, and fold in the stiffly beaten egg white.
4 Put into glasses and chill.

Apple custard

you will need for 4-5 servings:
METRIC/IMPERIAL
large can evaporated milk
milk
40 g/1½ oz (4 tablespoons) custard powder
40 g/1½ oz sugar
2 sharp dessert apples
2 tablespoons orange squash
to decorate:
grated chocolate

1 Make the evaporated milk up to 900 ml/1½ pints with milk.
2 Mix the custard powder into a smooth paste with a little of the milk, then stir into the rest.
3 Bring to the boil, stirring with a wire whisk, and boil for 1-2 minutes. Remove from the heat and stir in the sugar until dissolved. Allow to cool, stirring occasionally to prevent a skin forming on top.
4 Peel the apples and grate on a coarse grater into the orange squash. Stir into the custard.
5 Pour into a decorative bowl and chill.
6 Decorate with a scattering of grated chocolate.

Easy apple cream

you will need for 6 servings:
METRIC/IMPERIAL
450-550 g/1-1¼ lb cooking apples
50 g/2 oz granulated sugar
water
1 packet (135 g/4¾ oz) lemon jelly
150 ml/¼ pint double or whipping cream
to decorate:
extra whipping cream or wafer biscuits

1 Peel, core, and slice the apples.
2 Stew with the sugar and 3 tablespoons water until soft and mushy.
3 Meanwhile put the jelly cubes into 300 ml/½ pint water and heat until the jelly is completely dissolved.
4 Put the liquid and apple into a liquidiser and blend until smooth, or rub the apple through a sieve and mix with the dissolved jelly.
5 Allow to cool, then whisk in the softly whipped cream.
6 Pour into sundae glasses or into a decorative bowl and chill.
7 Decorate with extra whipped cream or with ice cream wafers.

Apple Marguerite

you will need for 4 servings:
METRIC/IMPERIAL
4 large (unblemished) dessert apples
½ bottle (400 ml/scant ¾ pint) white wine or cider or apple juice
25 g/1 oz soft brown sugar
3 teaspoons gelatine
75-100 g/3-4 oz apricot jam
to decorate:
150 ml/¼ pint whipping cream
toasted halved almonds and glacé cherries

1 Peel two of the apples first and remove cores with an apple corer. Cut in halves crosswise.
2 In a saucepan large enough to take the four apple halves lying flat, bring the wine and sugar to the boil, lower the apple halves into it, cover and simmer gently for 3 minutes. Turn the halves over and continue simmering for 3-4 minutes until tender but not soft.
3 Remove with a straining spoon to a shallow serving dish large enough to take the 8 cooked halves side by side.
4 Repeat with the remaining two apples.
5 As soon as all the apples have been removed, take the pan off the heat, sprinkle in the gelatine and stir occasionally until completely dissolved.
6 Stir 2 tablespoons of the jam into the wine.
7 Fill the centres of the apples with jam, strain the wine into the dish and leave to set.
8 Decorate with piped rosettes (or spoonfuls) of whipped cream between and around the apples and put an almond and a glacé cherry alternately on the rosettes.

Blackberry and apple zebras

you will need for 4 servings:

METRIC/IMPERIAL
450 g/1 lb blackberries
175 g/6 oz granulated
  sugar
2 teaspoons gelatine

0.75 kg/1½-1¾ lb
  cooking apples
1 tablespoon water

1 Reserve 4 blackberries for decoration. Wash the rest and stew with 50 g/2 oz of the sugar, stirring, until tender and the juice has run freely.
2 Pour some of the juice immediately onto the gelatine in a cup and stir occasionally until completely dissolved and smooth.
3 Stir into the blackberries and leave until cold and thickened.
4 Peel, core, and chop the apples and stew with the water and the rest of the sugar, stirring, until mushy. Mash with a potato masher and leave until cold.
5 Place in layers in tall glasses, blackberries first and ending with apple. Chill.
6 Serve decorated with the reserved blackberries.

Apple with apricot chiffon

you will need for 4 servings:

METRIC/IMPERIAL
175 g/6 oz dried
  apricots
300 ml/½ pint water
150 g/5 oz granulated
  sugar
1 large or 2 small egg
  whites

450 g/1 lb cooking
  apples
juice of 1 small lemon
to decorate:
ratafia biscuits or
  desiccated coconut

1 Soak apricots in the water for several hours or overnight, then stew with half the sugar until soft enough to blend in a liquidiser or rub through a sieve.
2 When the purée is cold fold in the stiffly beaten egg white.
3 Peel and core the apples, cut them into small pieces and stew with the rest of the sugar and the lemon juice until soft and mushy. Mash with a fork.
4 Put the apple into a serving dish, cover with the apricot chiffon and decorate the top with ratafia biscuits or desiccated coconut.

Uncle Fred's apple delight

you will need for 4-5 servings:

METRIC/IMPERIAL
450 g/1 lb cooking
  apples
3 tablespoons water
75 g/3 oz granulated
  sugar

4 tablespoons port
150 ml/¼ pint double
  or whipping cream
1 egg white

1 Peel, core and chop the apples.
2 Put them in a saucepan with the water and sugar and bring to the boil, stirring. Boil until soft and mushy.
3 Blend in a liquidiser or rub through a sieve. Stir in the port and allow to get cold.
4 Fold in the lightly whipped cream and stiffly beaten egg white.

5 Add a few drops of red colouring to give a pale rosy colour and turn into sundae glasses. Serve chilled, with shortbread or almond fingers, or tuiles dentelles.

Danish apple cake

you will need for 4-5 servings:

METRIC/IMPERIAL
0.5 kg/1¼ lb cooking
  apples after peeling
  and coring
50 g/2 oz granulated
  sugar
75 g/3 oz butter
75 g/3 oz soft
  breadcrumbs

50 g/2 oz macaroons
50 g/2 oz brown or
  castor sugar
to decorate:
150 ml/¼ pint double
  or whipping cream

1 Slice the apples and stew with the granulated sugar until soft and mushy, stirring to prevent sticking.
2 Remove from the heat, stir in 25 g/1 oz of the butter and beat with a fork.
3 Melt the rest of the butter in a frying pan and gently fry the breadcrumbs, macaroons broken into small pieces, and the brown or castor sugar until the crumbs are a golden brown.
4 When everything is cold, arrange in layers in a glass bowl – apple, crumbs, apple, and top with crumbs.
5 Decorate with whipped cream, or serve the cream separately.

Orange caramel

you will need per person:

METRIC/IMPERIAL
1 large orange
25 g/1 oz sugar
to decorate:
If desired, chopped

red and green
  glacé cherries,
  angelica

1 Peel the skin and pith from the oranges and slice thinly. Remove the pips.
2 Place in layers in a serving dish, scattering a little of the sugar between each layer.
3 Put the rest of the sugar in a small saucepan and just cover with water. Bring to the boil, stirring until the sugar is dissolved, then boil without further stirring until the caramel begins to turn a pale golden brown.
4 Pour immediately all over the orange evenly, covering every piece. Chill.
5 Decorate with chopped glacé cherries and angelica and serve with cream or custard.
Note:
The caramel should not be made and poured over the fruit more than 2-3 hours before serving, or it will begin to melt.

Moroccan oranges

you will need for 4 servings:

METRIC/IMPERIAL
4 medium or large
  oranges
175 g/6 oz granulated
  sugar

175 ml/6 fl oz water
1 tablespoon Grand
  Marnier, Cointreau,
  or lemon juice

1 Grate the peel of 3 of the oranges in long strips on a suet grater or special gadget, being careful not to go below the zest to the white pith. Slice off both ends from the four oranges and then with a sharp knife cut off all the peel and pith. Place standing upright in a decorative dish.
2 Discard any untidy pieces of the grated peel and place the rest in a saucepan and cover with cold water. Bring to the boil and drain immediately. Recover with cold water, bring to the boil again and boil for 15-20 minutes until the peel is tender. Drain, but keep the liquid.
3 Bring the sugar and 175 ml/6 fl oz of the liquid to the boil, stirring until the sugar is dissolved, add the peel and simmer in the syrup for 2-3 minutes until the peel looks glazed.
4 Remove from the heat and stir in the liqueur or lemon juice.
5 Strain the syrup over the oranges, then scatter the peel over each one. Serve chilled.

Mousse d'or

you will need for 4 servings:

METRIC/IMPERIAL

2 medium to large oranges	100 g/4 oz castor sugar
1 lemon	Boudoir sponge fingers
3 eggs, separated	

1 Grate the rinds of both the oranges and lemon finely.
2 Put in a bowl with the juice, egg yolks and sugar, and stir over hot but not boiling water until the mixture thickens, 10-15 minutes. Allow to cool.
3 Whip the egg whites stiffly and fold into the fruit mixture gently and thoroughly.
4 Pour into a decorative dish and surround with upstanding sponge fingers.

Angel's food

you will need for 5 servings:

METRIC/IMPERIAL

1 large or 2 small lemons	100 g/4 oz castor sugar
water	*to decorate:*
2 teaspoons gelatine	whipped cream (optional) and jellied lemon slices
3 eggs, separated	

1 Grate the lemon rind finely. Squeeze the juice and make up to 200 ml/7 fl oz with water.
2 Heat the rind and juice until really hot, remove from the heat, sprinkle with the gelatine and stir occasionally until completely dissolved and smooth.
3 In a basin beat the egg yolks and sugar together with a wooden spoon to a thick cream. Pour in the lemon liquid and leave until just beginning to set around the edges.
4 Whisk with a wire whisk and fold in the stiffly beaten egg whites.
5 Pour into sundae glasses and leave to set in a refrigerator.
6 Decorate with piped whipped cream and jellied lemon slices.

Banana orange moon

you will need for 4-5 servings:

METRIC/IMPERIAL

1 small orange	150 ml/¼ pint whipping or double cream
water	
450 g/1 lb bananas	
75 g/3 oz granulated sugar	*to decorate:*
3 teaspoons gelatine (or use ½ packet orange jelly cubes dissolved in 300 ml/½ pint water and omit the orange)	orange and lemon jelly slices

1 Grate the orange rind finely, mix with the juice and make up to 300 ml/½ pint with water.
2 Peel the bananas and blend in a liquidiser with some of the orange liquid, or rub through a sieve.
3 Bring the rest of the liquid and the sugar to the boil, stirring until the sugar is dissolved. Remove from the heat, sprinkle with the gelatine and stir occasionally until completely clear and smooth.
4 Stir into the banana pulp and leave until just beginning to set around the edges, then whisk with a wire whisk and stir in the lightly whipped cream.
5 Pour into a 900-ml/1½-pint ring mould rinsed out with cold water and leave to set in a refrigerator.
6 Turn out (see page 27) and decorate with orange and lemon jelly slices standing up all round the top.

Hammett flan

you will need for 4-5 servings:

METRIC/IMPERIAL

175 g/6 oz coconut or macaroon biscuits	4 small bananas
65 g/2½ oz butter or margarine, melted	lemon juice
½ packet orange jelly	*to decorate:*
150 ml/¼ pint water	black or green grapes or glacé cherries
150 ml/¼ pint single cream or evaporated milk	

1 Put the biscuits a few at a time into a bag and crush with a rolling pin. Stir in the melted butter.
2 Oil an 18-20.5-cm/7-8-inch loose-bottomed flan tin and spread the crumb mixture evenly over the base. Leave to harden.
3 Melt the jelly in the water over medium heat until completely dissolved. Leave to cool and whisk in the cream or milk and 3 of the mashed bananas.
4 Spread on top of the crumb base and leave to set.
5 Remove carefully to a serving dish and decorate just before serving with alternate slices of the remaining banana dipped into lemon juice, and halved stoned grapes or glacé cherries.

Fairy ring

you will need for 4-5 servings:

METRIC/IMPERIAL

150 ml/¼ pint water
juice of ½ small lemon
175 g/6 oz granulated sugar
3½ teaspoons gelatine

3 egg whites
450 g/1 lb fresh apricots (or a 425-g/15-oz can)
150 ml/¼ pint double cream

1 Bring the water, lemon juice, and half the sugar to simmering point, stirring until the sugar is dissolved.
2 Remove from the heat, sprinkle with the gelatine and stir occasionally until completely dissolved and clear.
3 Pour into a basin and leave until just beginning to set around the edges, then with a wire whisk, whisk in the stiffly beaten egg whites.
4 Pour into a 900-ml/1½-pint ring mould rinsed out with cold water and leave to set in a refrigerator.
5 Stew the stoned and chopped apricots with the rest of the sugar until very soft. Blend in a liquidiser or rub through a sieve.
6 Whip the cream and stir in the apricot purée.
7 To serve. Turn out the ring (see page 27) onto a serving dish and fill the centre with the apricot purée.

Apricot or fruit sponge flan

you will need for 4 servings:

METRIC/IMPERIAL

350 g/¾ lb fresh apricots
150 ml/¼ pint water
75 g/3 oz granulated sugar
1½ teaspoons arrowroot or cornflour

1 tablespoon sweet sherry (optional)
1 bought sponge flan case
to decorate:
whipped cream and/or flaked almonds if liked

1 Cut the apricots in halves and discard the stones. Keep 4 halves aside and cut the rest into 3 or 4 pieces each.
2 Bring the water and sugar to the boil, stirring until the sugar is dissolved, drop in the apricot pieces and simmer until tender.
3 Strain the syrup into a measuring jug and make up to 150 ml/¼ pint with water if necessary.
4 Make the arrowroot or cornflour into a smooth paste with a little cold water, add to the apricot syrup and bring to the boil, stirring. Boil for 2-3 minutes, remove from the heat and add the sherry if used.
5 Sprinkle a little over the flan case and reserve the rest.
6 Fill the flan case with the stewed fruit, pour the rest of the syrup over it and leave until cold and thickened.
7 Decorate with the reserved apricot halves and whipped cream and/or flaked almonds if liked.
Note:
Any fresh or tinned fruit can be treated in the same manner.

Golden cloud

you will need for 6 servings:

METRIC/IMPERIAL

160 g/6 oz dried apricots, or 225 g/8 oz apricots and prunes mixed
300 ml/½ pint water
50 g/2 oz granulated sugar
2 egg whites
25 g/1 oz (2 tablespoons) custard powder

750 ml/1¼ pints milk (some evaporated is good)
25 g/1 oz castor sugar
¼ teaspoon vanilla essence
to decorate:
whipped cream and/or chocolate vermicelli

1 Stew the apricots with the water and granulated sugar until very soft (if prunes are used, soak first for several hours and stone).
2 Put into a liquidiser and blend until smooth, or rub through a sieve.
3 When cold, fold in the stiffly beaten egg whites.
4 Mix the custard powder to a smooth paste with a little of the milk, add the rest and bring to the boil, stirring. Boil for 2-3 minutes, remove from the heat and stir in the castor sugar and vanilla essence.
5 Pour into a serving dish and leave until cold and thick.
6 Cover with the fruit mixture and decorate with whipped cream and/or chocolate vermicelli.

Jellied redcurrant sponge flan

you will need for 4 servings:

METRIC/IMPERIAL

225 g/8 oz redcurrants
1 bought sponge flan case
½ packet (135 g/4¾ oz) raspberry jelly

150 ml/¼ pint water
to decorate:
whipped cream

1 String the washed redcurrants and cover the base of the flan with some of the fruit. Reserve a few for decoration and roughly squash the rest.
2 Put the jelly and water in a small saucepan and heat until the jelly is completely dissolved. Stir in the squashed currants.
3 Leave the jelly until thick and beginning to set, then spoon it over the currants in the flan. Leave to set.
4 Decorate with whipped cream and the reserved currants.

Variations:

Use raspberries, strawberries, or blackberries in place of the currants, with the appropriate jelly.

Fluffy cherry rice creams

you will need for 4 servings:

METRIC/IMPERIAL

450 g/1 lb black or red cherries	150 g/¼ pint double or whipping cream
75 g/3 oz granulated sugar	1 egg white
5 tablespoons water	scant ¼ teaspoon almond essence
439-g/15½-oz can creamed rice pudding	*to decorate:*
	4 small meringue halves or rosettes

1 Wash and stone the cherries.
2 Bring the sugar and water to the boil, stirring until the sugar is dissolved, add the cherries and simmer gently, covered, for 4-5 minutes until the cherries are tender. Allow to cool.
3 Drain off any excess liquid from the rice pudding, pour into a basin and stir in the whipped cream and stiffly beaten egg white. Flavour to taste with almond essence.
4 Divide the mixture into 4 sundae glasses.
5 Spoon the drained cherries over the top, then pour in a little of the syrup which will run down the sides to give an attractive colour. Chill.
6 Just before serving place a meringue in the centre of each.
Note:
A can of cherries may be used in place of the fresh ones, in which case commence from stage 3.

Cranberry orange carnival

you will need for 4 servings:

METRIC/IMPERIAL

4 medium oranges	300 ml/½ pint soured cream
2 tablespoons soft brown sugar	
184-g/6½-oz jar cranberry sauce	

1 Grate the rind of 2 oranges. Cut off all the peel from all 4 oranges and slice the flesh thinly. Reserve 5 or 6 of the best slices for decoration.
2 Lay the rest of the slices in a shallow dish, scattering with the sugar.
3 Pick out 20-24 whole cranberries and spread the rest of the sauce over the orange. Spoon over the soured cream to cover the sauce completely.
4 Scatter the grated orange rind over the soured cream. Place the reserved orange slices on the cream and pile a few of the whole cranberries in the centre of each.

Banana ginger frou-frou

you will need for 6 servings:

METRIC/IMPERIAL

200-225 g/7-8 oz gingernut biscuits	300 ml/½ pint double cream
6 medium (about 0.75 kg/1¾ lb) bananas	2 tablespoons castor sugar

1 Put the biscuits, a few at a time, into a bag and with a rolling pin crush into crumbs.
2 Peel and mash the bananas.
3 Whip the cream fairly stiffly and fold in the bananas and sugar.
4 Sprinkle a generous third of the biscuit crumbs over the base of an ungreased 18-cm/7-inch cake tin.
5 Carefully cover with half the banana mixture. Repeat layers and top with the rest of the crumbs.
6 Place another tin or small plate with a weight on top and leave in a refrigerator or cold place for several hours or overnight.
7 Cut around the sides with a knife and turn out.

Sugarless dried fruit foam

you will need for 5 servings:

METRIC/IMPERIAL

225 g/8 oz dried apricots, prunes, peaches, or a mixture	150 ml/¼ pint double, single or soured cream
1 banana	*to decorate:*
1 tablespoon clear honey	chopped nuts (roasted hazelnuts if possible)

1 Cover the fruit well with water and leave to soak overnight. Drain but keep the liquid.
2 Put some of the fruit into a liquidiser with the sliced banana, honey, cream, and 4-5 tablespoons of the fruit liquid and blend until smooth, adding the rest of the fruit gradually. Alternatively, rub everything through a sieve.
3 Pour into sundae glasses and chill.
4 Sprinkle with chopped nuts to serve.

Fresh dates Wilberforce

you will need for 4 servings:

METRIC/IMPERIAL

450 g/1 lb fresh dates	1 tablespoon sweet sherry
250 ml/8 fl oz whipping or double cream	*to decorate:*
25 g/1 oz walnuts and hazelnuts or almonds, chopped	toasted flaked almonds or chopped glacé cherries
25 g/1 oz desiccated coconut	

1 Skin the dates by nicking off the stalk end and squeezing from the other end, then the whole date will pop out. Cut in halves and remove the stones.
2 Whip half the cream lightly and stir in the chopped nuts, coconut, and sherry. Stuff the dates with the mixture.
3 Place the dates in sundae glasses and pour the rest of the cream over them.
4 Decorate with toasted flaked almonds or chopped glacé cherries.

Melon stuffed with ginger

you will need for 4 servings:

METRIC/IMPERIAL

1 medium to small
honeydew melon
75 g/3 oz stem ginger
2–3 tablespoons
ginger syrup
4 tablespoons sweet
sherry or sweet
white wine

to decorate:
maraschino or glacé
cherries

1 Cut a thin slice off the bottom of the melon to allow it to stand upright firmly. Cut a slice off the top, less than one-third of the way down. Scoop out all the flesh (from the top piece also) and discard the seeds.
2 Cut the melon flesh into cubes and the ginger into thin slices. Replace in the melon shell.
3 Mix the ginger syrup with the sherry or wine and pour over the filling. Arrange the cherries decoratively over the top, replace the lid and chill.

Rhubarb apple biscuit flan

you will need for 4-5 servings:

METRIC/IMPERIAL

175 g/6 oz digestive
and Nice biscuits
mixed (or use all
digestives)
50 g/2 oz castor sugar
100 g/3½ oz butter or
margarine, melted

450 g/1 lb rhubarb
450 g/1 lb cooking
apples
175 g/6 oz granulated
sugar

1 Make the flan case. Put the biscuits, a few at a time, into a bag and with a rolling pin crush into crumbs. Stir in the castor sugar and melted butter.
2 Place a 20.5-cm/8-inch flan ring on a perfectly flat serving dish and press the biscuit crumbs over the base and up the sides. Leave to harden, then gently pull off the flan ring.
3 Wash and trim the rhubarb. Peel and core the apples and cut both into small pieces.
4 Bring to the boil with the granulated sugar, stirring. Boil until the fruit is soft and mushy. Mash with a potato masher and leave until cold.
5 Turn into the flan case and rough up the top, or decorate with whipped cream.

Blackcurrant summer pudding

you will need for 4 servings:

METRIC/IMPERIAL

7 slices bread from a
sandwich loaf
0.75 kg/1½ lb
blackcurrants

6 tablespoons water
175 g/6 oz granulated
sugar

1 First line a generous 1-litre/2-pint pudding bowl with the bread. Remove the crusts, cut a circle to fit the base of the bowl, reserve one slice for covering the pudding and line the bowl (but not quite to the top) with the rest, leaving no gaps.
2 Wash and stalk the blackcurrants. Stew with the water and sugar until tender.

3 Pour into the bowl, keeping back a little of the juice.
4 Cover with the reserved bread slice and fill in the gaps with off-cuts from the other slices. Pour the rest of the juice over the top.
5 Cover with a weighted plate or saucer and leave overnight.
6 Turn out onto a dish deep enough to hold the juice when the pudding is cut. Serve with cream or custard.

Jellied summer pudding

you will need for 4-5 servings:

METRIC/IMPERIAL

450 g/1 lb redcurrants
and raspberries,
mixed
7 slices bread
(preferably thin
ones) from a
sandwich loaf

1½ packets raspberry
jelly cubes
500 ml/18 fl oz water

1 Wash and stalk the redcurrants, but do not wash the raspberries.
2 Line a generous 1-litre/2-pint pudding bowl with bread as directed in the previous recipe.
3 Over medium heat melt the jelly cubes completely in the water.
4 Dip each piece of bread (including the reserved piece) into the liquid jelly and replace in the bowl.
5 Mix the fruit with the rest of the jelly and pour into the bowl.
6 Place the reserved bread slice on top, filling in the gaps with off-cuts from the other slices, and leave in a refrigerator or cold place to set.
7 Run a knife blade around the sides carefully and turn out.

Variations:
Blackberries Add a scant ¼ teaspoon each of ground cinnamon and nutmeg to the liquid. Use half cider and half water.
Blackcurrants Lightly stew the blackcurrants first, then use the juice to make up the liquid. Use a black-currant jelly.

Sussex pudding

you will need for 4 servings:

METRIC/IMPERIAL

7 slices bread from a
sandwich loaf
0.5 kg/1¼ lb
blackberries

250 ml/8 fl oz medium
cider
225 g/8 oz granulated
sugar

1 Line a generous 1-litre/2-pint pudding bowl with the bread as for Blackcurrant summer pudding (see page 38).
2 Wash and boil the blackberries with the cider and sugar until tender, 4-5 minutes. Pour into the lined bowl.
3 Proceed from stage 3 of Blackcurrant summer pudding (see page 38).

To clear jelly

you will need for 4-6 servings:

METRIC/IMPERIAL

shells and whites of 2 eggs
600-900 ml/1-1½ pints liquid

50-100 g/2-4 oz sugar
2-3 tablespoons gelatine

1 Wash the eggshells and crush them; beat the whites lightly to break up into liquid.
2 Put the liquid, sugar, and gelatine in a saucepan and add the egg shells and whites.
3 Place this mixture over a low heat and whisk to simmering point, but it must not boil. There should be a thick froth on the surface. Take out the whisk and allow the froth to rise and crack, then reduce the heat to minimum and leave for 5 minutes.
4 For straining, a jelly bag is ideal. You can use a clean cloth or several thicknesses of muslin over a sieve, but make sure the bowl is deep enough for the sieve to remain above and not in contact with the sieved liquid; the cloth can be tied to the legs of an upturned chair if necessary.
5 Before sieving, pour boiling water through the cloth into the bowl beneath, so that both are hot. Also have a second bowl ready for the next straining.
6 Empty the water from the bowl and then carefully pour the jelly through the cloth, allowing it to drip into the bowl, which takes 20-30 minutes. The egg shells and whites help to filter the jelly.
7 Pour hot water into the second bowl, or the jelly may begin to set before the straining is complete. Repeat the straining without shaking the jelly.
8 When straining is complete, pour into a wetted mould and leave to set.

Claret, port, or red wine jelly

you will need for 4 servings:

METRIC/IMPERIAL

300 ml/½ pint claret, port, or any red wine
300 ml/½ pint water
50 g/2 oz castor sugar
1 tablespoon redcurrant or cranberry jelly

2 tablespoons (21 g/¾ oz) gelatine
few drops red colouring

1 Turn the wine, water, sugar, jelly, and gelatine into a saucepan and heat slowly, stirring, until the sugar and gelatine have dissolved completely.
2 Remove and stir in enough red colouring to give a rich dark red. Pour into a 600-ml/1-pint mould, rinsed out with cold water, and leave to set in a refrigerator.
3 Turn out (see page 27) and serve with cream.

Orange (or fruit) jelly

you will need for 4 servings:

METRIC/IMPERIAL

450 g/1 lb oranges
1 lemon
water

75 g/3 oz granulated sugar
2 tablespoons gelatine

1 Grate the orange rinds and mix with the juice from the oranges and lemon. Make up to 600 ml/1 pint with water.
2 Bring to the boil with the sugar, stirring, and boil for 2 minutes.
3 Strain at once through two thicknesses of muslin or J-cloths.
4 Sprinkle with the gelatine and stir occasionally until completely dissolved and clear.
5 Pour into a 600-ml/1-pint mould, rinsed out with cold water, and leave to set.
6 Turn out (see page 27) and decorate if desired.

Variations:

Fruit jelly

If whole fruit, or pieces of fruit are added, leave the liquid in a basin and do not stir in the fruit until the jelly is beginning to thicken and set around the edges, or it will sink to the bottom.

To decorate the top of a jelly

Pour in enough liquid jelly to cover the base of the mould by at least 0.5 cm/¼ inch and allow to set. Dip the fruit or other decoration to be used into the liquid jelly and place in position on the layer of set jelly. Allow to set, then pour in the rest of the liquid jelly. A quantity of fruit may be set in layers in the same way, in which case the jelly mould must be placed in a refrigerator after each addition, or in a basin surrounded by ice cubes to speed the setting.

Packet jellies

These can be made according to pack instructions and set with fruit in the same way as above.

Variations:

Jelly froth

1 Pour a little liquid jelly into each sundae dish (glass is prettiest) and allow to set.
2 Pour the rest into a basin and when it begins to set around the edges, whisk with a rotary beater until frothy. Pile onto the set jelly.
3 Pieces of fruit may also be placed upon the layer of set jelly and then the rest added to the whisked froth.

Creamy froth

1 Make the liquid up to 450 ml/¾ pint and melt the jelly cubes in it.
2 When it begins to set, whisk 150 ml/¼ pint double cream or evaporated milk (best left in a refrigerator first), stir into the jelly and whisk the two together.
3 Pile into sundae glasses and when set decorate with grated chocolate or chopped nuts.

Milk jelly

you will need for 4 servings:

METRIC/IMPERIAL

568 ml/1 pint milk
thinly peeled rind of ½ orange or lemon
50 g/2 oz granulated sugar

5 teaspoons gelatine
4 tablespoons boiling water

1 Heat the milk, fruit rind, and sugar together, stirring until the sugar has dissolved. Remove from the heat and cool to blood heat.
2 Pour the boiling water over the gelatine in a cup and stir occasionally until completely dissolved and clear. Cool to blood heat also.
3 Pour the gelatine into the milk while stirring.
4 Strain into a wetted mould and leave to set.
5 Turn out (see page 27).
Note:
Fruit juice may be substituted for a part of the milk, but if an acid fruit is used it may curdle the milk. Be sure that the temperature of the milk and gelatine are both about blood heat when mixing together or the gelatine will curdle the milk.

Honeycomb mould

you will need for 4 servings:
METRIC/IMPERIAL
2 large or 3 small eggs vanilla essence
568 ml/1 pint milk 4 tablespoons boiling
2 tablespoons castor water
 sugar 2 tablespoons gelatine

1 Make a thin custard with the egg yolks, milk and sugar, then flavour with vanilla to taste.
2 Pour the boiling water over the gelatine in a cup and stir occasionally until completely dissolved and clear. Add to the custard whilst stirring.
3 When the custard is cool, whip the egg whites stiffly and fold into the mixture.
4 Turn into a generous 1-litre/2-pint mould, rinsed out with cold water, and leave to set in a refrigerator.
5 Turn out (see page 27) but do not cut around the edge, which is the frothy section, or it will look untidy. Serve with jam or a sweet sauce.
Note:
Instead of the vanilla essence, the rind of a lemon or orange can be heated with the milk and then left to infuse before making the custard.

Harvest jelly

you will need for 4 servings:
METRIC/IMPERIAL
1 packet (135 g/4¾ oz) 2 pears
 blackcurrant jelly 1 dessert apple
 cubes 100 g/4 oz blackberries
250 ml/scant ½ pint *to decorate:*
 boiling water 150 ml/¼ pint double
150 ml/¼ pint red cream and roasted
 wine hazel nuts (optional)

1 Melt the jelly thoroughly in the boiling water.
2 Stir in the wine and leave until cold but not set.
3 Peel the pears and apple and grate on a coarse suet grater into the jelly. Stir in the washed and drained blackberries.
4 Turn into a 900-ml/1½-pint mould, rinsed out with cold water, and leave to set.
5 Turn out (see page 27) and, if desired, decorate with rosettes of cream with a roasted hazel nut in the centre of each.

Autumn layer jelly

you will need for 4-5 servings:
METRIC/IMPERIAL
560-ml/19-fl oz can 50/2 oz sugar
 Jaffa orange juice, 2 tablespoons gelatine
 or can of frozen 225 g/8 oz blackberries
 juice made up to 2 small dessert apples
 quantity with water

1 Heat about one-third of the orange juice sufficiently to dissolve the sugar and gelatine in it thoroughly. Mix with the rest of the juice.
2 Pour a little into the bottom of a generous 1-litre/2-pint jelly mould (a tall shape is best) and stand the mould in a basin of cold water with ice cubes if possible. Place a plate on top of the mould to keep it level.
3 As soon as the jelly has set, cover with a layer of washed and drained blackberries and then thin slices of peeled and cored apple.
4 Pour in more juice just to cover the fruit (or it will float) and let that set.
5 Repeat all the layers once more and leave in a cold place to set.
6 Turn out to serve (see page 27).

Almond gooseberry mallow

you will need for 4 servings:
METRIC/IMPERIAL
0.5 kg/1¼ lb 75 g/3 oz ground
 gooseberries almonds
100 g/4 oz almond essence
 marshmallows green colouring
2 tablespoons water (optional)
150 g/5 oz granulated
 sugar

1 Keep aside 4 gooseberries or 2 marshmallows for decoration.
2 Wash the gooseberries and stew with the water and sugar until soft and mushy.
3 Rub through a sieve, return to the pan with the marshmallows and over gentle heat stir until melted.
4 Leave to cool a little, then stir in the ground almonds and flavour to taste with almond essence. Colour with a few drops of green colouring if liked.
5 Pour into sundae glasses and leave in a cold place for several hours or overnight.
6 Decorate with the reserved gooseberries or halved marshmallows.

Gooseberry fool

you will need for 4 servings:
METRIC/IMPERIAL
450 g/1 lb gooseberries green colouring
1 tablespoon water *to decorate:*
175-200 g/6-7 oz meringue rosettes, or
 granulated sugar halves, or
250 ml/8 fl oz double shortbread or wafer
 cream, or thick biscuits
 custard, or half and
 half

1 Wash the gooseberries and stew with the water and sugar, stirring, until soft and mushy.
2 Rub through a sieve, or put into a liquidiser and blend until smooth and then rub through a sieve. The purée should measure 300 ml/½ pint.
3 When cold, stir in the whipped cream or custard and colour a faint green with colouring.
4 Turn into sundae glasses and chill.
5 Decorate with meringue rosettes or small halves, or with shortbread or wafer biscuits.

Variations:
Blackcurrant 350 g/12 oz is sufficient with 3 table-spoons water.
Rhubarb 0.5-0.75 kg/1¼-1½ lb rhubarb, 200 g/7 oz sugar, no water.
Plum 450 g/1 lb plums, 125 g/4½ oz sugar, 1 table-spoon water.
Chestnut 450-g/15¾-oz can sweetened chestnut purée, 150 ml/¼ pint double cream, 1 egg white. Rub the purée through a sieve and fold in the lightly whipped cream and the stiffly beaten egg white. Decorate with grated chocolate. A little brandy or rum may be added if liked.

Rødgrød med fløde

you will need for 4-5 servings:

METRIC/IMPERIAL	
225 g/8 oz raspberries and/or strawberries	water
225 g/8 oz redcurrants	1 tablespoon (approx) arrowroot
225 g/8 oz blackcurrants	225 g/8 oz granulated sugar

1 Do not wash raspberries or strawberries unless necessary, but wash and stem the currants.
2 Stew gently with 150 ml/¼ pint water until soft and mushy.
3 Rub through a sieve, or blend in a liquidiser and then rub through a sieve. Measure the sieved fruit and allow 1 tablespoon arrowroot per 600 ml/1 pint juice.
4 Make the arrowroot into a smooth paste with 2 table-spoons water.
5 Bring the sieved fruit and the sugar to the boil slowly, stirring until the sugar is dissolved, stir in the arrow-root and return to the boil. Boil for 2-3 minutes until clear.
6 Allow to cool a little, then pour into a bowl or sundae glasses and chill.
7 Serve with cream, ice cream, or custard.

Greengage or plum whip

you will need for 4 servings:

METRIC/IMPERIAL	
450 g/1 lb greengages or plums	1 large egg white
300 ml/½ pint water	green or red colouring
75 g/3 oz granulated sugar	

1 Wash the fruit and keep 2 aside for decoration. Bring the rest to the boil with the water and sugar, stirring, and boil until soft and mushy.

2 Remove the stones, put the fruit in a liquidiser and blend until smooth or rub through a sieve.
3 Allow to get cold, then fold in the stiffly beaten egg white.
4 Add a few drops of colouring and pile into sundae dishes. Chill.
5 Decorate with the reserved fruit cut into halves.

David's plum special

you will need for 4-5 servings:

METRIC/IMPERIAL	
450 g/1 lb plums	4 teaspoons gelatine
water	small can evaporated milk (or half a large one)
75 g/3 oz granulated sugar	
4 tablespoons boiling water	

1 Wash the plums, cut a few into halves and reserve for decoration. Cut the rest into pieces, removing the stones.
2 Stew with 4 tablespoons water and the sugar until soft and mushy. Put them in a liquidiser and blend until smooth or rub through a sieve. The purée should measure 300 ml/½ pint, if not make up with water. Pour into a basin.
3 Pour the boiling water over the gelatine in a cup and stir occasionally until completely dissolved and clear.
4 Dilute the milk to 300 ml/½ pint with warm water.
5 Stir half the gelatine into the plum purée. Stir the other half into the milk and leave until just beginning to set around the edges, then whisk to a froth and stir into the plum purée.
6 Pour into a 900-ml/1½-pint ring or other mould, rinsed out with cold water, and leave to set.
7 Turn out (see page 27) and decorate with the reserved plums and whipped cream.

Eton mess

you will need for 4 servings:

METRIC/IMPERIAL	
350-450 g/¾-1 lb strawberries	50 g/2 oz castor sugar
300 ml/½ pint double cream	1 egg white

1 Hull the strawberries. Keep aside 4 good ones for decoration. Chop half the rest into small pieces and squash the remainder.
2 Whip the cream and fold in the sugar and stiffly beaten egg white.
3 Stir in the chopped and squashed strawberries and pile into sundae dishes.
4 Decorate each with a reserved strawberry.

Strawberry orange wheels

you will need for 4 servings:

METRIC/IMPERIAL

275-350 g/10-12 oz strawberries	3-4 tablespoons Grand Marnier
2 oranges or 298-g/10½-oz can mandarin segments	castor sugar
241-g/8½-oz can pineapple slices or 4 slices fresh pineapple	

1 Reserve 4 good strawberries and cut the rest in halves.
2 Remove skin and all the pith from the oranges, cut the fruit across into barely 0.5-cm/¼-inch thick slices, and cut those in halves.
3 Place a drained pineapple slice on the centre of each plate, arrange the halved orange slices or mandarin segments wheel fashion, overlapping the pineapple.
4 Fill between the slices and the centre with strawberry halves and place a whole strawberry on the centre of each.
5 Drizzle with Grand Marnier. Sprinkle the strawberries with castor sugar and leave to marinate for at least 30 minutes.

Boozy pears

you will need for 4 servings:

METRIC/IMPERIAL

piece of root ginger	175 ml/6 fl oz red wine
5-cm/1-inch stick cinnamon	5 tablespoons port
50 g/2 oz castor sugar	2 tablespoons water
	0.75 kg/1½ lb pears

1 Bruise the ginger with a hammer and put into a saucepan with the cinnamon, sugar, and liquids. Heat gently until the sugar is dissolved.
2 Peel and core the pears and if small cut into quarters, if large into eighths.
3 Place in a casserole and pour the liquid over them. Cover and bake in a moderate oven (170°C, 325°F, Gas Mark 3) for 35-45 minutes, or until the pears are tender, turning over the pieces once or twice. Serve cold or hot with cream or ice cream.

Chocolate mousse pears

you will need for 4 servings:

METRIC/IMPERIAL

4 ripe pears	3 tablespoons water
25 g/1 oz glacé cherries, chopped	25 g/1 oz butter
25 g/1 oz roasted hazelnuts or walnuts, chopped	1 tablespoons rum or brandy (optional)
115 g/4 oz plain chocolate	2 eggs, separated
	to decorate:
	halved blanched almonds

1 Peel the pears, cut in halves, scoop out the cores and press the chopped cherries and nuts into the cavities.
2 Place the pears, stuffed side down, in a shallow serving dish.

3 Melt the chocolate with the water in a bowl over hot but not boiling water, remove from the heat and stir in the butter and spirit, if used.
4 Beat the egg yolks into the mixture smoothly and then fold in the stiffly beaten egg whites. Spoon over the pears.
5 Chill in a refrigerator for several hours or overnight.
6 Decorate with halved almonds stuck into the pears.
Note:
For party presentation, peel the pears, leaving the stalks intact. Cut a thin slice off the base of each pear and scoop out as much of the core as possible. Push stuffing into the cavity. Stand the pears upright in a serving dish and spoon the sauce over them. Chill and decorate with the almonds.

Hobart sultana pears

you will need for 4 servings:

METRIC/IMPERIAL

150 g/5 oz sultanas	4 pears (the round shape are the best)
1 orange	4 tablespoons honey
water	

1 Pour boiling water over the sultanas to cover and leave for an hour or more to plump up. Drain.
2 Grate the orange rind finely, mix with the juice and make up to 300 ml/½ pint with water.
3 Peel the pears and cut in halves.
4 Bring the orange liquid and honey to the boil in a saucepan large enough to take 4 halves lying flat. Lower the halves into the syrup, cover, and simmer gently for 4-5 minutes each side, or until just tender. Repeat with the remaining 4 halves.
5 With a straining spoon remove the pears, scoop out the cores and place the halves, cut sides up, in a serving dish.
6 Add the sultanas to the pan and simmer for 4-5 minutes. Cool slightly and pour everything over the pears. Serve chilled, with cream.

Pear and prune medley

you will need for 4 servings:

METRIC/IMPERIAL

225 g/8 oz prunes	0·75 kg/1½ lb pears
300 ml/½ pint water	¾ teaspoon vanilla essence
1 small lemon	
75 g/3 oz granulated sugar	

1 Soak the prunes in the water overnight.
2 Cut the lemon (omitting the two ends) into very thin slices, remove the pips and cut each slice into quarters.
3 Tip the liquid from the prunes into a saucepan with the sugar and lemon. Bring to the boil and boil for 2 minutes.
4 Add the peeled, cored, and quartered pears with the prunes and vanilla essence and simmer, covered, for 20-30 minutes, according to the ripeness of the pears. Do not overcook. Serve chilled.

Peaches in Grand Marnier

you will need for 4 servings:

METRIC/IMPERIAL

4 peaches	1½ tablespoon lemon
50 g/2 oz granulated	juice
sugar	1 miniature bottle, or
40 g/1½ oz butter	2 tablespoons
juice of 1 small orange	Grand Marnier

1 Peel the peaches by dropping them into boiling water for 20-25 seconds, then plunge into cold water and carefully remove the skins.
2 In a small saucepan just large enough to hold the peaches, melt the sugar, butter, and juices together, stirring, and bring to the boil.
3 Lower the peaches into the pan, cover, and allow to simmer gently, turning them over once, for 4-8 minutes each side, or until just tender.
4 Remove the pan from the heat and with a straining spoon carefully place the peaches in a serving dish.
5 Stir the Grand Marnier into the syrup and pour it over the peaches. Serve chilled.

Peaches in Cinzano Rosso

you will need for 4 servings:

METRIC/IMPERIAL

4 peaches	5 tablespoons Cinzano
75 g/3 oz granulated	Rosso
sugar	150 ml/¼ pint water

1 Peel the peaches as in the previous recipe.
2 In a small saucepan only just large enough to take the peaches, bring the sugar, 4 tablespoons of the vermouth, and the water to the boil.
3 Lower the peaches into the pan, cover, and allow to simmer gently, turning them over once, for 4-8 minutes each side, or until just tender.
4 Remove carefully with a straining spoon and place in a serving dish.
5 Reduce the syrup to under half by boiling fast, uncovered. Cool a little, stir in the rest of the vermouth and pour over the peaches. Serve chilled.

Note:
The same recipe can be made with any sweet or dry vermouth.

Stewed fruit

you will need for 4 servings:

METRIC/IMPERIAL

Apples

0·75 kg/1½ lb cooking	150 ml/¼ pint water
apples (0·5 kg/1¼ lb	strip of lemon rind
after peeling and	and juice of ½ small
coring)	lemon, or 3 cloves
150 g/5 oz granulated	and 2·5-cm/1-inch
sugar	stick cinnamon

1 Bring the sugar, water and lemon juice or spices to the boil, stirring until the sugar is dissolved. Boil for 1-2 minutes.

2 Peel and core the apples and cut into 1-cm/½-inch slices.
3 Put into a 1·75-litre/3-pint casserole and pour the syrup over them immediately.
4 Cover and bake in a moderate oven (170°C, 325°F, Gas Mark 3) for 25 minutes, turn over the pieces carefully and continue cooking for a further 10-15 minutes or until the fruit is only just tender. Do NOT allow to boil.

Note:
Apples look a bit dull when stewed, so I prefer to stew them in a saucepan until they are mushy – the French call the dish, "Marmalade de pommes." ½ teaspoon of Angostura bitters can also be stirred in, which gives a subtle flavour.

Apricots (fresh)

0·75 kg/1½ lb apricots	150 ml/¼ pint water
175 g/6 oz granulated	
sugar	

1 Cut the apricots in halves and remove the stones. Crack the stones and add a few of the kernels, or a few sweet almonds, to the dish if liked.
2 Proceed from stages 1 and 3 for Stewed apples (see above).

Blackberries

0·75 kg/1½ lb	150 ml/¼ pint water or
blackberries	sweet cider
125 g/4½ oz	
granulated sugar	

1 Wash and drain the blackberries.
2 Proceed from stages 1 and 3 for Stewed apples (see above).

Cherries

0·75 kg/1½ lb cherries	200 ml/8 fl oz water
125 g/4½ oz	
granulated sugar	

1 Wash and stone the cherries.
2 Proceed from stages 1 and 3 for stewed apples (see above). Alternatively, cherries can be stewed in a saucepan without damage.

Damsons

0·75 kg/1½ lb	300 ml/½ pint water
damsons	
200-275 g/7-8 oz	
granulated sugar	

1 Cut the damsons in halves and remove the stones.
2 Proceed from stages 1 and 3 for Stewed apples (see above).

Dried fruit

450 g/1 lb dried fruit (apples, apricots, figs, peaches, or a mixture)
175 g/6 oz demerara or granulated sugar

750 ml/1¼ pints water
lemon peel or cinnamon

1 Soak the fruit in the water overnight.
2 Put in a saucepan with the water in which it was soaked and add the sugar.
3 Add a strip of lemon peel for all the fruit except the prunes. For prunes add a 2·5-cm/1-inch or longer stick of cinnamon or ¼ teaspoon ground cinnamon. Bring to the boil and simmer gently until the fruit is tender.
4 With a straining spoon remove the fruit to a serving dish. Boil the juice fast, uncovered, for a few minutes until syrupy and pour it over the fruit.

Greengages

0·75 kg/1½ lb greengages
100 g/4 oz granulated sugar

175 g/6 fl oz water

1 Treat as for apricots (see page 43).

Gooseberries

0·5 kg/1¼ lb gooseberries (these are best for stewing when slightly underripe)
200 g/7 oz granulated sugar
250 ml/8 fl oz water

1 Wash the gooseberries and top and tail them.
2 Proceed from stages 1 and 3 for Stewed apple (see page 43).
Note:
A spray of elderberry flowers may be stewed with the fruit for a subtle flavour.

Loganberries

0·5 kg/1¼ lb loganberries
175 g/6 oz granulated sugar

175 ml/6 fl oz water

1 Treat as for Stewed blackberries (see page 43).

Pears

(with cranberry jelly)

2 tablespoons cranberry jelly
1 tablespoon golden syrup

2 teaspoons water
0·75 kg/1½ lb pears

1 Bring the cranberry jelly, golden syrup and water to the boil.
2 Peel and core the pears and cut into halves or quarters.

3 Proceed from stage 3 for Stewed apples (see page 43).
4 Remove pears with a straining spoon to a serving dish. Pour the syrup into a saucepan and boil fast, uncovered, until reduced by about half. Cool a little and pour it over the pears.

(spiced)

50-75 g/2-3 oz granulated sugar
150 ml/¼ pint water
1-2·5-cm/½-1-inch piece root ginger, lightly crushed
2·5-cm/1-inch piece cinnamon stick

4 cloves
450 g/1 lb pears after peeling and coring, or 0·75 kg/1½ lb pears

1 Bring the sugar and water to the boil with the spices, stirring until the sugar is dissolved. Proceed from stage 2 above.

Plums

0·75 kg/1½ lb plums
150 g/5 oz granulated sugar

175 ml/6 fl oz water

1 Treat as for Stewed apricots (see page 43).

Rhubarb

0·75 kg/1½ lb rhubarb
225 g/8 oz granulated sugar
grated rind of ½ orange or less lemon

4 tablespoons orange juice or
2 tablespoons lemon juice
2 tablespoons water

1 Wash the rhubarb, trim and cut into 2·5-cm/1-inch lengths.
2 Proceed from stages 1 and 3 for Stewed apples (see page 43).

Compote Cardinale

you will need for 4 servings:

METRIC/IMPERIAL
225 g/8 oz black cherries
225 g/8 oz blackcurrants
50-75 g/2-3 oz redcurrants

225 g/8 oz granulated sugar
300 ml/½ pint water
100 g/4 oz raspberries

1 Stone the cherries and remove stalks from the black and red currants (keep separate). Wash and drain.
2 Bring the sugar and water to the boil, stirring until the sugar is dissolved. Boil for 2-3 minutes.
3 Add the cherries and blackcurrants and simmer for 3-4 minutes until just tender. Remove from the heat and gently stir in the redcurrants and raspberries. Chill.

Spiced prunes

you will need for 4 servings:

METRIC/IMPERIAL
450 g/1 lb prunes
100 g/4 oz granulated
  sugar
150 ml/¼ pint red
  wine
450 ml/¾ pint water

1 teaspoon Angostura
  bitters
⅛ teaspoon ground
  cinnamon
3 cloves

1 Put everything into a saucepan and bring to the boil slowly, stirring until the sugar is dissolved. Simmer gently, covered, for 35-45 minutes, until the prunes are really tender.
2 Chill, remove the cloves, and serve with cream or custard.

Note:
If the prunes are very dry, soak overnight in the water, then use the water for stewing.

Ananas au Kirsch

you will need for 4-5 servings:

METRIC/IMPERIAL
1 small pineapple
3-5 tablespoons Kirsch
maraschino cherries

1 Cut off the skin and remove the 'eyes' from the pineapple.
2 Cut the flesh into slices, and with an apple corer punch out the centre core from each.
3 Arrange the slices on plates, pour the Kirsch over them and fill the centre holes with chopped maraschino cherries for colour.

Fruit salads

Winter (or whole year) salad
you will need for 4 servings:

METRIC/IMPERIAL
125 g/4½ oz
  granulated sugar
300 ml/½ pint water
0·5-0·75 kg/1¼-1½ lb
  mixed fruit after
  preparation

choose from melon
  (when possible)
oranges, red
  skinned apples,
  grapes, bananas,
  pineapple

1 Bring the sugar and water to the boil, stirring. Boil for 3-4 minutes.
2 If melon is used, cut the flesh into 1-cm/½-inch pieces. Cut all the skin and pith from the oranges and cut the flesh into pieces about the same size as the melon. Cut the unpeeled but cored apples into wedges and slice the grapes in halves and remove the pips.
3 Put the fruit into a serving dish and immediately pour the syrup over it. Be careful to cover the apple and banana to prevent their becoming brown.

Summer fruit salad

Make the syrup as above and choose from gooseberries, strawberries, raspberries, red and black currants, cherries, loganberries, peaches, plums, blackberries. Leave all the small fruit whole; stone the cherries and cut the peaches and plums in halves or quarters. If strawberries or raspberries are used, scatter some on top as decoration.

Tropical fruit salad

you will need for 6 servings:

METRIC/IMPERIAL
312-g/11-oz can
  lychees
340-g/12-oz can
  pineapple slices
410-g/14½-oz can
  sliced mangos or
  guava halves

410-g/14½-oz can paw
  paw, melon, or
  goldenberries
150-175 g/5-6 oz fresh
  grapes, halved and
  stoned

1 Drain all the fruit, keeping the syrups separate.
2 Cut the lychees in halves and the pineapple into pieces of about the same size. If mangos or guavas are used, cut these in the same way. Leave paw paw, melon, and goldenberries (Cape gooseberries) as they are.
3 Put all the fruit into a serving dish and pour syrup over it to come nearly to the top of the fruit. Use lychee syrup and any other preferred.

Cold soufflés

The traditional way of serving a cold soufflé or mousse is as follows: Cut a strip of double greaseproof paper long enough to go right round the dish and to overlap slightly. It must be wide enough to reach from the bottom of the dish to 5-6·5 cm/2-2½ inches above the rim. Tie in place.
When the mixture is poured into the dish it should come at least 2·5-4 cm/1-1½ inches above the rim. It is, therefore, very important to have the correct size of soufflé dish for the quantity of mixture used. For a cold soufflé, the shallower type of soufflé dish is better.
To remove the paper when the soufflé has set, cut off the string, and with a knife dipped in hot water gently ease the paper away from the soufflé.

Blackberry soufflé

you will need for 4 servings:

METRIC/IMPERIAL
450 g/1 lb blackberries
50 g/2 oz granulated
  sugar
3 eggs, separated
50 g/2 oz castor sugar
3 tablespoons boiling
  water

2 teaspoons gelatine
to decorate:
finely chopped nuts or
  cake crumbs, and
  whipped cream if
  desired

1 Wash the blackberries, reserve several for decoration and bring the rest to the boil with the granulated sugar, stirring. Boil until soft and mushy.
2 Rub through a sieve, or blend in a liquidiser and then rub through a sieve. The pulp should measure a scant 300 ml/½ pint. If not, make up with water.
3 In a basin beat the egg yolks and castor sugar together with a wooden spoon until light coloured and like thick cream.

4 Pour the boiling water over the gelatine in a cup and stir occasionally until smooth and clear.
5 Stir the warm blackberry purée into the creamed egg yolk mixture with the gelatine.
6 Leave until just beginning to set around the edges, then whisk with a wire whisk and stir in the stiffly beaten egg whites.
7 Pour into the prepared (see above) 900-ml/1½-pint soufflé dish, or sundae glasses and leave to set in a refrigerator.
8 If in a soufflé dish, remove the paper band (see above), decorate around the sides of the soufflé with chopped nuts or cake crumbs and place the reserved blackberries on top. If liked, piped whipped cream can also be used for decoration.

Orange

2 oranges	to decorate:
50 g/2 oz granulated sugar	toasted desiccated coconut or chopped nuts, with whipped cream
2 teaspoons gelatine	
3 eggs, separated	
50 g/2 oz castor sugar	

1 Grate the orange rinds and mix with the juice of the oranges. Make up to 300 ml/½ pint with bottled or canned orange juice.
2 Heat with the granulated sugar, stirring until the sugar is dissolved. Remove from the heat sprinkle the gelatine over the top and stir occasionally until smooth and clear. Proceed from stage 3 for Blackberry soufflé (see page 45).

Blackcurrant

350 g/12 oz blackcurrants	2 teaspoons gelatine
5 tablespoons water	to decorate:
75 g/3 oz granulated sugar	chopped nuts or cake crumbs, and whipped cream if desired
3 eggs, separated	
50 g/2 oz castor sugar	
3 tablespoons boiling water	

1 Wash and string the blackcurrants and proceed from stage 1 for Blackberry soufflé (see page 45).

Raspberry

550 g/1¼ lb raspberries	2 teaspoons gelatine
3 eggs, separated	to decorate:
100 g/4 oz castor sugar	chopped nuts or cake crumbs, and whipped cream
4 tablespoons boiling water	

1 Do not wash the raspberries unless necessary. Proceed from stage 2 for Blackberry soufflé (see page 45).

Damson

350 g/12 oz damsons	2 teaspoons gelatine
5 tablespoons water	
75 g/3 oz granulated sugar	to decorate:
3 eggs, separated	chopped nuts, biscuit crumbs, desiccated coconut, and whipped cream if liked
50 g/2 oz castor sugar	
3 tablespoons boiling water	

1 Wash the damsons, keep 2 aside for decoration and stew the rest with the water and granulated sugar. Remove the stones, then proceed from stage 2 for Blackberry soufflé (see page 45).

Rhubarb

0·75 kg/1½ lb rhubarb	3 tablespoons boiling water
1 tablespoon orange or lemon juice, or water	2 teaspoons gelatine
100 g/4 oz granulated sugar	to decorate:
3 eggs, separated	chopped nuts or biscuit crumbs
50 g/2 oz castor sugar	

1 Wash and trim the rhubarb and cut into short lengths. Proceed from stage 1 for Blackberry soufflé (see page 45).

Gooseberry

450 g/1 lb gooseberries (slightly underripe)	2 teaspoons gelatine
4 tablespoons water	to decorate:
50 g/2 oz granulated sugar	desiccated coconut or chopped nuts, with whipped cream if liked
3 eggs, separated	
50 g/2 oz castor sugar	
3 tablespoons boiling water	

1 Wash the gooseberries and proceed from stage 1 for Blackberry soufflé (see page 45).

Chocolate

175 g/6 oz plain chocolate	to decorate:
175 ml/6 fl oz milk	chocolate vermicelli or chopped nuts, and chocolate drops and/or glacé cherries
3 eggs, separated	
75 g/3 oz castor sugar	
3 tablespoons boiling water	
2 teaspoons gelatine	

1 Melt the chocolate in the milk in a bowl over hot but not boiling water. Proceed from stage 3 for Blackberry soufflé (see page 45).

Coffee

6 tablespoons strong
  black coffee
1 tablespoon coffee
  essence
150 ml/¼ pint milk
3 eggs, separated
75 g/3 oz castor sugar
3 tablespoons boiling
  water

2 teaspoons gelatine

to decorate:
chocolate vermicelli or
  chopped nuts, with
  whipped cream

1 Warm the coffees and milk together. Proceed from stage 3 for Blackberry soufflé (see page 45).

Ginger

250 ml/8 fl oz water
2 teaspoons gelatine
75 g/3 oz preserved
  ginger, finely
  chopped
1 tablespoon ginger
  syrup
1 teaspoon ginger
  essence

3 eggs, separated
75 g/3 oz castor sugar

to decorate:
chopped nuts or cake
  crumbs mixed with
  finely chopped
  ginger, and slices of
  ginger for the top

1 Bring the water to the boil, remove from the heat, sprinkle the gelatine over the top and stir occasionally until smooth and clear.
2 Stir in the ginger, syrup, and essence. Proceed from stage 3 of Blackberry soufflé (see page 45).

Mousses

For the following quantities use a 900-ml/1½ pint soufflé dish or ring mould.
you will need for 4-5 servings:

Chestnut mousse or Bavarian

METRIC/IMPERIAL

450-g/15¾-oz can
  sweetened chestnut
  purée
5 tablespoons boiling
  water
4 teaspoons gelatine

250 ml/8 fl oz whipping
  or double cream
2 egg whites

to decorate:
chopped nuts

1 Rub the purée through a sieve into a basin.
2 Pour the boiling water over the gelatine in a cup and stir occasionally until completely smooth and clear. Stir vigorously into the chestnut purée.
3 Whip the cream lightly and the egg whites stiffly and fold into the purée. Proceed from stage 7 for Blackberry soufflé (see page 45).

Note:
1–2 tablespoons rum may be added to the mousse.

Chocolate

1 large egg, separated
1 egg yolk
75 g/3 oz castor sugar
250 ml/8 fl oz milk
150 g/5 oz plain
  chocolate
4 tablespoons warm
  water
3 tablespoons boiling
  water

2 teaspoons gelatine
150 ml/¼ pint
  whipping or double
  cream

to decorate:
chopped roasted hazel
  nuts or almonds,
  and chocolate drops

1 In a basin beat the egg yolks and sugar together with a wooden spoon until light coloured and creamy.
2 Bring the milk to simmering point and pour onto the creamed mixture.
3 Return to the pan and stir over a low heat until the custard thickens (be careful it does not boil or it will turn into scrambled eggs). Remove from the heat and pour into the basin.
4 Melt the chocolate with the warm water in a bowl over hot but not boiling water and stir into the custard.
5 Pour the boiling water over the gelatine in a cup and stir occasionally until completely dissolved and clear.
6 Stir into the chocolate mixture and leave until just beginning to set around the edges, then stir in the lightly whipped cream and stiffly beaten egg white. Proceed from stage 7 for Blackberry soufflé (see page 45).

Coffee

3 eggs, separated
75 g/3 oz castor sugar
150 ml/¼ pint strong
  black coffee
3 teaspoons gelatine
2 teaspoons coffee
  essence

4 tablespoons milk
150 ml/¼ pint double
  cream

to decorate:
chopped nuts and/or
  chocolate vermicelli

1 In a basin beat the egg yolks and sugar together with a wooden spoon to the colour and consistency of thick cream.
2 Bring the coffee to simmering point, remove from the heat, sprinkle with the gelatine and stir occasionally until completely dissolved and smooth. Add the coffee essence and milk.
3 Stir into the creamed mixture and leave until just beginning to set around the edges, then whisk with a wire whisk until frothy and whisk in the lightly whipped cream and stiffly beaten egg whites. Proceed from stage 7 for Blackberry soufflé (see page 45).
Note:
1 tablespoon Crème de Cacao, brandy, or rum may be added to the coffee.

Fruit

3 tablespoons boiling water	2 egg whites
3 teaspoons gelatine	*to decorate:*
scant 300 ml/½ pint sweetened fruit purée (see cold soufflé, page 45)	chopped nuts, biscuit or cake crumbs, angelica 'leaves' and the reserved fruit
150 ml/¼ pint whipping or double cream	

1 Pour the boiling water over the gelatine in a cup and stir occasionally until completely dissolved and clear.
2 Heat the fruit purée a little and stir in the gelatine.
3 Pour into a basin and leave until just beginning to set around the edges, then whisk with a wire or rotary whisk and stir in the lightly whipped cream and the stiffly beaten egg whites. Proceed from stage 7 for Blackberry soufflé (see page 45).

Lemon

2 large or 3 small lemons	250 ml/8 fl oz whipping or double cream
3 large eggs, separated	*to decorate:*
175 g/6 oz castor sugar	toasted almonds, chopped, and any lemon decoration for the top
4 tablespoons boiling water	
3 teaspoons gelatine	

1 Grate the lemon rinds finely and mix with the juice, egg yolks, and sugar in a bowl.
2 Place the bowl over hot but not boiling water and cook, stirring, to the consistency of thin cream, 8-10 minutes.
3 Meanwhile, pour the boiling water over the gelatine in a cup and stir occasionally until completely dissolved and clear, then stir into the lemon mixture.
4 Pour into a basin and leave until just beginning to set around the edges, then whisk with a wire whisk and stir in the lightly whipped cream and stiffly beaten egg whites. Proceed from stage 7 for Blackberry soufflé (see page 45).

Vanilla

2 eggs, separated	3 teaspoons gelatine
1 extra egg yolk	150 ml/¼ pint whipping or double cream
75 g/3 oz vanilla sugar, or castor sugar with a generous ¼ teaspoon vanilla essence	*to decorate:*
250 ml/8 fl oz diluted evaporated milk	chopped roasted hazelnuts or almonds
4 tablespoons boiling water	

1 In a basin beat the egg yolks and sugar together with a wooden spoon to the colour and consistency of thick cream.
2 Bring the milk to simmering point, stirring, and pour onto the yolks.
3 Add the essence (if used), return to the pan and stir over a low heat until the custard thickens. Remove from the heat and pour into the basin.
4 Pour the boiling water over the gelatine in a cup and stir occasionally until completely dissolved and clear.
5 Stir into the custard and leave until just beginning to set around the edges, then stir in the lightly whipped cream and stiffly beaten egg whites. Proceed from stage 7 for Blackberry soufflé (see page 45).

Sherry mousse

you will need for 4 servings:

METRIC/IMPERIAL

juice of 1 lemon	150 ml/¼ pint medium sherry
pinch of salt	
175 g/6 oz castor sugar	*to decorate:*
150 ml/¼ pint water	whipped cream, chopped glacé fruits, nuts
2 teaspoons gelatine	
1 large or 2 small eggs	
300 ml/½ pint double cream	

1 Bring the lemon juice, salt, sugar, and water to the boil, stirring, and boil for 5 minutes.
2 Remove from the heat and stir in the gelatine until completely dissolved and clear.
3 Beat the egg yolks in a basin and stir in the gelatine. Leave until just beginning to set around the edges.
4 Whip the cream lightly and stir in the sherry.
5 Whisk the gelatine mixture until frothy and then whisk in the cream.
6 Beat the egg whites stiffly and fold into the mixture. Turn into sundae glasses and leave to set in a refrigerator.
7 Decorate with more whipped cream, chopped fruits and nuts.

Mousse au chocolat

you will need for 4-5 servings:

METRIC/IMPERIAL

225 g/8 oz plain chocolate	3 eggs, separated
25 g/1 oz butter	2 extra egg whites
	15 g/½ oz castor sugar

1 Melt the chocolate in a bowl over hot but not boiling water.
2 Remove the bowl from the hot water and beat in the butter and egg yolks one after the other until perfectly smooth.
3 Whip the egg whites stiffly with the sugar and fold into the chocolate.
4 Pour into small pots or glasses and leave in a refrigerator or cold place overnight.

Mousse au chocolat à la facon du Moulin de Vey

you will need for 6 servings:

METRIC/IMPERIAL

5 eggs, separated	few drops vanilla essence
50 g/2 oz castor sugar	2-3 tablespoons brandy
125 g/4½ oz plain chocolate	

1 In a basin beat the egg yolks and sugar together with a wooden spoon until light coloured and creamy.
2 Melt the chocolate in a bowl over hot but not boiling water and stir into the egg yolk mixture with the vanilla essence and brandy.
3 Whip the egg whites stiffly and fold into the chocolate. Treat as above.

Chocolate fudge walnut pie

you will need for 6 servings:

METRIC/IMPERIAL

pie case:

200 g/7 oz gingernut biscuits	75 g/3 oz butter or margarine, melted
40 g/1½ oz soft brown sugar	1 tablespoon water

filling:

large can sweetened condensed milk	2 eggs, separated
¼ teaspoon salt	50 g/2 oz self-raising flour
100 g/4 oz plain chocolate	100 g/4 oz walnuts, coarsely chopped
½ teaspoon vanilla essence	25 g/1 oz castor sugar

1 Put the biscuits a few at a time into a bag and crush into crumbs with a rolling pin. Put into a basin and stir in the brown sugar, melted butter and water.
2 Press over the base and up the sides of a 21·5-cm/8½-inch loose bottomed sandwich tin or line the base with greaseproof paper. Leave to set for at least an hour.
3 To make the filling, in a bowl over gently simmering water heat the milk with the salt and chocolate broken into small pieces, until the chocolate has melted and the mixture is smooth. Remove from the heat and stir in the vanilla essence, egg yolks, flour and walnuts.
4 Whip the egg whites stiffly with the castor sugar and fold into the mixture.
5 Pour into the pie case and bake in a moderate oven (180°C, 350°F, Gas Mark 4) for 55-60 minutes. Leave in the tin until cold before turning out.

Chocolate peppermint mousse

you will need for 4 servings:

METRIC/IMPERIAL

2 eggs, separated	40 g/1½ oz mint crisps
75 g/3 oz castor sugar	
150 g/5 oz plain chocolate	*to decorate:*
250 ml/8 fl oz milk	4 mint crisps, chopped nuts or desiccated coconut
2 tablespoons boiling water	
2 teaspoons gelatine	
150 ml/¼ pint whipping or double cream	

1 Beat the egg yolks and sugar together with a wooden spoon until light coloured and creamy.
2 Over a low heat melt the chocolate with a little of the milk, adding the rest gradually, until perfectly smooth.
3 Pour the boiling water over the gelatine in a cup and stir occasionally until completely dissolved and clear.
4 Stir the chocolate and gelatine into the creamed mixture and leave until just beginning to set around the edges, then whisk with a wire whisk and stir in the lightly whipped cream and stiffly beaten egg whites.
5 Fold in the mint crisps broken into small pieces, turn into sundae glasses and leave to set in a refrigerator.
6 Before serving, decorate with a mint crisp in the top of each, surrounded by chopped nuts or desiccated coconut.

Australian summer Christmas pudding

you will need for 8 servings:

METRIC/IMPERIAL

75 g/3 oz prunes	250-g/8½-oz can crushed pineapple
200 g/7 oz mixed dried fruit	4 tablespoons boiling water
25 g/1 oz soft browm sugar	2 tablespoons gelatine
1¼ teaspoons mixed cake spice	100 g/4 oz glacé cherries, quartered
¼ teaspoon ground cinnamon	miniature bottle (5 tablespoons) rum
700 ml/1¼ pints warm medium tea	
75 g/3 oz chopped mixed peel	*to decorate:*
1 tablespoon lemon juice	150 ml/¼ pint whipping or double cream, and toasted almonds
1 medium orange	

1 Chop the prunes, discarding the stones.
2 Put into a basin with the dried fruit, sugar, and spice and the strained warm tea. Leave overnight.
3 Transfer to a saucepan with the mixed peel, lemon juice, grated rind and half the juice of the orange, and the can of pineapple. Bring to the boil and boil for 4 minutes. Remove from the heat.
4 Pour the boiling water over the gelatine in a cup and stir occasionally until completely dissolved and smooth. Stir into the fruit with the cherries and rum.
5 Pour into a generous 1-litre/2-pint mould (fluted looks pretty) rinsed out with cold water and leave in a refrigerator to set.
6 Turn out (see page 27) and decorate if liked with piped rosettes of whipped cream all round with a toasted almond in the centre of each. Serve with Sabayon sauce (see page 91), or cream or custard lightly flavoured with rum.

Note:
If no refrigerator is available to set this pudding, increase the gelatine by half.

Equinox pudding

you will need for 5-6 servings:

METRIC/IMPERIAL
450 g/1 lb mixed dried fruit
600 ml/1 pint water
4 tablespoons boiling water
4 teaspoons gelatine
15 g/½ oz (1 tablespoon) cocoa powder

1 teaspoon mixed cake spice
25 g/1 oz soft brown sugar
1 tablespoon sweet or medium sherry

to decorate:
whipped cream

1 Bring the fruit to the boil in the water and boil for 5 minutes.
2 Pour the boiling water over the gelatine in a cup and stir occasionally until completely dissolved and clear, then stir into the fruit.
3 Mix the cocoa powder, mixed spice and sugar into a paste with the sherry and add to the fruit.
4 Turn into a generous 1-litre/2-pint ring or other mould rinsed out with cold water and leave to set in a refrigerator.
5 Turn out (see page 27) and fill the centre or decorate with whipped cream if liked.

Note:
If no refrigerator is available, increase the gelatine by half.

Chocolate log

you will need for 6 servings:

METRIC/IMPERIAL
175 g/6 oz plain chocolate
1½ tablespoons water
100 g/4 oz butter or margarine
100 g/4 oz icing sugar
2 egg yolks
5 tablespoons milk

225 g/8 oz Nice biscuits

to decorate:
glacé cherries, crystallised violets, nuts, or any decoration desired

1 Melt the chocolate with the water in a bowl over hot but not boiling water.
2 Cream the butter and sugar together until light and fluffy. Beat in the egg yolks and chocolate.
3 Pour the milk into a saucer and dip each biscuit into it on both sides.
4 Arrange 4 biscuits on a flat dish, spread with a layer of the chocolate mixture and continue the layers until all the biscuits are used.
5 Cover the top and sides with the remaining chocolate.
6 Decorate the surface all over with a fork, or tip of a knife, and with any other decoration desired.

Continental chocolate cake

you will need for 5-6 servings:

METRIC/IMPERIAL
225 g/8 oz plain chocolate
225 g/8 oz butter or margarine
2 eggs
50 g/2 oz castor sugar
1 teaspoon strong coffee
few drops vanilla essence

225 g/8 oz boiled potato, sieved
225 g/8 oz plain cake or biscuits, broken roughly into 1-cm/¼-inch pieces
225 g/8 oz marzipan

to decorate:
chocolate drops

1 Line a 450-g/1-lb loaf tin with greased greaseproof paper.
2 Melt the chocolate in a bowl over hot but not boiling water. Melt the butter separately.
3 In a basin beat the eggs and sugar together thoroughly, pour in the butter slowly, stirring continuously, then beat in the chocolate, coffee and vanilla essence.
4 Fold in the potato and cake or biscuit pieces and put the mixture into the tin.
5 Leave in a refrigerator or cold place to harden. Turn out.
6 Roll out the marzipan between sheets of greaseproof paper and cover the top and sides of the cake with it.
7 Mark in criss-cross lines for decoration and place chocolate drops or any othe decoration on top if desired.

Rich uncooked mocha-chocolate cake

you will need for 6-7 servings:

METRIC/IMPERIAL
175 g/6 oz semi-sweet biscuits
175 g/6 oz plain chocolate
175 g/6 oz butter or margarine
1 egg yolk
2 teaspoons rum or brandy
½ teaspoon vanilla essence
2 tablespoons evaporated milk or cream

1 tablespoon instant coffee
50 g/2 oz almonds, chopped
175 g/6 oz icing sugar

to decorate:
150 ml/¼ pint whipped cream, and grated chocolate or crumbled flake chocolate

1 Break the biscuits into small pieces.
2 Melt the chocolate in a bowl over hot but not boiling water. Add the butter by degrees, stirring until smooth after each addition. Remove the bowl from the water.
3 Beat the egg yolk with the rum and vanilla essence and stir into the chocolate.
4 Heat the evaporated molk or cream sufficiently to dissolve the instant coffee and add to the chocolate with the chopped almonds, sifted icing sugar and biscuits.

5 Lightly oil a generous 450-g/1-lb loaf tin. Lay a long piece of oiled greaseproof paper from one long end to the other, extending above the rim at each end.
6 Turn the cake mixture into the tin, level the top and press down with a spatula. Leave in a cold place to set.
7 Cut along the two unlined sides and pull out the cake by the protruding paper.
8 Decorate with whipped cream and grated chocolate or crumbled flake chocolate, or, for use as a cake, with butter or glacé icing.

Mocha biscuit log

you will need for 5-6 servings:

METRIC/IMPERIAL
150 g/5 oz butter or margarine
75 g/3 oz icing sugar
3 tablespoons drinking chocolate powder
1 tablespoon coffee essence

1½-2 tablespoons rum
6 tablespoons strong black coffee
16-24 (depending upon size) petit beurre biscuits

1 Cream the butter until soft, then beat in the sugar, chocolate powder and coffee essence.
2 Mix the rum and coffee and pour into a soup plate or saucer.
3 Dip each biscuit into the liquid for 10-15 seconds.
4 Lay (large ones 4 end to end, small ones 6 in an oblong) on a serving dish.
5 Spread with a layer of mocha icing. Repeat layers (4 layers of biscuits in all), and cover the top and sides with the remaining icing.
6 Decorate with a fork or knife tip and add any other decoration if desired. Leave in a refrigerator or cold place to harden.

Pies, Tarts, and Flans

Pastry dishes, both sweet and savoury, are great favourites with many people. They also enhance a variety of foods to give a contrast in texture and a marriage of flavours.

I do not intend to describe the full range of pastries because recipes for making these can be found in any comprehensive cookery book. Also modern housewives can buy and store frozen puff and flaky pastry at home. There are also packets of pastry mixes which save some preparation time.

However, I will give an unusual and unorthodox method for making flaky pastry which I learned in New Zealand and have used with pleasure ever since. There are various mixtures for shortcrust pastry which I think are worth giving as a choice for different dishes. Recipes for suet crust pastry are given in the chapter on Steamed Puddings (see page 23).

Hints for making pastry

1 Always roll pastry on a floured board, and flour the rolling pin also. Try to roll as evenly as possible without stretching the dough.
2 It is best, if possible, to leave all pastry for 15-30 minutes to 'rest' before rolling, but it is not essential.
3 There is no need to grease any tin for pastry. It will not stick because of the fat incorporated in the mixture.
4 When any quantity is given for pastry in a recipe, e.g. 225 g/8 oz, it is for pastry made from that quantity of flour etc. Bought pastry will require about twice as much.

Standard shortcrust pastry

Self-raising flour can be used, but the cooked pastry will be spongier and not as crisp. Decrease the fat by 15 g/½ oz.

METRIC/IMPERIAL
225 g/8 oz plain flour
¼ teaspoon salt
115 g/4 oz fat (butter or margarine and cooking fat or lard)
cold water

1 Sift the flour and salt into a basin and rub in the fats until the mixture resembles fine breadcrumbs.
2 With a knife or fork and then the fingertips, add only just sufficient cold water to make the dough bind. Knead for a few seconds to give a smooth dough.
3 Lightly flour the board and the rolling pin (they should not need a lot of flour to prevent sticking).
4 Roll out to the required thickness, lifting the dough lightly and turning it around to keep it light and even.
5 Bake according to each recipe, but as a general rule bake in a hot oven (220°C, 425°F, Gas Mark 7).

Note:
For a sweet pastry, stir in 1 tablespoon castor sugar after the fat has been rubbed in.

Rich shortcrust

Use 75 g/3 oz butter or margarine and 50 g/2 oz lard to 225 g/8 oz flour. It will require very little water to make the mixture bind.

Crusty shortcrust

Use above quantities for either standard or rich shortcrust, but substitute 25 g/1 oz ground rice for 25 g/1 oz of the flour.

Flan pastry

you will need for one 18-cm/7-inch flan:

METRIC/IMPERIAL
115 g/4 oz plain flour   1 egg yolk
pinch of salt
65-75 g/2½-3 oz butter
   or margarine and
   lard, mixed

1 Sift the flour and salt together and rub in the fat as above.
2 Stir in the egg yolk until the ingredients begin to stick together (it may be necessary to add a teaspoon of cold water), then with the hands knead very lightly to give a smooth dough.
3 Roll out and use to line the flan tin or ring (see below).

Note:
For a sweet flan, add 1 teaspoon castor sugar after the fat has been rubbed in.

Páte sucrée

you will need for one 20-cm/8-inch flan:

METRIC/IMPERIAL
150 g/5 oz plain flour   2 egg yolks
75 g/3 oz butter or   50 g/2 oz castor sugar
   margarine, softened

1 Put the flour on a cold surface (marble is the ideal) and make a large well in the centre. Tip in the butter, egg yolks and sugar.
2 With the tips of the fingers of one hand, squeeze the fat, yolks, and sugar together while incorporating the flour little by little from the sides with the aid of a knife blade or spatula.
3 Mix it to a soft dough, kneading lightly (you may have to add a teaspoon of water, depending on the size of the egg yolks). Put aside in a cold place for 1-2 hours before rolling out on a well-floured board.

New Zealand flaky pastry

METRIC/IMPERIAL
225 g/8 oz plain flour   1 teaspoon lemon
¼ teaspoon salt   juice
125 g/4½ oz butter or   cold water
   margarine   ¾-1 teaspoon cream
65 g/2½ oz hard white   of tartar
   fat

1 Sieve the flour and salt onto a pastry board.
2 With a long bladed knife chop the fat into the flour until the pieces are the size of small peas.
3 Sweep into a basin and with a fork stir in the lemon juice and just sufficient cold water to make the dough stick together.

4 Roll out on the floured board to an oblong about 28 cm/11 inches by 15 cm/6 inches. Sprinkle the cream of tartar through a sieve evenly all over.
5 Fold up by folding the two long sides to meet in the centre; then the two short ends to meet in the centre; and finally over in half. Press the edges lightly with the rolling pin to seal in the air.
6 Give a half turn, roll out again and fold up in the same way. Repeat once more. Leave, covered, in a cold place for an hour or more, although it may be used immediately if necessary.
7 Bake in a hot oven (230°C, 450°F, Gas Mark 8).

Choux pastry

The most important point for lightness of this pastry is the accuracy with which each ingredient is weighed or measured. And the eggs must be beaten into the mixture very thoroughly.

METRIC/IMPERIAL
65 g/2½ oz plain flour   130 ml/¼ pint water
pinch of salt   2 eggs, beaten
50 g/2 oz butter

1 Sift the flour and salt together.
2 In a small saucepan melt the butter in the water and bring to the boil. Tip in the flour all at once and over a more gentle heat carefully beat it in with a wooden spoon until completely smooth and the paste comes away from the sides of the pan.
3 Remove from the heat, allow to cool slightly, then gradually beat in sufficient egg to give a smooth glossy paste of piping consistency (if too much egg is added the mixture will become too soft to keep its shape when piped).
4 Use as required for each recipe, but the usual temperature for baking is in a moderately hot oven (200°C, 400°F, Gas Mark 6).

To make a flan case and bake 'blind'

Use flan pastry, pâte
   sucrée, standard or
   rich shortcrust (using
   115 g/4 oz flour, etc.).

1 Roll out the pastry on a floured board, and as an aid to lifting the dough onto the flan tin or ring, fold the half section from the further end over the rolling pin, and holding the two together, carefully lift into position over the flan tin.
2 Line an 18-cm/7-inch flan tin or place a flan ring on a baking sheet and line that. Be careful not to stretch the dough, and to press it lightly into the right angle at the base of the tin all round making sure there are no air pockets, or the air will expand with the heat and blow up a bubble in the pastry. Trim the edge.
3 Prick the base all over with a fork, then leave in a cold place for at least 30 minutes to 'rest' before cooking, to prevent the pastry shrinking unevenly from the sides.
4 Place a smaller tin in the centre and bake in a moderately hot oven (200°C, 400°F, Gas Mark 6) for 15 minutes, then remove the smaller tin from the inside and continue baking for 5-10 minutes to dry out the

pastry.
Note:
If the flan is to be filled and used without further baking, give it another 5-10 minutes, until lightly browned.

Apple pie or tart

you will need for 4-5 servings:

METRIC/IMPERIAL

0·75 kg/1½-1¾ lb cooking apples	water
125 g/4½ oz granulated sugar	175 g/6 oz any shortcrust pastry (see page 51)
grated rind of ½ small lemon	beaten egg or milk
2 cloves	castor sugar

1 Peel and core the apples and cut into thick slices.
2 Pack into a 900-ml/1½-pint pie dish, mounding the centre to above the level of the rim. Sprinkle each layer with the sugar and lemon rind. Put in one clove at either end. Less than half fill with water.
3 Roll out the pastry a little larger than the dish. Cut off a narrow strip all round and roll out thinly.
4 Brush the edge of the pie dish with cold water and press the band of pastry onto it. Brush that also with water and cover the whole dish with the pastry. Trim with a sharp knife and decorate the edge by scalloping or pressing with the handle of a knife.
5 Brush all over with beaten egg or milk. Cut several slits to allow the steam to escape and bake in a moderately hot oven (200°C, 400°F, Gas Mark 6) for 35-40 minutes until golden brown and the fruit is cooked. Dredge with castor sugar to serve.

Variation:
Fruit pie or tart

Use 0·75 kg/1½ lb any fruit prepared as for Stewed fruit (see page 43–4) and using the same quantity of sugar. Add only 2-3 tablespoons water. Proceed from stage 2 above.

Note:
If puff or flaky pastry is used, flake the edge all round with a knife before scalloping, and bake in a hot oven (230°C, 450°F, Gas Mark 8) for 15 minutes, then lower heat to moderately hot (190°C, 375°F, Gas Mark 5) and continue baking for a further 20–30 minutes, until the fruit is cooked and the pastry nicely browned.

Apple plate pie

you will need for 4 servings:

METRIC/IMPERIAL

0·5 kg/1¼ lb cooking apples, after peeling and coring	⅛ teaspoon ground cinnamon pinch of ground cloves
1 tablespoon water	
150-175 g/5-6 oz granulated sugar	225 g/8 oz rich or crispy shortcrust pastry (see page 51)
50 g/2 oz sultanas	
½ teaspoon Angostura bitters (optional)	beaten egg or milk castor sugar

1 Slice or chop the apples roughly and stew with the water and granulated sugar until the apple is mushy.
2 Remove from the heat, mash with a potato masher and stir in the sultanas, Angostura and spices.
3 Roll out over half the pastry and line a 23-cm/9-inch pie plate or 18-cm/7-inch flan tin with it. Trim the edges. Spread with the apple.
4 Roll out the rest of the pastry including the trimmings. Brush round the edges of the pastry-lined plate with water, place the second piece on top and press the edges together to seal firmly. Decorate around the edge with the handle of a knife or as desired.
5 Brush with beaten egg or milk, sprinkle liberally with castor sugar and prick all over with a fork. Bake in a hot oven (220°C, 425°F, Gas Mark 7) for 30-35 minutes, until golden brown.

Note:
If preferred, flaky or bought puff pastry may be used in place of shortcrust.

Variation:
Blackberry and apple plate pie

450 g/1 lb dessert or cooking apples (375-400 g/13-14 oz after peeling and coring)	225 g/8 oz blackberries
	225 g/8 oz any shortcrust pastry (see page 51)
125 g/4½ oz granulated sugar	

1 Peel and core the apples and cut into small pieces. Bring to the boil with three-quarters of the sugar (no water), stirring continuously, and boil to a mash. Wash the blackberries and drain thoroughly.
2 Roll out over half the pastry and line a 23-cm/9-inch pie plate with it, trimming the edges. Spread with the apple, then cover with the blackberries and sprinkle the remaining sugar over them. Proceed from stage 4 above.

Bilberry plate pie

450 g/1 lb bilberries	cinnamon
150 g/5 oz granulated sugar	225 g/8 oz any shortcrust pastry (see page 51)
½ teaspoon ground	

1 Mix the washed and drained bilberries with the sugar and cinnamon and proceed from stage 3 for Apple plate pie above.

Rhubarb and raisin plate pie

450 g/1 lb rhubarb	⅛ teaspoon ground cinnamon
100 g/4 oz seedless raisins	225 g/8 oz any shortcrust pastry (see page 51)
175 g/6 oz granulated sugar	
2 teaspoons lemon juice	

1 Wash and trim the rhubarb and cut into small pieces. Put into a saucepan with the raisins, sugar, and lemon juice. Bring to the boil, stirring, and boil until the rhubarb is soft. Remove from the heat, stir in the

cinnamon and leave until cold. Proceed from stage 3 for Apple plate pie (see page 53).

Apple almond lattice flan

you will need for 4 servings:

METRIC/IMPERIAL
175 g/6 oz plain flour
¼ teaspoon salt
50 g/2 oz ground
  almonds
25 g/1 oz castor sugar
75 g/3 oz butter or
  margarine
1 egg yolk
water

350-400 g/12-14 oz
  cooking apples
  (275 g/10 oz after
  peeling and coring)
50 g/2 oz brown sugar
1 teaspoon ground
  cinnamon
300 ml/½ pint soured
  cream

1 Make the pastry. Mix together the flour, salt, ground almonds and castor sugar. Rub in the butter. Beat the egg yolk with 1 tablespoon water and stir into the flour, adding a little more water if necessary to make the dough stick together.
2 Roll out and line an 18-cm/7-inch flan tin with it. Keep remaining pastry aside for decoration.
3 Peel, core, chop, and stew the apple with the brown sugar until mushy. Mash with a potato masher and stir in the cinnamon.
4 When cold spread the apple in the flan case and pour the soured cream over it.
5 Roll out remaining pastry and cut into strips. Lay these across the flan to form a lattice pattern, brushing the ends with water to make them stick onto the flan case. Bake in a moderately hot oven (190°C, 375°F, Gas Mark 5) for 30 minutes, or until the pastry is golden.

La tarte Annette

you will need for 5-6 servings:

METRIC/IMPERIAL
75 g/3 oz granulated
  sugar
water
1½ tablespoons
  brandy
75 g/3 oz sultanas
200 g/7 oz butter
213 g/7½ oz plain flour

2 egg yolks
icing sugar
50 g/2 oz soft
  breadcrumbs
350-400 g/12-14 oz
  dessert or cooking
  apples, after peeling
  and coring

1 Bring the granulated sugar and 5 tablespoons water to the boil, stirring until the sugar is dissolved. Boil for 3 minutes, remove, stir in the brandy and sultanas and leave for several hours.
2 Rub 175 g/6 oz of the butter into the flour. Beat the egg yolks together and mix into the dough until smooth. Leave covered for 2 hours.
3 Roll out over half the pastry and line a 23-cm/9-inch pie plate or 20-cm/8-inch flan tin with it. Sieve about 25 g/1 oz icing sugar over the base.
4 Fry the breadcrumbs in the remaining butter until golden and scatter them over the icing sugar. Cut the apples into very thin slices and lay in overlapping circles on the breadcrumbs. Spread the sultanas over the top and pour in the syrup.
5 Roll out the rest of the pastry and cover the tart with it, sealing the two edges together firmly with cold

water. Trim, prick the top with a fork and bake in a moderately hot oven (190°C, 375°F, Gas Mark 5) for 20 minutes, then lower the heat to moderate (180°C, 350°F, Gas Mark 4) and continue baking for a further 30-40 minutes. Sprinkle with icing sugar to serve.

Apple dumplings

you will need for 4 servings:

METRIC/IMPERIAL
225 g/8 oz any
  shortcrust pastry
  (see page 51)
4 large cooking apples

granulated sugar (or
  brown)
4 cloves (optional)
beaten egg or milk

1 Cut the pastry into 4 pieces. Roll out each piece into 20-25·5-cm/8-10-inch diameter circles.
2 Peel and core the apples with an apple corer. Place one on each pastry circle and fill the centres with sugar, and a clove if liked.
3 Pull up the pastry to meet on top of the apples and seal well with cold water. Trim the edges. Turn upside-down and place on a baking sheet. Decorate the tops with pastry 'leaves' or 'petals' cut from the trimmings.
4 Make one small hole or 2 or 3 small cuts on top, brush all over with beaten egg or milk and bake in a hot oven (220°C, 425°F, Gas Mark 7) for 30-35 minutes, until golden brown.

Fruity apple slices

you will need for 4 servings:

METRIC/IMPERIAL
225 g/8 oz bought puff
  or flaky or 110 g/4 oz
  New Zealand pastry
  (see page 52)
175-200 g/6-7 oz
  cooking apples,
  after peeling
50 g/2 oz seedless
  raisins and currants,
  mixed

25 g/1 oz desiccated
  coconut
40 g/1½ oz cut mixed
  peel
40-50 g/1½-2 oz soft
  brown sugar
milk
castor sugar

1 Roll out the pastry thinly to an oblong 30 by 15 cm/12 by 6 inches, with edges trimmed. Cut in half across.
2 Cut the apples into quarters and cut out all the core. Slice each quarter thinly and cover one half of the pastry with overlapping slices. Sprinkle one with the fruit, coconut, mixed peel, and a liberal amount of sugar.
3 Cover with the second piece of pastry and press down firmly. Brush with milk, sieve over castor sugar and mark into 4 without cutting through.
4 Bake in a hot oven (230°C, 450°F, Gas Mark 8) for 15-20 minutes until golden brown. Cut through while hot and serve hot or cold.

Tart of several sweetmeats

you will need for 6-7 servings:

METRIC/IMPERIAL

368-g/13-oz packet bought puff, flaky, or 225 g/8 oz New Zealand pastry (see page 52)
175 g/6 oz currants
350 g/12 oz apples

castor sugar
225-350 g/8-12 oz plums or grapes

to decorate:
cut mixed peel and angelica

1 Roll out the pastry thinly and cut into 4 oblongs of about 23 by 15 cm/9 by 6 inches, or into squares. Trim the edges.
2 Lay one piece on a baking sheet and scatter the currants over it, pressing them in lightly. Cover with a second piece of pastry.
3 Lay thin slices of peeled and cored apple all over it and sprinkle with sugar to taste. Cover with a third piece of pastry.
4 Lay slices of stoned plums or halved and seeded grapes over it and sweeten as necessary. Cover with the last piece of pastry, and with a small pastry cutter cut out 5 holes to show the fruit beneath.
5 Brush with beaten egg or milk and bake in a hot oven (220°-230°C, 425°-450°F, Gas Mark 7-8) for 25-30 minutes until golden brown.
6 Fill the holes with chopped mixed peel and arrange small half 'leaves' of angelica all round each to suggest posies. Serve hot or cold.

Cherry pie

you will need for 4-5 servings:

METRIC/IMPERIAL

175 g/6 oz rich shortcrust pastry (see page 51)
0·75 kg/1½ lb black cherries (preferably morello)
1 tablespoon lemon juice

200 g/7 oz granulated sugar (100 g/4 oz for sweet cherries)
25 g/1 oz cornflour
¼ teaspoon almond essence
15 g/½ oz butter

1 Roll out the pastry and line a 23-cm/9-inch pie plate with it, leaving a little over, with the trimmings, for lattice strips. Trim the edge.
2 Stone the cherries.
3 Mix the cherries thoroughly with the lemon juice, sugar, cornflour, and essence and pack into the pastry case. Dot with flakes of butter.
4 Criss-cross with narrow strips of pastry, sticking the ends onto the pastry edge firmly with cold water, and bake in a hot oven (220°C, 425°F, Gas Mark 7) for 15 minutes, then lower heat to moderate (180°C, 350°F, Gas Mark 4) and continue baking for a further 25-30 minutes. Serve warm or cold.

Cherry cream pie

you will need for 4 servings:

METRIC/IMPERIAL

450 g/1 lb cherries
18-cm/7-inch baked flan case
1 tablespoon flour
75 g/3 oz castor sugar

pinch of salt
1 egg yolk
1½ teaspoons lemon juice

1 Wash and stone the cherries. Pack as tightly as possible into the flan case in one layer.
2 Mix the flour, sugar, and salt together and beat in the egg yolk and lemon juice until creamy.
3 Spread over the cherries and bake in a moderately hot oven (190°C, 375°F, Gas Mark 5) for 35-40 minutes, until lightly browned.

Cherry shortcake

you will need for 6 servings:

METRIC/IMPERIAL

225 g/8 oz plain flour and 3 teaspoons baking powder (or self-raising flour with 1 teaspoon baking powder)
50 g/2 oz butter or margarine

castor sugar
1 large egg
2-3 tablespoons milk
450 g/1 lb black cherries

1 Sieve the flour and baking powder into a basin, rub in the butter until the mixture resembles fine breadcrumbs, then stir in 75 g/3 oz castor sugar.
2 Beat the egg with 2 tablespoons milk and stir into the dough, adding a little more milk if necessary to give a soft spreading consistency.
3 Spread the dough evenly in a 20-cm/8-inch sandwich tin. Press in the stoned cherries all over the top and dredge well with castor sugar.
4 Bake in a moderately hot oven (200°C, 400°F, Gas Mark 6) for 35-40 minutes. Dredge again with sugar and serve hot with cream or custard.

Cherry ring

you will need for 4 servings:

METRIC/IMPERIAL

225 g/8 oz self-raising flour
pinch of salt
50 g/2 oz margarine or vegetable fat

100 g/4 oz castor sugar
milk
450 g/1 lb cherries

1 Sieve the flour and salt into a basin and rub in the fat until it resembles fine breadcrumbs. Stir in 25 g/1 oz of the sugar and sufficient milk to give a soft dough.
2 Roll out to an oblong a scant 0·5 cm/¼ inch in thickness. Trim the edges.
3 Stone the cherries and spread all over the dough to within 1 cm/½ inch of the edge. Sprinkle over the rest of the sugar.
4 Roll up like a Swiss roll, starting from the long side. Brush the edge with cold water and seal onto the roll.
5 Place on a baking tray and bend round to form a complete circle, joining the ends together with cold water.

6 Brush with milk and cut radiating slits half way through the ring at about 2·5-cm/1-inch intervals. Bake in a hot oven (220°C, 425°F, Gas Mark 7) for 30 minutes, or until the pastry is a golden brown.

Fruit cobbler

you will need for 4 servings:

METRIC/IMPERIAL

175 g/6 oz self-raising flour	5-6 tablespoons milk
pinch of salt	0·75 kg/1½ lb stewed fruit
50 g/2 oz margarine	
40 g/1½ oz castor sugar	

1 Sieve the flour and salt into a basin, rub in the margarine until the mixture resembles fine breadcrumbs and stir in the sugar.
2 Make a well in the centre and add sufficient milk to give a soft dough.
3 Turn out onto a floured board and roll to about 1 cm/½ inch in thickness. Cut into rounds with a 4·5-5cm/1¾-2-inch fluted pastry cutter.
4 Turn the fruit into a generous 1-litre/2-pint heat-proof dish and arrange the rounds, overlapping, around the perimeter of the dish. Brush with milk to glaze.
5 Bake above centre in a hot oven (220°C, 425°F, Gas Mark 7) for 15 minutes, or until the topping is golden brown.

Fruit flan

you will need for 4 servings:

METRIC/IMPERIAL

450 g/1 lb strawberries, raspberries, loganberries, redcurrants, blackberries, greengages, plums	1 teaspoon arrowroot or cornflour
	4 tablespoons water
	3 tablespoons redcurrant jelly or seived apricot jam
18-cm/7-inch baked flan case	castor sugar

1 Prepare the fruit as for stewing (see page 43–4) and fill the flan case with it.
2 Make the syrup. Make the arrowroot or cornflour into a smooth paste with the water, bring to the boil with the jam, stirring, and boil for 2-3 minutes. Add sugar to taste, and stir until dissolved.
3 Leave until just beginning to thicken before pouring over the fruit.

Variation:

If gooseberries, blackcurrants, or damsons are used, it is better to stew them lightly first, and use the juice in place of the water.

Grape flan

you will need for 8 servings:

METRIC/IMPERIAL

2 egg whites	almond essence
175 g/6 oz ground almonds and hazelnuts (optional), mixed	23-25·5-cm/9-10-inch flan pastry flan case made from 225 g/8 oz flour (see page 52)
100 g/4 oz castor sugar	
75 g/3 oz soft breadcrumbs	175 g/6 oz each black and white grapes

Apricot sauce:

½ teaspoon arrowroot or cornflour	2 tablespoons sieved apricot jam
5 tablespoons water	

1 Whip the egg whites stiffly, stir in the ground nuts, sugar, breadcrumbs, and enough almond essence to give a good flavour. Spread evenly in the flan case.
2 Cut the grapes in halves and remove the seeds.
3 Arrange them neatly over the mixture to form 4 alternate triangles of black and white.
4 To make the sauce, mix the arrowroot or cornflour into a smooth paste with a little of the water, add the rest and the jam.
5 Bring to the boil, stirring, and boil for 2 minutes.
6 Pour over the warm apricot sauce and leave until cold.

Cranberry pie or tart

you will need for 4-5 servings:

METRIC/IMPERIAL

450 g/1 lb fresh cranberries	225 g/8 oz granulated sugar
225 g/8 oz cooking or dessert apples	4 tablespoons water
1 small (75-100-g/3-4-oz) orange	225 g/8 oz any shortcrust pastry (see page 51)

1 Wash and drain the cranberries. Peel and core the apples and chop into small pieces. Wash the orange and cut (peel included) into very small pieces.
2 Mix all the fruit with the sugar and pack into a generous 1-litre/2-pint pie dish, mounding the centre. Pour in the water.
3 Cover the dish with pastry as for Apple pie (see page 53) and bake in a hot oven (220°C, 425°F, Gas Mark 7) for 15 minutes, then lower the heat to moderately hot (190°C, 375°F, Gas Mark 5) and continue baking for 30 minutes, or until the pastry is a golden brown. Sprinkle with castor sugar to serve.

Evesham tart

you will need for 5-6 servings:

METRIC/IMPERIAL

0·5 kg/1¼ lb plums	150 ml/¼ pint single cream
275 g/10 oz any shortcrust pastry (see page 51)	2 eggs
125 g/4½ oz castor sugar	¼ teaspoon grated nutmeg

1 Wash the plums, cut in halves and remove the stones.
2 Roll out the pastry and line a 30 by 20-cm/12 by 8-inch Swiss roll tin. Crimp the edges for decoration.
3 Arrange the plums, cut sides up, on the pastry and sprinkle over half the sugar. Bake in a moderately hot oven (200°C, 400°F, Gas Mark 6) for 15 minutes.
4 Meanwhile beat together the cream, eggs, nutmeg, and the rest of the sugar and pour this mixture over the plums.
5 Continue baking in a moderate oven (180°C, 350°F, Gas Mark 4) for a further 30 minutes until the custard is set. Best served hot but may also be served cold.

Switzen plum flan

you will need for 4-5 servings:

METRIC/IMPERIAL

0·5 kg/1¼ lb Switzen (purple) plums	1 teaspoon cold water
175 g/6 oz plain flour	25 g/1 oz roasted hazelnuts, finely chopped
100 g/4 oz butter or margarine	50 g/2 oz cake crumbs
50 g/2 oz castor sugar	icing sugar
1 egg yolk	

1 Wash the plums, cut in halves and discard the stones.
2 Sift the flour into a basin. Rub in the butter until resembling fine breadcrumbs, stir in half the sugar and then the egg yolk beaten with the water. Knead lightly until smooth.
3 Roll out and line a 20-cm/8-inch flan tin, trimming the edges.
4 Mix the rest of the sugar with the nuts and cake crumbs. Scatter over the base of the flan, and arrange the plum halves in overlapping circles on top.
5 Bake in a moderately hot oven (200°C, 400°F, Gas Mark 6) for 40-45 minutes, until the plums are just soft and the pastry golden.
6 Scatter icing sugar generously over the top and serve hot or cold.

Gooseberry meringue pie

you will need for 4 servings:

METRIC/IMPERIAL

0·5 kg/1¼ lb gooseberries	2 eggs, separated
1 tablespoon water	100 g/4 oz castor sugar
125 g/4½ oz soft brown sugar	18-cm/7-inch baked flan case (see page 52)
25 g/1 oz butter	

1 Wash, top and tail the gooseberries. Stew with the water and brown sugar until mushy.
2 Remove from the heat and stir in the butter until melted. Beat in the egg yolks and turn into the flan case.
3 Whip the egg whites stiffly with a little of the castor sugar and fold in the rest. Pile over the gooseberries to touch the pastry all round and bake in a moderate oven (180°C, 350°F, Gas Mark 4) for 15-20 minutes, until the meringue is golden on top.

Nutty gooseberry flan

you will need for 5-6 servings:

METRIC/IMPERIAL

115 g/4 oz plain flour	2 teaspoons wine vinegar
50 g/2 oz potato flour (or 175 g/6 oz plain flour)	2 teaspoons cold water
⅛ teaspoon salt	2 egg whites
115 g/4 oz butter or margarine	65 g/2½ oz ground almonds
125 g/4½ oz castor sugar	450 g/1 lb gooseberries

1 Sift the flours and salt into a basin and rub in the butter. Stir in 40 g/1½ oz of the sugar and then the vinegar and water and knead lightly until smooth.
2 Line a 20-cm/8-inch flan tin, pressing out the pastry evenly with the hands, and prick the bottom. Bake in a moderately hot oven (200°C, 400°F, Gas Mark 6) for 10 minutes.
3 Whip the egg whites stiffly with a little of the remaining sugar, then fold in the rest with the ground almonds. Spread evenly in the re-cooked flan case.
4 Place the washed, dried, and topped and tailed gooseberries all over the top (some will sink into the mixture), and bake in a moderately hot oven (190°C, 375°F, Gas Mark 5) for 40 minutes. Serve hot or cold, sprinkled with castor sugar.

Old English pumpkin pie

you will need for 4-5 servings:

METRIC/IMPERIAL

1·75 kg/4 lb pumpkin (1·25 kg/2½ lb after peeling)	¼ teaspoon ground cinnamon
75 g/3 oz sultanas	2 cloves
25 g/1 oz currants	225 g/8 oz any shortcrust pastry (see page 51)
75 g/3 oz demerara sugar	
¼ teaspoon grated nutmeg	

1 Cut the peeled pumpkin into 2-2·5-cm/¾-1-inch pieces and mix thoroughly with the dried fruit, sugar, and spices.
2 Pack tightly into a generous 1-litre/2-pint pie dish, mounding the top. Proceed from stage 3 for Apple pie (see page 53).
3 After baking for 35-40 minutes, cover the pastry with a double thickness of greaseproof paper and continue baking until the pumpkin is tender when tested with a skewer through the hole in the top, 15-20 minutes.

American pumpkin pie

you will need for 6 servings:

METRIC/IMPERIAL

225 g/8 oz flan or rich shortcrust pastry (see page 51 or 52)	¾ teaspoon ground cinnamon
2·25 kg/5 lb pumpkin (350 g/12 oz cooked or canned pulp)	½ teaspoon grated nutmeg
75 g/3 oz dark soft brown sugar	¼ teaspoon ground cloves
¼ teaspoon salt	150 ml/¼ pint milk
1½ teaspoons ground ginger	2 large eggs

1 Roll out the pastry and line a 20-cm/8-inch flan tin with it. Crimp the edges.
2 Peel the pumpkin, cut the flesh into small pieces, drop into boiling water and boil, covered, for 10-15 minutes until tender. Drain thoroughly, then blend in a liquidiser or rub through a sieve.
3 Mix the dry ingredients into the pulp. Stir in the milk and lastly the well-beaten eggs.
4 Pour into the pie case and bake in a hot oven (230°C, 425°F, Gas Mark 7) for 10 minutes, then lower the heat to moderate (180°C, 350°F, Gas Mark 4) and continue baking for a further 30-35 minutes, until the filling is set and firm.

Treacle or golden tart

you will need for 4 servings:

METRIC/IMPERIAL
225 g/8 oz any shortcrust pastry (see page 51)
40 g/1½ oz soft breadcrumbs
4-5 tablespoons golden syrup

1 Cut off about a quarter of the pastry. Roll out the rest and line a 22-23-cm/8½-9-inch (across the top) pie plate with it. Trim the edge.
2 Sprinkle the base with the breadcrumbs, then pour over the golden syrup. Alternatively, these may be mixed together first.
3 Roll out the remaining pastry with the trimmings and cut into narrow strips. Lay these, flat or twisted, criss-cross across the top, sticking the ends firmly onto the pastry edge with cold water.
4 Bake in a moderately hot oven (200°C, 400°F, Gas Mark 6) for 30-35 minutes, until the pastry is golden.

Custard tart or pie

you will need for 4 servings:

METRIC/IMPERIAL
115 g/4 oz shortcrust pastry (preferably rich, see page 51)
2 eggs
25 g/1 oz castor sugar
300 ml/½ pint milk
grated nutmeg

1 Roll out the pastry and line a deep 18-cm/7-inch flan tin with it, or make the pastry stand above the rim of a flan ring by pinching it up all round. Make sure the pastry is not stretched and is well pressed into the right angle at the bottom of the tin so no air bubbles can form beneath. Prick the base all over.
2 Beat the eggs with the sugar, pour on the warmed milk and strain into the flan case. Sprinkle with a little grated nutmeg.
3 Bake in a moderately hot oven (220°C, 425°F, Gas Mark 7) for 10 minutes, until the pastry begins to colour, then lower the heat to moderate (180°C, 350°F, Gas Mark 4) and continue baking for a further 20-25 minutes, until the custard is set.

Old Dutch milk tart

you will need for 5 servings:

METRIC/IMPERIAL
40 g/1½ oz sugar
generous 25 g/1¼ oz flour
pinch of salt
450 ml/¾ pint milk
15 g/½ oz butter
5-cm/2-inch stick cinnamon
1 tablespoon ground almonds
few drops almond essence
2 eggs
350 g/12 oz bought puff or 175 g/6 oz New Zealand flaky pastry (see page 52)

1 Mix the sugar, flour, and salt together and make into a smooth paste with a little of the milk.
2 Bring the rest of the milk to simmering point with the butter and cinnamon stick.
3 Remove the cinnamon stick and slowly stir the milk into the flour paste. Return to the pan, bring to the boil, stirring, and simmer for 5 minutes. Remove from the heat and stir in the ground almonds, almond essence, and the well-beaten eggs. Allow to cool.
4 Roll out the pastry and line a deep 20-cm/8-inch pie plate with it. Trim the edge.
5 Pour in the custard and bake in a hot oven (230°C, 450°F, Gas Mark 8) for 5-7 minutes, then lower the heat to moderately hot (200°C, 400°F, Gas Mark 6) and continue baking for a further 20-25 minutes. Serve hot or cold.

Quick cream pie

you will need for 5-6 servings:

METRIC/IMPERIAL
175 g/6 oz cream cheese
150 ml/¼ pint single cream
150 ml/¼ pint milk
397-g/14-oz can cherry, apricot, strawberry, or blackcurrant pie filling
½ packet Instant whip
20-cm/8-inch baked flan case (see page 52)

1 Cream the cream cheese in a basin, then beat in the cream, milk, about three-quarters of the pie filling and the Instant whip powder until creamy and thick.
2 Turn into the flan case, level the top and chill for 1 hour or more. Pour the remaining pie filling in the centre on top to decorate.

Cream Horns

you will need for 5 servings (10 horns):

METRIC/IMPERIAL
212-g/7½-oz packet frozen puff pastry
1 egg yolk
raspberry jam
150 ml/¼ pint double cream
icing sugar

1 Roll out the pastry to an oblong 20 cm/8 inches wide and about 38 cm/15 inches in length. Trim the edges. Cut into 10 long strips, 2 cm/¾ inch in width.
2 Beat the egg yolk with a teaspoon of water and brush

58

one edge of each strip before winding it, egg side outwards, round a cone-shaped tin mould from the pointed end, slightly overlapping at the moistened edge.

3 Bake in a hot oven (220°C, 425°F, Gas Mark 7) for 10-15 minutes until crisp and lightly golden.

4 Carefully slip off the cones with a gentle rotating movement and leave to cool on a wire cake rack.

5 When cold, half fill with jam and top with whipped cream. Dredge with icing sugar.

Mille feuilles or vanilla slices

you will need for 4 servings (8 'slices'):

METRIC/IMPERIAL

212-g/7½-oz packet puff pastry	to decorate: pink or white glacé icing
raspberry jam	
250 ml/8 fl oz double cream whipped, thick Crème pâtissière (see page 89) or thick vanilla flavoured custard	

1 Roll out the pastry into a strip about 10 cm/4 inches wide after trimming, and 0·5 cm/¼ inch in thickness. Cut into 12 fingers.

2 Bake in a hot oven (230°C, 450°F, Gas Mark 8) for 12-15 minutes, until well risen and golden. Cool on a wire cake rack.

3 When cold, slice each in half horizontally. Sandwich three pieces together for each 'slice', spreading first with jam, then the chosen filling.

4 Ice the tops with pink or white glacé icing.

Strawberry mille feuilles

you will need for 4 servings:

METRIC/IMPERIAL

212-g/7½-oz packet puff pastry	150 ml/¼ pint double cream
225 g/8 oz strawberries	
2-3 tablespoons castor sugar	to decorate: icing or castor sugar
85-g/3-oz packet Philadelphia cream cheese	

1 Roll out the pastry to a rectangle 30 by 23 cm/12 by 9 inches after trimming the edges. Cut into 8 fingers.

2 Bake in a hot oven (230°C, 450°F, Gas Mark 8) for 12-15 minutes until well risen and golden brown. Leave on a wire cake rack to cool.

3 Hull the strawberries, keep 4 good ones aside and slice the rest.

4 Beat the sugar into the cream cheese and stir in the whipped cream. Fold in the sliced strawberries.

5 Sandwich two slices together at a time with half of the cream mixture, spread the tops with the rest and place a reserved strawberry in the centre of each. Sprinkle the strawberries with icing or castor sugar to decorate.

Strawberry tartlets

you will need for 2 servings:

METRIC/IMPERIAL

175-225 g/6-8 oz strawberries	50 g/2 oz granulated sugar
4 home-made or bought tartlet cases, about 7·5 cm/3 inches across the top	4 tablespoons water few drops red colouring
1 teaspoon arrowroot or cornflour	

1 Place one good strawberry in the centre of each case and arrange the rest of the strawberries cut in halves or quarters around it.

2 Make a paste of the arrowroot or cornflour and sugar with the water, bring to the boil, stirring, and boil for 2-3 minutes until clear. Remove from the heat, add red colouring to give an attractive colour and leave until almost cold and well thickened, then spoon it over the fruit to glaze and sweeten.

Variation:

Fill the tartlet cases with raspberries, cherries, gooseberries or redcurrants. Glaze in the same way using appropriate colouring.

Strawberry or raspberry shortcake

you will need for 6 servings:

METRIC/IMPERIAL

225 g/8 oz self-raising flour	4 tablespoons milk
¼ teaspoon salt	350-450 g/12-16 oz strawberries or raspberries
75 g/3 oz butter or margarine	150 ml/¼ pint double cream
50 g/2 oz castor sugar	
1 egg	

1 Sift the flour and salt into a basin. Rub in the butter, mix in the sugar, and then the egg and milk beaten together. The dough should be rather stiff. Add a little more milk if necessary.

2 Turn into a 20-cm/8-inch sandwich tin, smooth evenly and bake in a hot oven (220°C, 425°F, Gas Mark 7) for 25-30 minutes, until light golden brown.

3 Turn out immediately onto a wire cake rack and leave until cool, but not cold, before cutting in half horizontally.

4 Keep some of the fruit aside for decoration and crush the rest roughly.

5 Cover the bottom half of the shortcake with the crushed fruit, spread with under half of the cream, whipped, and cover with the second half of the shortcake.

6 Swirl the rest of the cream over the top and decorate with the reserved fruit.

Sweetheart flan

you will need for 4 servings:

METRIC/IMPERIAL

175 g/6 oz flan or rich shortcrust pastry (see page 51 or 52)	raspberry jam 150 ml/¼ pint double cream
lemon curd	

1 Roll out and line an 18-cm/7-inch flan tin with the pastry (see page 52). There should be a lot of trimmings over. Roll these out thinly and cut into heart shapes (14-16) with a small heart shaped cutter, with one larger one for the centre.
2 Place them on a tin, brush with beaten egg or milk and bake with the flan, but for 8-10 minutes only, to a light golden brown.
3 Fill the cold flan case by spreading lemon curd over the base. Whip the cream stiffly and fold in as much raspberry jam as necessary to give a good pink colour. Spread over the lemon curd.
4 Place the small hearts all round the perimeter with the larger one in the centre.

Caramel candy pie

you will need for 4 servings:

METRIC/IMPERIAL

2 tablespoons boiling water	150 ml/¼ pint double cream
2 teaspoons gelatine	18-cm/7-inch baked flan case (see page 52)
175 g/6 oz caramels	
5 tablespoons milk	

caramelized almonds to decorate:

25 g/1 oz halved blanched almonds	1½ tablespoons castor sugar

1 Pour the boiling water over the gelatine in a cup and stir occasionally until completely dissolved and clear.
2 In a bowl over gently boiling water melt the caramels with the milk, stirring until smooth. Allow to cool to blood heat and then stir in the gelatine.
3 Leave until cold and thick, but before it sets stir in the stiffly whipped cream and turn into the flan case.
4 To make the caramalized almonds, place almonds and sugar in a thick-bottomed pan and over a low heat keep stirring until the sugar and almonds are a golden brown.
5 Turn at once onto a well oiled tin, separating the almonds as much as possible.
6 Cool, then break apart.
7 Decorate the pie with caramelized almonds, but do not place them in position more than an hour or so before serving or the sugar may begin to melt.

Butterscotch pie

you will need for 4 servings:

METRIC/IMPERIAL

175 g/6 oz soft dark brown sugar	2 eggs, separated
40 g/1½ oz butter or margarine	18-cm/7-inch baked flan case (see page 52)
50 g/2 oz flour	100 g/4 oz castor sugar
150 ml/¼ pint milk	

1 Put sugar, butter, flour, milk, and egg yolks into a bowl over simmering water and stir occasionally until the mixture thickens, 12-15 minutes.
2 Spread in the flan case and bake in a moderate oven (180°C, 350°F, Gas Mark 4) for 15 minutes.
3 Whip the egg whites stiffly with a little of the castor sugar and fold in the rest. Pile on top of the butterscotch mixture, making sure that the meringue touches the pastry all round, and continue baking for 15-20 minutes until lightly browned. Serve hot or cold.

Lemon meringue pie

you will need for 4 servings:

METRIC/IMPERIAL

2 large lemons	2 eggs, separated
40 g/1½ oz custard powder	18-cm/7-inch baked flan case (see page 52)
250 ml/8 fl oz milk	
100 g/4 oz granulated sugar	100 g/4 oz castor sugar

1 Grate the lemon rinds and mix with the juice.
2 Make a paste of the custard powder and lemon with a little of the milk. Add the rest of the milk and bring slowly to the boil stirring. Boil for 1-2 minutes. Remove from the heat, stir in the granulated sugar until dissolved, and then the egg yolks.
3 Return to the heat and stir over a low heat until the custard thickens, but without allowing it to boil. Pour into the flan case.
4 Whip the egg whites stiffly with a little of the castor sugar and fold in the rest. Pile on top of the custard, making sure that the meringue touches the pastry all round, and bake in a moderate oven (180°C, 350°F, Gas Mark 4) for 15-20 minutes, until lightly browned.

Variations:

2 lemons	75 g/3 oz granulated sugar
water	
3 tablespoons cornflour	

Proceed with rest of ingredients and method as above.

American lemon pie

you will need for 4 servings:

METRIC/IMPERIAL

2 large lemons	175 g/6 oz castor sugar
water	2 eggs, separated
2 teaspoons flour	18-cm/7-inch baked flan case of flaky or shortcrust pastry (see page 51 or 52)
15 g/½ oz butter	
50 g/2 oz biscuit crumbs	
pinch of salt	

1 Grate the lemon rinds, mix with the juice and make up to 150 ml/¼ pint with water.
2 Put into a thick-bottomed saucepan with the flour, butter, biscuit crumbs, salt, and half the sugar. Stir over a low heat until thick, remove from the heat and beat in the egg yolks. Proceed from stage 3 for Lemon meringue pie (see above).

Bob Hope's lemon pie

you will need for 6 servings:

METRIC/IMPERIAL

225 g/8 oz rich sweet shortcrust pastry (see page 51)
3 medium lemons
water
3 tablespoons cornflour
15 g/½ oz flour
150 g/5 oz castor sugar
15 g/½ oz butter
3 eggs

1 Cut off less than a quarter of the pastry and roll out the rest. Line a 21·5-23-cm/8½-9-inch pie plate with it. Trim the edge. Paint the inside with a little of the egg white from the filling.
2 Make the filling. Grate the lemon rinds and squeeze the juice. Make up to 300ml/½ pint with water.
3 Make the flours into a smooth paste with a little of the liquid and stir in the rest. Bring to the boil, stirring, and boil for 2-3 minutes.
4 Remove from the heat and stir in the sugar, butter, and lightly beaten eggs. Allow to cool before pouring into the pie case.
5 Roll out the reserved pastry with the trimmings, cut into strips and lay criss-cross across the filling, sticking the ends onto the pastry edge with cold water.
6 Bake in a moderately hot oven (200°C, 400°F, Gas Mark 6) for 10 minutes, then lower the heat to moderate (180°C, 350°F, Gas Mark 4) for a further 25-30 minutes, until the pastry is lightly browned.

Slice-o-lemon pie

you will need for 5 servings:

METRIC/IMPERIAL

225 g/8 oz any shortcrust pastry (see page 51)
1 lemon
175 g/6 oz castor sugar
2 tablespoons flour
2½ tablespoons (35 g/1¼ oz) butter
2 eggs
6 tablespoons water

1 Cut off over half the pastry, roll out and line a 20-cm/8-inch flan tin with it. Trim the edge.
2 Grate the lemon rind, then carefully peel the lemon free from pith and cut the flesh into paper-thin slices, discarding the pips.
3 Make the filling. Mix the sugar and flour together, then blend in the softened (not melted) butter.
4 Reserve 1 teaspoon of egg white, beat the rest of the beaten eggs into the sugar mixture until smooth. Stir in the water, grated rind, and slices of lemon. Pour into the flan case.
5 Roll out the rest of the pastry with the trimmings. Brush both edges with cold water, place the second piece on top and press the edges together well. Trim off and decorate the edge.
6 Brush the top with the reserved egg white lightly beaten, sprinkle liberally with castor sugar and prick with a fork.
7 Bake in a moderately hot oven (220°C, 425°F, Gas Mark 7) for 30-35 minutes.

Lime (or lemon) chiffon pie

you will need for 4-5 servings:

METRIC/IMPERIAL

2 eggs, separated
small can sweetened condensed milk
2 limes or 1 large lemon
18-cm/7-inch baked shortcrust pastry flan case (see page 52)

1 Beat the egg yolks and gradually stir in the condensed milk and the grated rind and juice of the limes or lemon.
2 Fold in the stiffly beaten egg whites and colour a very pale green if liked.
3 Pour into the flan case and bake in a moderate oven (170°C, 325°F, Gas Mark 3) for 15-20 minutes. Serve cold.

Eccles cakes

you will need for 16 cakes:

METRIC/IMPERIAL

368-g/13-oz packet puff or 225 g/8 oz New Zealand flaky pastry (see page 52)
25 g/1 oz butter or margarine
175 g/6 oz currants
50 g/2 oz brown sugar
75 g/3 oz cut mixed peel
½ teaspoon mixed cake spice
⅛ teaspoon grated nutmeg
beaten egg or milk
castor sugar

1 Roll out the pastry thinly and cut into 16 rounds with each of two pastry cutters, 7·5 cm/3 inches and 8·25 cm/3¼ inches, so you have 32 pastry circles in all.
2 Melt the butter in small saucepan, remove from the heat and stir in the currants, sugar, mixed peel and spices.
3 Place about 1 tablespoon of the fruit mixture in the centre of the smaller pastry circles, brush all round the edges with cold water, and brush the edges of the larger circles with water also. Cover the fillings with the larger circles, pressing the edges together to seal firmly.
4 Flatten the tops lightly with a rolling pin, and if possible leave for 30 minutes or so, then brush with beaten egg or milk, dredge well with castor sugar and make 3 incisions in each with a sharp pointed knife.
5 Bake in a hot oven (230°C, 450°F, Gas Mark 8) for 12-15 minutes, until golden brown.

Note:
These cakes will keep in a box for weeks, but should be refreshed in a hot oven on the day of consumption.

Mince pies

you will need for 18 mince pies:

METRIC/IMPERIAL

225 g/8 oz New Zealand flaky (see page 52) or 450 g/1 lb bought puff pastry
0·5-0·75 kg/1¼-1½ lb mincemeat
1 tablespoon brandy, sherry or whisky (optional)
beaten egg or milk
castor sugar

1 Roll out the pastry thinly and cut into 18 circles with each of two pastry cutters, 7·5 cm/3 inches and 8·25 cm/3¼ inches, so you have 36 circles in all.
2 Line patty pans with the larger rounds. Prick the bottoms with a fork and fill with mincemeat mixed with the liquor if used.
3 Brush around the edges of both circles with cold water. Place the smaller circles on top and press the edges together to seal firmly. Leave for 30 minutes or so if possible.
4 Brush with beaten egg or milk, dredge well with castor sugar and make 3 incisions in each with a sharp pointed knife.
5 Bake above centre in a hot oven (230°C, 450°F, Gas Mark 8) for 22-25 minutes, until golden brown.

Note:
If for serving hot or warm, flaky type pastry is preferable, but for serving cold, shortcrust (use 25% more) may be used instead. Bake in a moderately hot oven (220°C, 425°F, Gas Mark 7).

Plaited mince pie

you will need for 6 servings:

METRIC/IMPERIAL

275-350 g/10-12 oz mincemeat	2 teaspoons lemon juice
75 g/3 oz glacé cherries, quartered	
1 tablespoon brandy or sherry	*to decorate:* blanched almond halves and glacé cherries (mixed colours if possible)
368-g/13-oz packet puff pastry	
75 g/3 oz icing sugar	

1 Mix together the mincemeat, quartered cherries and brandy or sherry.
2 Roll out the pastry to an oblong about 30 by 33-35 cm/12 by 13-14 inches and trim the edges. Mark lightly into 3, lengthways, and place on a baking sheet. At 2·5-cm/1-inch intervals on both sides, make cuts at a 45° angle but only 7·5 cm/2½ inches in length.
3 Place the mincemeat down the centre third evenly, to within 2·5 cm/1 inch of each end. Fold these two ends up, then draw up the two sides and fold the cut pieces over the top alternately to give a plaited effect.
4 Brush with beaten egg or milk and bake in a hot oven (230°C, 450°F, Gas Mark 8) for 20-25 minutes, or until golden brown.
5 When cold, sift the icing sugar, stir in the lemon juice, and then just enough boiling water to give a smooth glacé icing. Spoon it over the plait and decorate with almonds and halved glacé cherries.

Mincemeat marshmallow flan

you will need for 4 servings:

METRIC/IMPERIAL

1½ tablespoons stout	8 marshmallows (pink and white)
350 g/12 oz mincemeat	
18-cm/7-inch baked flan case (see page 52)	

1 Mix the stout into the mincemeat thoroughly and spread in the flan case.
2 Heat through in the oven, then place 7 marshmallows, pink and white alternately, in a circle on the mincemeat, with one in the centre.
3 Place under a low grill until the marshmallows are lightly browned.

Variation:
Mincemeat meringue flan
Fill the flan case with mincemeat as above. Whip 2 egg whites stiffly with a little of 100 g/4 oz castor sugar and fold in the rest. Add a few drops of red colouring and swirl around with a fork to give a marbled effect. Spread the meringue all over the mincemeat, flicking it up decoratively, and bake in a moderate oven (180°C, 350°F, Gas Mark 4) for 15-20 minutes, until lightly browned.

Kentish pudding pies

you will need for 4 servings:

METRIC/IMPERIAL

40 g/1½ oz ground rice	generous pinch of salt
450 ml/¾ pint milk	currants
50 g/2 oz castor sugar	100 g/4 oz shortcrust pastry (see page 51)
25 g/1 oz butter	
1-2 egg yolks	
¼ teaspoon mixed cake spice, or grated rind of ½ lemon	

1 Make a paste of the ground rice with a little of the milk, add the rest and bring to the boil, stirring. Boil until the rice is cooked, 6-7 minutes.
2 Remove from the heat and beat in the sugar, butter, egg yolks, spice or lemon rind and salt.
3 Roll out the pastry thinly and line 4 saucers with it. Pour in the rice mixture to three-quarters fill each saucer. Sprinkle liberally with currants and bake in a moderately hot oven (200°C, 400°F, Gas Mark 6) for 25-30 minutes, or until the pastry and filling are a light golden brown.

Maids of Honour

you will need for 12 tarts:

METRIC/IMPERIAL

568 ml/1 pint rich milk (not homogenized)	1 egg, beaten
1 tablespoon rennet	15 g/½ oz butter, melted
212-g/7½-oz packet puff pastry	50 g/2 oz castor sugar

1 Make the junket. Heat the milk to blood heat only, stir in the rennet and leave in a warm place to set. When set, tie in muslin and leave to drain overnight, then squeeze out any liquid remaining and rub the curd through a sieve into a basin.
2 Roll out the pastry thinly and cut into 12 circles with an 8·25-cm/3¼-inch cutter.
3 Brush 7·5-cm/3-inch deep patty pans with cold water and line with the pastry, pressing it from the base up the sides, so that the base is paper thin. Prick the base well.

4 Stir the egg, butter, and sugar into the curd and pour into the patty pans only to half fill each.

5 Bake in a moderately hot oven (200°C, 400°F, Gas Mark 6) for 20-25 minutes, until the filling is well risen and the pastry lightly browned.

Grandmother's leg or baked jam roll

you will need for 4-5 servings:

METRIC/IMPERIAL

225 g/8 oz plain flour	50 g/2 oz lard
⅛ teaspoon salt	jam
50 g/2 oz margarine	

1 Sift the flour and salt into a basin and rub in the fats. Stir in sufficient cold water to make the dough stick together. Knead lightly.

2 Roll out to a rectangle about 33 cm/13 inches by 25·5 cm/10 inches. Spread with jam to within 2·5 cm/1 inch of the edges. Wet the edges and roll up, sealing the edge firmly onto the roll and also the ends.

3 Place on a baking sheet and bake in a hot oven (220°C, 425°F, Gas Mark 7) for 30 minutes to a golden brown.

Dutch Kerst Krans

you will need for 6 servings:

METRIC/IMPERIAL

368-g/13-oz packet puff or 225 g/8 oz New Zealand flaky pastry (see page 52)	¼-½ teaspoon almond essence
175 g/6 oz ground almonds	1 egg
175 g/6 oz castor sugar	to decorate:
juice of ½ small lemon	apricot jam, glacé fruits, angelica, nuts

1 Roll out the pastry into a long strip 10-12·5 cm/4-5 inches in width and not less than 0·3 cm/⅛ inch in thickness.

2 Make the almond paste. Mix together the ground almonds and sugar, stir in the lemon juice and almond essence, and only just sufficient beaten egg to make the paste bind. Knead until smooth.

3 Turn onto a board and with the hands roll into a long sausage just shorter than the length of the pastry. Place along the centre of the pastry, bring up the two sides and press one firmly onto the other, brushing with some of the remaining egg.

4 Bend into a circle and seal the ends together. Place on a baking sheet, seal side down, brush with the rest of the egg and bake in a hot oven (220°C, 425°F, Gas Mark 7) for 30-35 minutes, until golden brown.

5 Remove and brush immediately with sieved apricot jam. Cover with any glacé fruit and nuts for colour and leave until cold on a wire cake rack.

Danish pastry layer cake

you will need for 5-6 servings:

METRIC/IMPERIAL

115 g/4 oz plain flour	50 g/2 oz blanched almonds, chopped
¼ teaspoon baking powder	300 ml/½ pint double cream
115 g/4 oz butter	
115 g/4 oz castor sugar	
25 g/1 oz skinned hazelnuts, chopped	

chocolate icing

50 g/2 oz plain chocolate	2 tablespoons water
	40 g/1½ oz icing sugar

1 Sieve the flour and baking powder into a basin, rub in the butter, add the sugar and knead lightly until the dough holds together. Leave to rest for 20-30 minutes.

2 Shape into a roll and cut into 4 equal pieces. Roll out each piece into a circle and cut neatly with a 15-cm/6-inch saucepan lid.

3 Place the circles on baking sheets, sprinkle evenly all over with the nuts, pressing them in lightly, and bake in a moderate oven (180°C, 350°F, Gas Mark 4) for 12-15 minutes until pale gold. Cool on a wire cake rack.

4 To make the chocolate icing, break the chocolate into pieces and melt with the water over a very low heat until smooth. Bring just to boiling point, remove from the heat and stir in the sieved icing sugar.

5 Beat until smooth and the right consistency for spreading.

6 When the layers are cold, sandwich together with lightly whipped cream and spread the chocolate icing over the top circle.

Note:
Fruit in season can be placed on the layers of cream.

Chocolate pie

you will need for 4 servings:

METRIC/IMPERIAL

100 g/4 oz plain chocolate	50 g/2 oz chocolate cake crumbs
150 ml/¼ pint milk	2 eggs, separated
25 g/1 oz butter	18-cm/7-inch baked flan case (see page 52)
25 g/1 oz flour	
25 g/1 oz granulated sugar	100 g/4 oz castor sugar

1 Over a low heat melt the chocolate with a little of the milk until smooth, remove from the heat and stir in the rest of the milk.

2 In another saucepan melt the butter, blend in the flour with a wooden spoon, pour in the chocolate milk and granulated sugar and stir with a wire whisk until beginning to thicken. Add the cake crumbs and stir until really thick.

3 Remove from the heat and stir in the egg yolks. Spread in the flan case and bake in a moderate oven (180°C, 350°F, Gas Mark 4) for 20 minutes.

4 Whip the egg whites stiffly with a little of the castor sugar and fold in the rest. Pile on top of the chocolate, making sure that the meringue touches the pastry all round and continue baking for 15-20 minutes, until lightly browned.

Bakewell tart

you will need for 4 servings:

METRIC/IMPERIAL
115 g/4 oz shortcrust
  or flan pastry (see
  page 51 or 52)
50 g/2 oz butter or
  margarine
50 g/2 oz castor sugar

1 egg yolk
few drops almond
  essence
50 g/2 oz ground
  almonds
raspberry jam

1 Roll out the pastry and line an 18-cm/7-inch flan tin or ring with it.
2 Cream the butter and sugar together, beat in the egg yolk, a few drops of almond essence, and the ground almonds.
3 Spread a thin layer of jam over the bottom of the flan case, and cover evenly with the almond mixture.
4 Bake in a moderately hot oven (220°C, 400°F, Gas Mark 6) for 25-30 minutes, until lightly browned. Serve cold.

Chessboard tart

you will need for 4 servings:

METRIC/IMPERIAL
175 g/6 oz any
  shortcrust pastry
  (see page 51)

red jam
desiccated coconut

1 Roll out the pastry and line a 23-cm/9-inch pie plate with it. Trim and decorate the edge.
2 Spread a layer of any red or dark jam over the centre.
3 Roll out the trimmings and cut into narrow strips. Place across the pastry to form fairly large squares, sticking the ends down onto the pastry with cold water.
4 Bake in a moderately hot oven (200°C, 400°F, Gas Mark 6) for 25-30 minutes, until lightly browned.
5 When cold, sprinkle desiccated coconut carefully into each alternate square to give the effect of a chessboard.

Quick and Easy Desserts

There can't be a cook in the world who doesn't upon many occasions long for a quick and easy dessert with which to round off a meal.
Here are some ideas.

Jellied blackcurrant cartwheels

you will need for 4 servings:

METRIC/IMPERIAL
225 g/8 oz Swiss roll
1 packet blackcurrant
  jelly cubes
water

425-g/15-oz can
  blackcurrants or
397-g/14-oz can pie
  filling

1 Cut the Swiss roll into thin slices and line a 900-ml/1½-pint pudding bowl with them, reserving 3 slices for the top.
2 Split up the jelly cubes, put into a measuring jug and make up to 300 ml/½ pint with boiling water. Stir until completely dissolved.
3 Mix with the contents of the can of blackcurrants and pour into the lined bowl. Place the reserved slices on top and press down a little until covered with juice.
4 Leave in a refrigerator or cold place to set, then turn out (see page 27) and serve with cream or custard.

Five minute blackcurrant fool

you will need for 4-5 servings:

METRIC/IMPERIAL
1 packet blackcurrant
  Instant Whip
300 ml/½ pint milk
397-g/14-oz can
  blackcurrant pie
  filling

to decorate:
whipped cream or
  Dream Topping
  (optional)

1 Make up the Instant Whip with the milk as directed on the packet.
2 When thick beat in the pie filling and turn into sundae glasses.
3 Decorate with whipped cream or Dream Topping if desired, or serve with finger biscuits.

Yogurt nut cream

you will need for 4 servings:

METRIC/IMPERIAL
454-g/16-oz carton
  natural yogurt
3 tablespoons clear
  honey

1 crunchie sweet bar
50 g/2 oz mixed nuts,
  coarsely chopped

1 Pour the yogurt into a basin and mix in the honey until well blended.
2 Crush the crunchie bar with a rolling pin and stir in with the nuts.
3 Spoon into sundae dishes and leave in a refrigerator or cold place for 30 minutes or more.

Treacle cream

you will need for 4-5 servings:

METRIC/IMPERIAL

568 ml/1 pint milk	3 tablespoons boiling
2 tablespoons black	water
treacle	150 ml/¼ pint single
1 tablespoon golden	cream
syrup	
4 teaspoons	
(15 g/½ oz) gelatine	

1 Warm the milk, treacle, and golden syrup together to about blood heat.
2 Turn the gelatine into a cup, pour the boiling water over it and stir occasionally until completely dissolved and clear. When blood heat also, stir it into the milk.
3 Pour into sundae glasses and leave to set in a refrigerator. Before serving, cover the surface in each glass with the cream.

Ginger-up whip

you will need for 4 servings:

METRIC/IMPERIAL

300 ml/½ pint	to decorate:
evaporated milk	slices of stem ginger,
2 tablespoons boiling	chocolate drops, or
water	wafer biscuits
scant 2 teaspoons	
gelatine	
127-g/4·5-oz jar	
Ginger-up sauce	

1 Chill the evaporated milk (to thicken it). Whip until well increased in volume and much thicker.
2 Pour the boiling water over the gelatine in a cup and stir occasionally until completely dissolved and clear. Whip into the milk.
3 Stir in the Ginger-up and turn into sundae dishes. Leave to set.
4 Decorate with slices of stem ginger, or chocolate drops or wafer biscuits.

Tutti frutti inspiration

you will need for 4 servings:

METRIC/IMPERIAL

65 g/2½ oz (12) glacé	1 packet Dream
cherries	Topping
50 g/2 oz almonds and	750 ml/1¼ pints milk
walnuts, mixed	1 packet vanilla
15-25 g/½-1 oz	Instant Whip
angelica (or green	
glacé cherries)	

1 Cut the cherries into quarters and chop the nuts and angelica.

2 Make up the Dream Topping as directed on the packet with 150 ml/¼ pint of the milk. Make up the Instant Whip also as directed with the rest of the milk and leave to thicken.
3 Whisk the two cream mixtures together and fold in the fruit and nuts.
4 Turn into sundae glasses and chill.

Pineapple lemon fluff

you will need for 6 servings:

METRIC/IMPERIAL

1 packet lemon jelly	1 packet Dream
cubes	Topping
water	150 ml/¼ pint milk
1 small can crushed	
pineapple	

1 Place the jelly cubes in a saucepan with 150 ml/¼ pint water and heat until the jelly is dissolved. Pour into a basin.
2 Press out as much of the juice from the pineapple as possible into a measuring jug and make up to 300 ml/½ pint with cold water. Mix into the jelly liquid and leave until just beginning to set around the edges.
3 Make up the Dream Topping with the milk as directed on the packet. Whisk into the jelly with the crushed pineapple, pour into sundae glasses and leave to set.
4 Decorate as desired or serve with finger biscuits.

Yellow moon

you will need for 5 servings:

METRIC/IMPERIAL

2 tablespoons boiling	150 ml/¼ pint double
water	cream
2 teaspoons gelatine	brandy snaps
large can crushed	
pineapple	
one 15 or 18-cm/6 or	
7-inch sponge	
sandwich cake	

1 Pour the boiling water over the gelatine in a cup and stir occasionally until completely dissolved. Add to the pineapple gradually whilst stirring vigorously and leave until thick and nearly set.
2 For a 15-cm/6-inch bought cake separate the halves and cut one across horizontally, leaving 3 layers of cake. For a home-made 18-cm/7-inch cake cut both halves across to make 4 layers.
3 Sandwich the smaller cake layers with the pineapple, leaving sufficient to spread over the top. But for the larger cake, use all the pineapple between the layers. Place in a refrigerator to set.
4 To serve, spread whipped cream over the top and scatter generously with crushed brandy snaps.
Note:
If no refrigerator is available, use 3 teaspoons gelatine.

Jersey lemon cream

you will need for 4 servings:

METRIC/IMPERIAL
2 lemons
150 ml/¼ pint double cream
small can sweetened condensed milk

to decorate:
angelica 'leaves' and mimosa balls or jellied lemon slices

1 Grate the lemon rinds and mix with the strained juice.
2 Whip the cream fairly lightly, then beat in the condensed milk and the lemon rind and juice.
3 Turn into wine glasses and chill.
4 Decorate with angelica 'leaves' and mimosa balls or jellied lemon slices.

Sunshine lemon whisk

you will need for 4 servings:

METRIC/IMPERIAL
1 packet lemon pie filling
2 eggs, separated
25 g/1 oz sugar
grated rind and juice of 1 small lemon
water
large can crushed pineapple or 340-g/12-oz can pineapple pieces

to decorate:
whipped cream or Dream Topping and glacé cherries and angelica

1 Make up the lemon pie filling as directed on the packet, using the egg yolks, sugar, and the lemon rind and juice made up to 450 ml/¾ pint with water. Allow to cool.
2 Drain the pineapple and, if using pieces, chop them finely, and stir into the lemon mixture.
3 Whip the egg whites stiffly and fold in. Turn into a decorative bowl.
4 Decorate with whipped cream or Dream Topping and glacé cherries and angelica for colour.

Butterscotch prune whip

you will need for 4-5 servings:

METRIC/IMPERIAL
225 g/8 oz prunes (not too dry) (175 g/6 oz pitted)
large can evaporated milk
milk
packet butterscotch Instant Whip

½ teaspoon almond essence
¼ teaspoon vanilla essence

to decorate:
grated chocolate or chocolate vermicelli

1 Soften and plump up the prunes by steaming over boiling water for 30-45 minutes. Remove stones and cut the flesh into small pieces.
2 Make up the evaporated milk to 600 ml/1 pint with fresh milk and whip in the Instant Whip powder with the essences.
3 When the mixture is thick and creamy, stir in the prunes and turn into a bowl or individual sundae dishes. Chill.

4 Scatter with a little grated chocolate or chocolate vermicelli to decorate.

Variation:

Raspberry banana whip

Substitute for the prunes, 1 banana and 100 g/4 oz raspberries or a small can, drained. Use raspberry whip in place of butterscotch.

1 Slice the peeled banana and cut each slice in half. Proceed from stage 2 above.

Fruit pie crispie

you will need for 4 servings:

METRIC/IMPERIAL
410-g/14½-oz can fruit pie filling
75 g/3 oz butter or margarine

50 g/2 oz soft brown sugar
100 g/4 oz porridge oats

1 Spread the pie filling in a shallow heatproof dish.
2 Cream the butter and sugar together and work in the oats.
3 Sprinkle the mixture over the fruit and bake in a moderate oven (180°C, 350°F, Gas Mark 4) for 25 minutes or until golden brown.

Marshmallow crumb pie

you will need for 4 servings:

METRIC/IMPERIAL
115 g/4 oz digestive biscuits
25 g/1 oz castor sugar
50 g/2 oz butter or margarine
115 g/4 oz marshmallows

175 ml/6 fl oz double or whipping cream or Dream Topping
370-379-g/13-14-oz can cherry, blackcurrant, or raspberry pie filling

1 Put the biscuits, a few at a time, into a bag and with a rolling pin crush into crumbs.
2 Put into a basin and stir in the sugar and melted butter until well blended.
3 Take out 2 tablespoons and reserve. Press the rest into a 20-cm/8-inch fluted china flan dish, or an 18-20-cm/7-8-inch cover of a glass casserole. Leave to get cold.
4 Cut the marshmallows into about 0·5-cm/¼-inch pieces and stir into the lightly whipped cream.
5 Spread less than half over the pie crust, cover with the pie filling and spread the rest of the cream over it.
6 Sprinkle the reserved crumbs all over the top.

Marshmallow coffee dessert

you will need for 4 servings:

METRIC/IMPERIAL
175 g/6 oz marshmallows
150 ml/¼ pint strong black coffee
150 ml/¼ pint whipping or double cream

to decorate:
flaked almonds, toasted

1 Over a low heat melt the marshmallows in the coffee until completely dissolved. Leave until cold.
2 Whip the cream lightly and stir into the coffee mixture. Turn into sundae glasses and leave to set in a refrigerator.
3 Sprinkle toasted almonds over the top to decorate.

Piccaloes

you will need for each serving:

METRIC/IMPERIAL
25 g/1 oz butter or margarine
25 g/1 oz castor sugar
1 teaspoon cocoa powder
1 teaspoon coffee essence

3 brandy snaps (bought)

to decorate:
2 tablespoons double cream
thin slices stem ginger

1 Cream the butter and sugar together and stir in the cocoa and coffee essence.
2 Fill the brandy snaps with the mixture (a piping bag and plain nozzle is easiest) and stand upright in a tall glass.
3 Whip the cream, place a teaspoonful at the top end of each snap and the rest in the centre of the glass. Decorate the cream with thin slices of stem ginger.

Striped zebras

you will need for 4 servings:

METRIC/IMPERIAL
225 ml/8 fl oz double cream
4 tablespoons milk
6 tablespoons marmalade, finely cut

½ teaspoon ground cinnamon
9 digestive biscuits, crushed into crumbs

1 Whip the cream and milk together until it will form soft peaks.
2 Reserve sufficient marmalade to place a teaspoonful on the top of each glass for decoration and stir the rest into the cream.
3 Stir the cinnamon into the biscuit crumbs and spoon in layers into 4 tall glasses.
4 Decorate with the reserved marmalade.

Creamed rice lemon meringue

you will need for 4 servings:

METRIC/IMPERIAL
grated rind of 1 lemon
2 eggs, separated
439-g/15½-oz can creamed rice

lemon curd
100 g/4 oz castor sugar

1 Stir the lemon rind and egg yolks into the rice and pour into a 900-ml/1½-pint pie or other heat proof dish.
2 Bake in a cool oven (150°C, 300°F, Gas Mark 2) for 20 minutes, then lower heat to 140°C, 275°F, Gas Mark 1 and continue baking for a further 20-25 minutes until lightly set.

3 Allow to cool for a few minutes then spread lemon curd all over the top.
4 Whip the egg whites stiffly with a little of the sugar and fold in the rest. Spread over the lemon curd to touch the dish all round and return to a cool oven (150°C, 300°F, Gas Mark 2) for 20-25 minutes, until the meringue is lightly browned.

Quick trick

you will need for 4 servings:

METRIC/IMPERIAL
439-g/15½-oz can creamed rice
397-g/14-oz can any fruit pie filling
100-g/3½-oz packet baby meringues

to decorate:
glacé cherries (optional)

1 Pour the contents of the can of rice into a generous 1-litre/2-pint pie dish or casserole.
2 Spread the pie filling all over the top, and cover with baby meringues.
3 Heat through in a moderate oven (170°C, 325°F, Gas Mark 3) for 25-30 minutes.
4 To decorate for guests, place halved glacé cherries between the meringues before serving.

Geoffrey's dream

you will need for 4 servings:

METRIC/IMPERIAL
6 tablespoons bitter marmalade
300 ml/½ pint double cream
¼ teaspoon instant coffee powder

to decorate:
4 meringue rosettes or small halves

1 Finely chop the pieces of peel in the marmalade.
2 Whip the cream, not too stiffly, and stir in the marmalade and coffee powder. Spoon into sundae glasses and chill.
3 To serve, decorate each with a meringue rosette or small half meringue, sprinkled with coffee powder.

Variation:
Use 6-8 tablespoons Rose's lime marmalade, or ginger marmalade, chopping the pieces finely.

Lemon whip

you will need for 4 servings:

METRIC/IMPERIAL
300 ml/½ pint evaporated milk
50 g/2 oz castor sugar
1 lemon
3 tablespoons boiling water
2 teaspoons gelatine

to decorate:
whipped cream, toasted almonds or crushed chocolate flake

1 The milk whips more easily if the can is left in a refrigerator for several hours.
2 Whip the milk with the sugar to blend, then stir in the grated rind and juice of the lemon and continue

whisking until thick. The lemon will thicken the milk considerably.

3 Pour the boiling water over the gelatine in a cup and stir occasionally until completely dissolved and clear.

4 Whisk into the milk and pour into sundae glasses. Leave in a refrigerator to set.

5 Decorate with whipped cream, chopped toasted almonds, or crushed flake chocolate.

Dorothy's surprise

you will need for 6-7 servings:

METRIC/IMPERIAL

1 packet orange jelly cubes	to decorate: any fresh or canned fruit, or jellied orange slices
500 ml/18 fl oz orange juice (frozen or bottled)	
family block (450 g/1 lb) vanilla ice cream	

1 Place the jelly cubes in a saucepan with under half the orange juice. Heat, stirring, until the jelly is completely dissolved.

2 Pour into a large basin, stir in the rest of the orange juice and leave until cold.

3 With a wire whisk or fork, whip in the melted ice cream, pour into a decorative dish and leave to set in a refrigerator or cold place.

4 Decorate with fresh or canned fruit, or jellied orange slices.

Instant orange sweet

you will need for 6 servings:

METRIC/IMPERIAL

568 ml/1 pint milk	grated rind of 1 orange (optional)
1 packet orange Instant Whip	
1 packet Dream Topping	to decorate: 312-g/11-oz can mandarin segments
2-3 tablespoons Orange Curaçao or Grand Marnier (optional)	

1 Pour the milk into a basin. Sprinkle the powders from both packets over the milk and whisk with an electric or rotary beater until thick. Whisk in the liqueur and the grated orange rind if used.

2 Turn into sundae glasses and leave for 10-15 minutes, then decorate with the mandarin segments.

Orange compote

you will need for each serving:

METRIC/IMPERIAL

1 orange	2-3 glacé cherries, chopped
2 teaspoons honey	
2 teaspoons marmalade, finely chopped	

1 Remove the skin and all the pith from the orange. Cut a thin slice off each end and then cut slices across the orange a scant 0·5 cm/¼ inch in thickness.

2 Arrange the slices on a plate and pour the honey and then the marmalade over them, and top with a scattering of chopped cherries.

Orange harmony

you will need for 4 servings:

METRIC/IMPERIAL

3 large oranges or 4 small	4-6 macaroons
castor sugar	to decorate: glacé cherries (optional)
rum (optional)	
3 bananas	

1 Cut the oranges free from skin and pith. Slice across thinly.

2 Arrange the slices on 4 plates, sprinkle with castor sugar and rum to taste and leave to marinate for 30 minutes or more.

3 Shortly before serving, peel and slice the bananas fairly thinly and spread over the oranges.

4 Scatter with crumbled macaroons and top with chopped glacé cherries for colour.

Andrew's citrus delight

you will need for 4 servings:

METRIC/IMPERIAL

1 packet lemon pie filling	150 ml/¼ pint water
2 eggs, separated	2 tablespoons sugar
150 ml/¼ pint tangerine or orange juice (bottled)	to decorate: coloured jellies or halved green grapes

1 Put the lemon pie filling into a saucepan with the egg yolks, tangerine or orange juice, water and sugar.

2 Stir over medium heat until the mixture thickens, remove and allow to cool, stirring occasionally.

3 Whip the egg whites stiffly, fold into the mixture and spoon into sundae glasses. Chill.

4 Decorate with coloured jellies or halved green grapes.

Mandarin jellies

you will need for 18 paper cases:

METRIC/IMPERIAL

312-g/11-oz can mandarin segments	2 packets orange jelly cubes
water	

1 Make up the strained juice from the can to a generous 1 litre/2 pints with water.

2 In a saucepan melt the jelly cubes with half the liquid. Remove and add the rest of the liquid. Two-thirds fill the cases and allow to set.

3 Arrange the mandarin segments on the jellies, wheel fashion, and nearly cover with more liquid jelly. Leave to set.

Butterscotch crunch

you will need for 4 servings:

METRIC/IMPERIAL
75 g/3 oz peanut brittle   300 ml/½ pint milk
1 packet butterscotch
   Angel Delight

1 Crush the peanut brittle, not too finely, in a bag with a rolling pin.
2 Make up the Angel Delight with the milk as directed on the packet. Stir in most of the brittle, reserving some for decoration.
3 Spoon into sundae glasses and sprinkle with the reserved brittle.

Banana quickie

you will need for 4 servings:

METRIC/IMPERIAL
5 (0·5-0·75 kg/1¼-1½ lb)   to decorate:
   bananas   chopped glacé
lime marmalade   cherries
150 ml/¼ pint single
   cream

1 Peel the bananas and slice them on the slant.
2 Lay half the slices overlapping in a shallow dish.
3 Spread with lime marmalade and pour over half the cream. Repeat layers.
4 Decorate by sprinkling with chopped glacé cherries.

Variation:

Use pineapple or raspberry jam in place of the lime marmalade.

Gray's glory

you will need for 8 servings:

METRIC/IMPERIAL
600 ml/1 pint natural   225 g/8 oz fresh fruit or
   yogurt   350-g/12-oz can
300 ml/½ pint double   castor sugar
   cream   demerara sugar

1 Whip the yogurt and cream together until thick.
2 Place the fruit (drained if canned) in a large shallow bowl, sprinkling with castor sugar if fresh.
3 Pour the cream mixture over the fruit, sprinkle liberally with demerara sugar and leave in a refrigerator overnight.

Melon fling

you will need for 4 servings:

METRIC/IMPERIAL
450 g/1 lb melon flesh   to decorate:
1 teaspoon castor   chopped stem ginger
   sugar   and chopped
½ teaspoon ground   walnuts
   ginger
150 ml/¼ pint soured
   cream

1 Cut the melon flesh into cubes.
2 Stir the sugar and ground ginger into the soured cream and mix with the melon.

3 Spoon into sundae glasses and sprinkle the tops with chopped stem ginger and walnuts.

Nest cake

you will need for 4 servings:

METRIC/IMPERIAL
150 ml/¼ pint   75 g/3 oz plain
   whipping or double   chocolate
   cream   8 marzipan eggs or
18-cm/7-inch sponge   411-g/14½-oz can
   flan (bought or   pear halves
   home-made)

1 Whip the cream until stiff enough to spread. Coat the flan inside and out with the cream (reserving a little if pears are used.)
2 Grate the chocolate coarsely and press into the cream all over to resemble a nest.
3 Place the marzipan eggs in the 'nest' and stand a fluffy chicken on top. Or, if pears are used, fill the 'nest' with the drained pear halves, but sides down, decorate with spoonfuls of the reserved cream and scatter with a little grated chocolate.

Last minute offering

you will need for 4 servings:

METRIC/IMPERIAL
1 dessert apple   to decorate:
538-g/1 lb 3-oz can   glacé or maraschino
   grapefruit segments   cherries
1 tablespoon sweet or
   medium sherry

1 Peel, core, and cut the apple into fairly small pieces.
2 Mix with the grapefruit, stir in the sherry and divide into sundae dishes.
3 Scatter the tops with chopped glacé cherries, or place a whole one in the centre of each. If for a first course, use maraschino cherries.

Sweet mince-cap

you will need for 4 servings:

METRIC/IMPERIAL
1 packet butterscotch   to decorate:
   Angel Delight   Dream Topping,
300 ml/½ pint milk   whipped cream, or
225 g/8 oz (approx)   chopped nuts
   mincemeat

1 Whip the Angel Delight with the milk as directed on the packet. Leave to thicken.
2 Place a layer of the Angel Delight in each sundae glass. Spoon a layer of mincemeat over it. Cover with more Angel Delight and top with mincemeat.
3 Decorate with a swirl of Dream Topping, whipped cream, and/or chopped nuts.

69

Meringue nests sunny-side-up

you will need for 4 servings:

METRIC/IMPERIAL
425-g/15-oz can
  apricot halves
275 g/10 oz mincemeat
grated rind of 1
  orange (optional)
8 meringue nests
  (bought)

to decorate:
150 ml/¼ pint
  whipping or double
  cream (optional)

1 Drain the apricots. Keep 8 aside and chop the rest.
2 Mix the chopped apricots into the mincemeat with the grated orange rind if used.
3 Fill the meringue nests with the mincemeat and place a reserved apricot half on the top of each.
4 Decorate with a piped rosette of whipped cream.

Sweets for special occasions

Special occasion sweets, whether for a dinner party or a larger buffet party, tend to be rather expensive because of the more unusual ingredients, but it is satisfying and fun to prepare more elaborate desserts for guests. Many of these recipes, although they sometimes require more time and trouble than other sweets, are not particularly extravagant.

Coronet soufflé

you will need for 4-5 servings:

METRIC/IMPERIAL
100 g/4 oz mixed glacé
  cherries (red, green,
  yellow, or red with
  angelica)
2 tablespoons gelatine
200 ml/7 fl oz golden
  syrup

5 eggs, separated

sauce:
65-75 g/2½-3 oz
  golden syrup
scant 400 ml/13-14 fl oz
  single cream

1 Chop the cherries and line the base of a scant 1·5-litre/2½-pint ring mould with them.
2 Sprinkle the gelatine over the water in a small saucepan and heat, stirring, until the gelatine is completely dissolved and clear. Stir in the golden syrup.
3 Carefully spoon a little over the cherries just to cover, and pour the rest into a basin.
4 Leave until just beginning to set around the edges, then whisk with an electric or rotary beater until frothy. Lightly whisk in the stiffly beaten egg whites and pour into the mould. Leave to set in a refrigerator.
5 To make the sauce, put the golden syrup, cream, and the egg yolks into a bowl over gently simmering water and cook, stirring, to the consistency of runny custard (it will thicken a little when cold). Stir occasionally while cooling, or place a piece of dampened greaseproof paper on top to prevent a skin from forming.
6 Turn out (see page 27) onto a large round dish and fill the centre with some of the sauce. Hand the rest separately.

Profiteroles au chocolat

you will need for 4 servings:

METRIC/IMPERIAL
1 recipe Choux pastry
  (see page 52)
250 ml/8 fl oz double
  cream whipped with
  25 g/1 oz icing sugar
    OR
1 recipe thick Crème
  pâtissière (see page
  89) with a little
  whipped cream

French chocolate
  sauce (see page 90)

1 Turn the paste into a piping bag with a 1-cm/½ inch plain nozzle and pipe small walnut-sized balls (20) onto a greased baking sheet, leaving room for spreading.
2 Bake above centre in a moderately hot oven (200°C, 400°, Gas Mark 6) for 20-25 minutes. Remove and make a small slit in the side of each to allow the air to escape, and return to the oven for 2-3 minutes. Remove to a wire cake rack to cool.
3 When cold, fill each with the chosen filling (easiest with a piping nozzle). Pile onto a serving dish and pour the chocolate sauce over them.

Zabaione

you will need for 2 servings:

METRIC/IMPERIAL
3 egg yolks
1½ tablespoons
  castor sugar

3 tablespoons Marsala

1 Beat the yolks and sugar together in a bowl until well blended.
2 Add the Marsala and place the bowl over medium hot water. Whisk until the mixture froths up and at least trebles in quantity, 5-7 minutes.

3 Pour into tall glasses and serve immediately with sponge fingers.

Note:

If no Marsala is available, use a little less sweet sherry.

Melon crescents

you will need for 6 servings:

METRIC/IMPERIAL
1 honeydew melon
312-g/11-oz can
  mandarin oranges

1 packet raspberry
  jelly cubes
water

1 Cut the melon in half lengthways and remove the seeds. Cut as much of the flesh as possible with a ball cutter, then scoop out the remaining flesh with a spoon to leave the shells trim and even.
2 Refill the shells with the melon balls and drained mandarin segments.
3 Make up the mandarin syrup to 300 ml/½ pint with water.
4 Put the jelly cubes with the liquid into a sauce pan and heat sufficiently to melt the jelly completely. Pour over the fruit and leave to set in a refrigerator.
5 To serve, cut each melon half into 3 pieces.

Note:

If the melon is a large one, it may need half as much again of the filling, or 2 cans mandarins, 1½ packets jelly, 450 ml/¾ pint liquid.

Old melon face

you will need for 4–5 servings:

METRIC/IMPERIAL
1 honeydew melon
450 g/1 lb fresh or
  canned fruit

2 black grapes
glacé cherries

1 To make the face, cut a thin slice off the bottom of the melon to allow it to stand upright firmly. Then cut a wider slice off the top.
2 With an apple corer cut through the skin only, to make two eyes, and gently run the blade of a small knife under the skin to remove the circles.
3 Cut the shape of a nose (triangular), but leaving it attached at the top, and cut under the skin so as to be able to raise it.
4 Cut a mouth in a half moon shape and again remove the skin only.
5 After tipping out the seeds, scoop out all the flesh, being careful to leave a good wall behind the 'face'.
6 Now serrate the top edge if liked with a sharp pointed knife.
7 Cut the melon flesh into cubes and mix with sufficient fresh or canned fruit to fill the melon shell.
8 To complete the face, stick black grapes into the eye holes (a half cocktail stick stuck into one end and into the melon keeps them firm). Lever up the skin from the nose and wedge it up, and fill the mouth cavity with halved and quartered glacé cherries.

Strawberries cardinal

you will need for 4 servings:

METRIC/IMPERIAL
125–175 g/4½–6 oz
  raspberries
50 g/2 oz castor sugar
150 ml/¼ pint double
  cream
25 g/1 oz icing sugar
1 egg white

0·75 kg/1½
  strawberries

to decorate:
40 g/1½ oz flaked
  almonds, toasted

1 Rub the raspberries through a sieve, stir in the castor sugar and leave until the sugar is dissolved.
2 Whip the cream fairly stiffly, stir in the icing sugar and the stiffly beaten egg white. Mix 4–5 tablespoons into the raspberry purée.
3 Hull the strawberries and place in sundae glasses. Pour the raspberry sauce over them and chill.
4 To serve, place a spoonful of the whipped cream on top of each and sprinkle with the nuts.

Strawberry Romanoff

you will need for 4 servings:

METRIC/IMPERIAL
0·5–0·75 kg/1¼–1½ lb
  strawberries
3 tablespoons
  Curaçao
2 tablespoons orange
  juice

150 ml/¼ pint
  Chantille cream (see
  page 89)

1 Hull the strawberries and marinate in the Curaçao and orange juice in a refrigerator for several hours or overnight, turning them over occasionally.
2 Serve in sundae glasses with the cream piped on top.

Strawberry Mont Blanc

you will need for 8–10 servings:

METRIC/IMPERIAL
0·75 kg/1½ lb
  strawberries
225 g/8 oz small
  meringue halves
castor sugar

600 ml/1 pint double
  cream

to decorate:
angelica 'leaves'

1 Hull the strawberries. Keep about 225 g/8 oz aside for decoration and cut the rest into halves or quarters.
2 On a large round dish place some of the meringues radiating from the centre to form an 18cm/7-inch diameter circle. Spread a little of the whipped cream over them with a spatula. Place a layer of cut strawberries on it and scatter generously with castor sugar.
3 Build up to a cone in this manner. Pipe rosettes of cream (using a large star nozzle) between the meringues outside, to cover the strawberries.
4 When all the meringues, cut strawberries, and cream have been used, decorate with the reserved whole strawberries and angelica 'leaves'.

Strawberry almond meringue

you will need for 6 servings:

METRIC/IMPERIAL

3 egg whites
75 g/3 oz castor sugar
100 g/3½ oz ground
  almonds
⅛ teaspoon almond
  essence

350 g/12 oz
  strawberries
300 ml/½ pint double
  cream

1 Mark a 20-cm/8-inch circle on two sheets of Bakewell non-stick silicone parchment. Brush the four corners of two baking sheets (to help prevent the parchment from sliding about) and place the parchment on the baking sheets. Brush very lightly with oil.
2 Whisk the egg whites until stiff with up to half of the sugar, then fold in the rest with the ground almonds and essence.
3 With a 0·9-cm/⅜-inch piping nozzle, pipe evenly over the marked circles and bake in a very cool oven (120°C, 250°F, Gas Mark ½) for 50–60 minutes, until set and very lightly coloured. Slide one circle carefully off the parchment onto a serving dish.
4 Hull the strawberries, keep a number of good ones aside for decoration and slice the rest.
5 Whip the cream, spread half over the meringue circle on the dish and cover with the sliced strawberries. Place the second circle on top, cover with the rest of the cream and decorate with the reserved strawberries.

Fruit cruncher

you will need for 4 servings:

METRIC/IMPERIAL

65 g/2½ oz butter or
  margarine
100 g/4 oz castor sugar
75 g/3 oz rice krispies
  or cornflakes
225–350 g/8–12 oz
  strawberries,
  raspberries,
  loganberries, or
  redcurrants

250–300 ml/8–fl oz
  double cream

1 Melt the butter and sugar together over a low heat, remove and stir in the rice krispies or lightly crushed cornflakes, until all are coated.
2 Press into a shallow serving dish and leave to harden, or overnight.
3 Prepare the fruit. If strawberries, hull, keep several good ones aside for decoration and cut the rest into halves or quarters.
4 Cover the crunchy base with the fruit, pile the whipped cream on top and decorate with the reserved fruit. Scatter with a little castor sugar.

Variation:
Canned pineaple, peaches or apricots
Drain the fruit well and treat as for fresh fruit above.

Coeur à la crème

you will need for 4 servings:

METRIC/IMPERIAL

3 tablespoons double
  or canned cream
175 g/6 oz Philadelphia
  cream cheese or
225 g/8 oz fresh
  cream cheese
scant ½ teaspoon
  lemon juice

25 g/1 oz icing sugar
350–450 g/¾–1 lb
  strawberries,
  raspberries, or
  blackberries

1 Prepare 4 small foil cases (or use special china ones) 7·5–10 cm/3–4 inches across the top. With a metal skewer prick good holes in the base and sides of the foil cases and then bend the cases into heart shapes. Line with pieces of muslin.
2 Beat the cream into the cheese until smooth, then stir in the lemon juice and icing sugar.
3 Pack firmly into the prepared cases, stand on a grid over a plate and leave in a refrigerator to drain overnight.
4 Turn out onto places, surround the hearts with the chosen fruit and serve with cream.

Rainbow peaches

you will need for 4 servings:

METRIC/IMPERIAL

3 medium to large
  peaches
castor sugar
2–3 tablespoons
  redcurrant jelly

150 ml/¼ pint double
  cream
4 meringue halves

1 Skin the peaches as for Pêches Melba (see page 88). Cut the flesh into slices, discarding the stones, and divide the slices equally into sundae glasses. Sprinkle with a little castor sugar.
2 If the redcurrant jelly is very stiff, moisten with a little warm water or port. Pour 2 teaspoons into each glass over the peaches.
3 Whip the cream lightly and place in mounds over the jelly. Chill.
4 Just before serving, place a meringue half on top of the cream and dribble a little of the jelly across the centre of each for colour.

Crème Marjorie

you will need for 4 servings:

METRIC/IMPERIAL

0·75 kg/1½ lb grapes,
  or 4 large peaches,
  or 4 small ones and
225 g/8 oz fresh or
  frozen raspberries

300 ml/½ pint double
  cream
100–150 g/4–5 oz soft
  brown sugar

1 Peel and de-seed the grapes, or peel the peaches as for Pêches Melba (see page 88) and cut the flesh into thin slices.
2 Place the fruit in the bottom of a 900-ml/1½-pint soufflé dish (if raspberries are used, scatter a little castor sugar over them).

3 Whip the cream stiffly and spread all over the fruit. Leave in a refrigerator or cold place for several hours or days.
4 Before serving, sprinkle the brown sugar thickly and evenly over the top and place under a hot grill for a few minutes until the sugar has caramelized, but be careful it does not burn.

Alonso's cold caramel apple

you will need for 4 servings:

METRIC/IMPERIAL
450 g/1 lb cooking apples, after peeling and coring
4 tablespoons water
juice of ½ small lemon
75 g/3 oz castor sugar
50 g/2 oz cream cheese
300 ml/½ pint double cream
demerara sugar

1 Cut the apples into small pieces and stew with the water, lemon juice, and castor sugar until soft and mushy. Mash with a potato masher. When cold, chill in a refrigerator for at least an hour.
2 Rub the cheese through a sieve into the apple. Whip the cream and stir in.
3 Fill fairly large individual soufflé dishes to within 0·5 cm/¼ inch of the top, and when required sprinkle with demerara sugar until level with the rim and place under a hot grill to caramelize the sugar.

Poires Josephine

you will need for 4 servings:

METRIC/IMPERIAL
750 ml/1¼ pints milk
1 vanilla pod
65 g/2½ oz short-grain rice
100 g/4 oz castor sugar
150 ml/¼ pint water
2 pears (preferably round shaped)
4 tablespoons strawberry jam
300 ml/½ pint double cream

to decorate:
pistachio nuts, chopped

1 Bring the milk to the boil slowly with the vanilla pod, stir in the rice and simmer gently for about 30 minutes or until the rice is tender and creamy. Stir occasionally at first and continuously when the mixture becomes thick. Remove the vanilla pod, stir in half the sugar and leave until cold.
2 Bring the rest of the sugar and the water to the boil in a saucepan large enough to take the 4 pear halves. Boil for 1–2 minutes.
3 Peel the pears, cut in halves and scoop out the cores. Drop into the syrup and simmer, covered, for 6–10 minutes until just tender, turning over once. Drain.
4 Rub the jam through a sieve. Whip the cream lightly and stir half into the rice.
5 On 4 plates make oval beds of the rice just larger than the pear halves, and place a pear half on each. Coat with the jam.
6 Whip the rest of the cream to piping consistency and pipe around each pear. Sprinkle with chopped pistachios to decorate.

Crimson cranberry ring

you will need for 4–5 servings:

METRIC/IMPERIAL
1 small orange
225 g/8 oz fresh cranberries
1 packet strawberry jelly cubes
300 ml/½ pint water
125 g/4½ oz granulated sugar
150 ml/¼ pint whipping or double cream

1 Scrub the orange, cut into quarters and remove the pips and centre pith. Put through a 'parsmint' or mincer with the cranberries.
2 Put the jelly cubes and water into a saucepan and heat, stirring occasionally, until the jelly is completely dissolved.
3 Remove from the heat, stir in the sugar and pour into a basin.
4 Leave until just beginning to set around the edges, then stir in the orange cranberry mixture and pour into a scant 1·5-litre/2½-pint ring mould and leave to set.
5 Turn out (see page 27) and fill the centre with lightly whipped cream.

Pashka

Pashka used to be a traditional Easter sweet in Russia. There are many variations, but this uncooked version is both easy and excellent and freezes perfectly.

you will need for 7–8 servings:

METRIC/IMPERIAL
115 g/4 oz butter
125 g/4½ oz icing sugar
340 g/12 oz cream cheese
150 ml/¼ pint soured cream
100 g/3½ oz mixed nuts, chopped
100 g/3½ oz seedless raisins
100 g/3½ oz cut mixed peel
100 g/3½ oz glacé cherries, roughly chopped

to decorate:
150 ml/¼ pint double cream
glacé cherries, angelica

1 Prepare the mould first. Use a well-washed flower pot or any mould with holes in the base. Line with muslin, leaving enough protruding to fold over the top for ease of removal.
2 Cream the butter until soft. Beat in the sugar, cream cheese and soured cream. Stir in the fruit and nuts.
3 Press into the prepared pot evenly, fold the muslin over, place a weighted saucer on top and stand the pot on a grid with a soup or tin plate beneath. Leave in a refrigerator overnight for any liquid to drain out.
4 Turn out and decorate with piped rosettes of cream around the base and top. Decorate the rosettes with glacé cherries and angelica 'leaves'.

Easter flower pot pudding

you will need for 6–7 servings:

METRIC/IMPERIAL

2 egg yolks
150 g/5 oz castor sugar
150 ml/¼ pint double cream
450 g/1 lb curd cheese
75 g/3 oz butter
75 g/3 oz blanched almonds, roughly chopped

75 g/3 oz sultanas

to decorate:
glacé cherries, angelica

1 Prepare a 12·5-cm/5-inch flower pot as for Pashka (see page 73).
2 Cream the egg yolks and sugar and stir in half the cream. Place the bowl over a pan of simmering water and stir occasionally until the custard is fairly thick, 20–25 minutes.
3 Rub the cheese through a sieve. Cream the butter until soft and stir into the cheese with the almonds and sultanas.
4 When the custard is cold, stir it into the cheese mixture and turn into the prepared flower pot. Proceed from stage 3 for Pashka (see page 73).

Melon basket with blackberries

you will need for 6 servings:

METRIC/IMPERIAL

1 honeydew melon
225 g/8 oz blackberries
castor sugar
2 tablespoons Madeira, sweet sherry or sweet cider

2 tablespoons Cointreau (optional)

to decorate:
maraschino or glacé cherries

1 Cut a thin slice off the bottom of the melon to allow it to stand upright firmly. Then cut two segments (nearly a quarter each) from the top of the melon, leaving a straight strip about 1-cm/½-inch wide between them to form the 'handle' of the basket.
2 Discard the seeds, scoop out all the flesh and cut into dice.
3 Serrate the edge of the 'basket' with a pair of scissors or sharp knife.
4 Mix the melon flesh and blackberries together, sweeten to taste (but be sparing with the sugar if Cointreau is included), stir in the liquors and pile into the melon shell.
5 Decorate around the edge with maraschino or halved glacé cherries.

Chinese stuffed melon

you will need for 6 servings:

METRIC/IMPERIAL

1 honeydew melon
1–2 peaches
1 pear
lemon juice
280-ml/½-pint jar cumquats (tiny oranges)
312-g-11-oz can lychees

sweet white wine or Framboise liqueur

to decorate:
red and green glacé cherries

1 Cut the top off the melon less than a quarter of the way down. Remove the seeds. With a small ball cutter scoop out the melon flesh into balls. Scoop out the remaining flesh with a spoon and chop it. Serrate the edge with a pair of scissors or sharp knife.
2 Peel and chop the peaches and pear and mix with lemon juice to prevent discolouration. Mix with the melon and drained cumquats (cut any larger ones in halves), and the syrup from the lychees. Flavour to taste with wine or liqueur.
3 Fill the melon with the fruit. Place a cherry in the hollow of each lychee and pack them alternately on top of the fruit filling.

Nutali

you will need for 4–5 servings:

METRIC/IMPERIAL

4 tablespoons water
50 g/2 oz granulated sugar
1½ tablespoons brandy
2 teaspoons sweet vermouth
10 Boudoir sponge fingers
300 ml/½ pint double cream
1 tablespoon castor sugar

1 egg white
1 large or 2 small bananas
1 large soft apple
1 pear

to decorate:
25 g/1 oz flaked almonds, toasted
ground cinnamon

1 Bring the water and granulated sugar to the boil and boil for 4–5 minutes. Allow to cool, then stir in the brandy and vermouth.
2 Dip the sponge fingers into the syrup slowly, one after the other, and place in two lines on a serving dish. Pour the remaining syrup over them.
3 Whip the cream with the castor sugar until fairly thick and fold in the stiffly beaten egg white. Spread less then half over the sponge fingers.
4 Place the thinly sliced banana over the cream, then cover with thin slices of peeled and cored apple, and finally with thick slices of peeled and cored pear.
5 Cover the whole lot with the rest of the cream and leave in a refrigerator for at least 1 hour.
6 Before serving, sprinkle the nuts all over the cream and then sieve a light sprinkling of ground cinnamon over it.

Sweet tiger

you will need for 4–5 servings:

METRIC/IMPERIAL

75 g/3 oz butter or margarine
175 o/6 oz castor sugar
2 egg yolks
grated rind of 1 lemon
5 tablespoons lemon juice (2 lemons)
1 packet (8) trifle sponge cakes

to decorate:
150 ml/¼ pint whipping cream
mimosa balls (optional)

1 Cream the butter and sugar together, beat in the egg yolks, lemon rind and juice.

2 Cut each sponge cake into 3 horizontally.

3 Lay 6 slices neatly over the bottom of a 1-kg/2-lb loaf tin. Spread with one-third of the creamed mixture. Repeat layers twice and top with remaining 6 sponge slices.

4 Place another tin on top with a weight in it and leave overnight.

5 Turn out and decorate with piped or swirled whipped cream, and mimosa balls if liked.

Beignets soufflé

you will need for 4 servings:

METRIC/IMPERIAL	
150 ml/¼ pint water	1 large egg and 1 egg
15 g/½ oz sugar	yolk, or 2 small eggs
pinch of salt	castor sugar and
40 g/1½ oz butter	ground cinnamon,
65 g/2½ oz plain flour	or jam

1 Bring the water, sugar, salt, and butter to the boil in a small saucepan.

2 Throw in the sifted flour all at once and stir vigorously until the dough is so thick that it leaves the sides of the pan.

3 Remove and allow to cool a little, then beat in the whole egg and the egg yolk.

4 Drop small teaspoons of the batter into deep hot fat (160°–180°C/325°–350°F) and fry until puffed up and golden brown.

5 Have ready some castor sugar mixed with a little ground cinnamon on a piece of kitchen paper and tip the fritters straight onto it as soon as they are removed from the fat. Toss them about until nicely coated and serve piled up on a hot dish. Alternatively, omit the sugar and cinnamon and serve with hot diluted jam.

New England baked fruit pudding

you will need for 9–10 servings:

METRIC/IMPERIAL	
115 g/4 oz semi-sweet biscuits	175 g/6 oz black treacle
900 ml/1½ pints milk	2 eggs
50 g/2 oz granulated sugar	450 g/1 lb seedless raisins
¼ teaspoon ground cloves	225 g/8 oz sultanas and currants, mixed
¼ teaspoon grated nutmeg	75 g/3 oz cut mixed peel
½ teaspoon ground cinnamon	¾ teaspoon bicarbonate of soda
¼ teaspoon salt	50 g/2 oz butter, melted

1 Put the biscuits a few at a time into a bag and with a rolling pin crush into crumbs. Soak in the milk for at least 2 hours.

2 Stir in thoroughly the sugar, spices, salt, treacle, beaten eggs, fruit, and lastly the bicarbonate dissolved in the melted butter.

3 Pour into a 2·25-litre/4-pint casserole and bake uncovered in a moderately hot oven (200°C, 400°F, Gas Mark 6) for 40 minutes. Remove and stir round thoroughly.

4 Turn into a 23-cm/9-inch cake tin, greased and lined at the bottom with greaseproof paper, and bake in a moderate oven (160°C, 325°F, Gas Mark 3) for 1½–1¾ hours, until firm to the touch. Run a knife around the edge, but leave in the tin until cold before turning out. Serve with Brown brandy butter (see page 92.)

Note:
This pudding will keep for months wrapped in film and then in foil. After the first baking the mixture will be almost runny, but will be solid after the second baking.

Grand Marnier walnut charlotte

you will need for 6 servings:

METRIC/IMPERIAL	
100 g/4 oz walnuts	150 ml/¼ pint milk
165 g/5½ oz butter	3 tablespoons Grand Marnier
150 g/5 oz castor sugar	2 75-g/3-oz packets
1 egg yolk	Boudoir sponge
½ teaspoon instant coffee powder	fingers
15 g/½ oz flour	

1 Put the walnuts through a mincer or 'parsmint'.

2 Beat 150 g/5 oz of the butter and the sugar together until light and fluffy, beat in the egg yolk, nuts, and coffee powder.

3 Melt the remaining butter in a small saucepan, blend in the flour, add half the milk gradually and stir hard until the mixture is so thick that it leaves the sides of the pan. Remove from the heat and allow to cook, then beat it into the nut mixture with 2 tablespoons of Grand Marnier.

4 Roll 17 sponge fingers quickly, one after the other, in the rest of the milk and Grand Marnier mixed, and place in position standing up all round a 15-cm/6-inch (across the top) charlotte mould or cake tin. Line the bottom also with more dipped fingers cut to fit.

5 Turn half of the nut mixture into the tin, cover with a layer of dipped fingers, and put the rest of the nut mixture on top. Trim the ends of the fingers level with the filling.

6 Leave for several hours or overnight before turning out onto a dish.

Biskotten torte

you will need for 6 servings:

METRIC/IMPERIAL	
175 g/6 oz Boudoir sponge fingers	115 g/4 oz castor sugar
25 g/1 oz margarine	2 teaspoons instant coffee powder
25 g/1 oz flour	115 g/4 oz walnuts,
150 ml/¼ pint milk	ground or finely
115 g/4 oz butter	minced

1 Cut the sponge fingers in halves and line the sides and base of a 15-cm/6-inch square cake tin with the biscuits touching each other, sugar sides against the tin.

2 Melt the margarine in a small saucepan, blend in the flour with a wooden spoon, add the milk and stir with a wire whisk until boiling and very thick. Remove and allow to cool, stirring occasionally.

3 Cream the butter and sugar together until fluffy, stir in the coffee powder, sauce, and nuts. Turn into the lined tin and leave overnight in a refrigerator.

4 Turn out and serve with whipped cream.

Satan's delight

you will need for 10–12 servings:

METRIC/IMPERIAL

350 g/12 oz Nice biscuits	150 g/5 oz red and green glacé cherries, cut into quarters or eighths (or angelica if no green cherries are available)
325 g/11½ oz plain chocolate	
325 g/11½ oz butter or margarine	
1 large egg	
50 g/2 oz castor sugar	50 g/2 oz mixed nuts, coarsely chopped
1 tablespoon rum or brandy	

1 Break the biscuits roughly into 0·5–1-cm/¼–½-inch pieces.

2 Break up the chocolate into a small saucepan, add the butter and over a low heat stir until completely melted and smooth.

3 Beat the egg and sugar together in a basin, pour in the chocolate and the rum or brandy and mix thoroughly. Add the biscuits and stir until all the pieces are well coated.

4 Brush a 1-kg/2-lb loaf tin with oil and line the bottom with greaseproof paper. Turn in the chocolate mixture and level the top.

5 Mix the fruit and nuts together, spread over the top of the loaf and press in lightly. Leave in a refrigerator to harden.

Uncooked chocolate refrigerator cake

you will need for 8–10 servings:

METRIC/IMPERIAL

225 g/8 oz Nice biscuits	175 g/6 oz butter or margarine
115 g/4 oz mixed nuts (almonds, walnuts, hazelnuts)	75 g/3 oz castor sugar
	2 eggs
50 g/2 oz glacé cherries, quartered	3 tablespoons brandy and sherry, mixed
100 g/3½ oz seedless raisins	to decorate:
75 g/3 oz cut mixed peel	150 ml/¼ pint double cream or ice cream if desired
225 g/8 oz plain chocolate	

1 Put the biscuits a few at a time into a bag and with a rolling pin crush into crumbs. Chop the nuts fairly coarsely.

2 Mix the nuts, fruit, and peel into the crumbs.

3 Put the chocolate, butter, sugar, and eggs into a bowl over gently simmering water and stir occasionally until the chocolate has melted and the mixture is smooth. Stir in the other ingredients and the brandy and sherry.

4 Turn into an 18-cm/7-inch cake tin with a loose bottom, or line completely with foil, and place in a refrigerator to harden.

5 Turn out and decorate with piped whipped cream, or serve with a bowl of ice cream.

Devil angel pie

you will need for 6–7 servings:

METRIC/IMPERIAL

Meringue shell

3 egg whites	50 g/2 oz roasted hazelnuts or walnuts, chopped (optional)
175 g/6 oz castor sugar	
1 teaspoon cornflour	
¼ teaspoon vanilla essence	

Chocolate filling:

200 g/7 oz unsweetened cooking chocolate	to decorate: silver balls, crystallized violets, angelica or as desired
3 tablespoons hot water	
¼ teaspoon vanilla essence	
300 ml/½ pint whipping or double cream	

1 Mark a 20-cm/8-inch circle (with a saucepan lid) on a piece of non-stick silicone parchment. Brush the underside corners with oil (to stop it from slipping) and place on a baking sheet. Brush very lightly with oil. Alternatively brush a 21·5–23–cm/8½–9–inch deep pie plate with oil and line the bottom with the same parchment and brush that with oil also.

2 Whip the egg whites with a little of the sugar until fairly stiff, add the cornflour and essence and continue whipping, gradually adding up to half of the sugar, then fold in the rest.

3 Either spread about 3 tablespoons over the marked circle, then with a forcing bag and star nozzle, pipe small circles touching each other all round the perimeter, and repeat with another layer; or, fold the nuts into the meringue, turn into the prepared tin and build up the sides as evenly as possible.

4 For the piped case, bake in a very cool oven (110°C, 225°F, Gas Mark ¼) for 2½–3 hours. Remove and gently lift off the parchment onto a wire cake rack. For the tin, raise the heat after 1 hour to 120°C, 250°F, Gas Mark ½ and continue baking for a further 1½–2 hours. Leave in the tin, or if to be removed, cut around the sides with a knife and gently ease the case onto a wire rack, but the sides are sure to break.

5 To make the filling, over a low heat melt the chocolate with the hot water until smooth, remove from the heat and stir in the vanilla essence.

6 Allow to cool before gradually stirring in the lightly whipped cream.

7 When cold, pour in the chocolate filling and leave that to set before decorating.

Note:

For an anniversary or birthday, it is fun to write the name or number in silver balls on the chocolate. First mark out with a pin, then carefully drop the balls into place with a small pair of tweezers.

Pavlova cake

you will need for 6 servings:

METRIC/IMPERIAL

3 egg whites
175 g/6 oz castor sugar
1 teaspoon wine
  vinegar
¼ teaspoon cream of
  tartar

300 ml/½ pint double
  cream
350–450 g/1 lb fresh or
  canned fruit

1 Mark a 20-cm/8-inch circle (with a saucepan lid) on a piece of non-stick silicone parchment. Brush the underside corners with oil to prevent slipping, then brush over the marked circle very lightly with oil.
2 Whip the egg whites with a little of the sugar until fairly stiff, stir in the vinegar and cream of tartar and continue whipping, gradually adding up to half the sugar until the meringue is stiff enough to stand up in a straight peak when the whisk is lifted. Fold in the rest of the sugar.
3 Spread evenly over the marked circle and bake in a moderate oven (170°C, 325°F, Gas Mark 3) for 20 minutes, then decrease the heat to very cool (110°C, 225°F, Gas Mark ¼) and continue baking for a further 40–50 minutes. The case should be puffed up and tinged with brown, but soft on the underside with a marshmallow centre.
4 Remove and turn out onto a dish. Gently depress the centre with the back of a spoon. The case will keep for weeks unfilled.
5 To serve, whip the cream, spread a little in the meringue case, keep some good fruit aside for decoration and pile the rest over the cream. Cover with the rest of the cream and decorate with the reserved fruit.

Chocolate meringue roll

you will need for 5–6 servings:

METRIC/IMPERIAL

2 eggs, separated
½ teaspoon vanilla
  essence
115 g/4 oz castor and
  granulated sugar,
  mixed
100 g/3½ oz packet
  unsweetened
  cooking chocolate
  (or plain)

50 g/2 oz butter or
  margarine
1 tablespoon water
to decorate:
150 ml/¼ pint double
  cream
grated or flake
  chocolate

1 Line a Swiss roll tin with non-stick silicone parchment and brush lightly with oil.
2 Whip the egg whites stiffly with a little of the sugar, add the vanilla essence and gradually beat in up to half the sugar, then fold in the rest.
3 Spread over the prepared tin and bake in a cool oven (150°–155°C, 300°–320°F, Gas Mark 2–2½) for 30 minutes until firm. Remove from the oven, place a piece of greaseproof paper on top and gently turn upsidedown onto the paper, then carefully pull off the parchment.
4 Make the filling. Melt the chocolate, butter, and water over a very low heat (or in a bowl over hot water) until quite smooth, remove and beat in the egg yolks.
5 Leave to cool to spreading consistency, then spread all over the meringue. Immediately roll up like a Swiss roll. The meringue will crack on the outside but will retain its softness inside.
6 Before serving, spread with the whipped cream and scatter with grated or broken up flake chocolate.

Lemon schaum torte (Angel pie)

you will need for 6 servings:

METRIC/IMPERIAL

Meringue case
Make and bake as for 'Devil angel pie' (see page 76) but without nuts.

Filling

4 egg yolks
100 g/3½ oz
  granulated sugar
1 tablespoon grated
  lemon rind (2 large
  lemons)

2 tablespoons lemon
  juice
300 ml/½ pint double
  cream

1 In a bowl beat the egg yolks with a wooden spoon, gradually beat in the sugar until cream coloured and thick. Stir in the grated lemon rind and juice.
2 Place the bowl over a pan of very hot but not boiling water and stir until the mixture is like thick cream, 10–12 minutes. Leave until cold.
3 Whip the cream fairly stiffly. Spread less than half in the meringue case, cover with the lemon mixture, then with the rest of the cream. Leave in a refrigerator overnight and serve cut in wedges.

Cheesecakes

Cheesecakes have been a special favourite in the United States for many years, and now they are catching up in popularity in the United Kingdom. The richest and perhaps the nicest are those made with the smooth Philadelphia cream cheese, but this makes them rather pricey. However, you will find many in this chapter that are delicious and much cheaper.

It does help enormously to have a flan tin with a loose bottom, so that there is no fear of breaking the cheesecake when it is removed from the tin.

Mrs. America's cream cheese pie

you will need for 7–8 servings:

METRIC/IMPERIAL

base:
150 g/5 oz digestive biscuits
50 g/2 oz castor sugar
75 g/3 oz butter, melted

filling:
4 78-g/3-oz packets Philadelphia cream cheese
2 eggs, beaten
125 g/4½ oz castor sugar
1 teaspoon vanilla essence
¾ teaspoon lemon juice

topping:
300 ml/½ pint soured cream
40 g/1½ oz castor sugar
¼ teaspoon vanilla essence

to decorate:
halved grapes, green or mixed, de-seeded

1 Put the biscuits, a few at a time, into a bag and with a rolling pin crush into crumbs. Stir in the sugar and melted butter.
2 Press lightly onto the base of a loose-bottomed 21·5-cm/8½-inch deep sandwich tin (or line the tin completely with foil, allowing sufficient length to fold over the outside of the tin to make easier the removal of the pie when cold and set). Leave to harden.
3 Beat the cheese until creamy, then mix in the rest of the filling ingredients, beating until smooth.
4 Pour onto the biscuit base and bake in a moderate oven (180°C, 350°F, Gas Mark 4) for 30 minutes.
5 Remove from the oven and cool for 5 minutes, then pour on the beaten topping and return to the oven for 10 minutes. When cold, place in a refrigerator overnight.
6 Remove from the tin and decorate with halved de-seeded grapes.

Note:
It is important that the baking times are followed precisely.

Fluffy cheesecake

you will need for 6–7 servings:

METRIC/IMPERIAL

base:
Proceed as for Mrs. America's cream cheese pie above.

filling:
4 78-g/3-oz packets Philadelphia cream cheese
2 eggs, separated
150 ml/¼ pint soured cream
75 g/3 oz castor sugar
¾ teaspoon vanilla essence
½ teaspoon lemon juice
3 tablespoons boiling water
2 teaspoons gelatine

to decorate:
halved de-seeded grapes

1 Cream together until smooth the cheese, egg yolks, soured cream, sugar, essence and lemon juice.
2 Pour the boiling water over the gelatine in a cup and stir occasionally until completely dissolved and clear. Beat into the cheese mixture gradually.
3 Fold in the stiffly beaten egg whites, pour onto the biscuit base and leave to set in a refrigerator.
4 Remove from the tin and decorate with halved deseeded grapes.

Economical lemon cheesecake

you will need for 9–10 servings:

METRIC/IMPERIAL

base:
175 g/6 oz digestive and Nice biscuits, mixed
65 g/2½ oz castor sugar
75 g/3 oz butter or margarine

Proceed as for base for Mrs. America's pie (see above) with a 23-cm/9-inch tin.

filling:
2 packets lemon jelly cubes
500 ml/scant 1 pint water
1 large or 2 small lemons
2 eggs, separated
450 g/1 lb cottage cheese

to decorate:
halved de-seeded grapes, lemon jelly slices, or chocolate drops

1 Turn the jelly cubes and water into a saucepan and heat, stirring, until the jelly is completely dissolved.
2 Pour into a large basin and whisk in the grated rind and juice of the lemon, and the egg yolks.
3 Rub the cheese through a sieve into the liquid and mix thoroughly.
4 Leave until just beginning to set around the edges, then whisk in the stiffly beaten egg whites and pour over the biscuit base. Leave to set in a refrigerator or cold place.
5 Cut around the edges and turn out of the tin. Decorate as desired.

Raspberry cheesecake

you will need for 6 servings:

METRIC/IMPERIAL

base:

50 g/2 oz butter or margarine
40 g/1½ oz golden syrup
175 g/6 oz Country Store or other muesli

300 ml/½ pint water
2 78-g/3-oz packets Philadelphia cream cheese
150 ml/¼ pint double cream
225 g/8 oz fresh or frozen raspberries

filling:

1 packet raspberry jelly cubes

1 Melt the butter and golden syrup together, remove from the heat and stir in the muesli.
2 Press over the base of a 20–21·5-cm/8–8½–inch sandwich tin with a loose bottom and leave to harden.
3 Put the jelly cubes and water into a saucepan and heat, stirring, until the jelly is completely dissolved. Remove from the heat and leave until cold.
4 Beat the cheese and gradually stir in the cream.
5 Keep aside some good raspberries for decoration, squash the rest and stir into the cheese.
6 Mix into the cold jelly, pour over the base and leave to set in a refrigerator or cold place.
7 Remove from the tin and decorate with the reserved raspberries.

Variation:
Blackcurrant filling

225 g/8 oz fresh or frozen blackcurrants
100 g/4 oz granulated sugar
300 ml/½ pint water
1 packet blackcurrant jelly cubes

2 78-g/3-oz packets Philadelphia cream cheese
150 ml/¼ pint double cream

1 Keep aside some blackcurrants for decoration. Stew the rest with the sugar and water until tender.
2 Strain the juice and dissolve the jelly cubes in it.
3 Beat the cheese and gradually stir in the cream, then mix into the cold jelly with the blackcurrants. Proceed from stage 4 above.

Pineapple cheesecake

you will need for 6 servings:

METRIC/IMPERIAL

base:

125 g/4½ oz digestive biscuits
25 g/1 oz desiccated coconut

25 g/1 oz castor sugar
75 g/3 oz butter or margarine

Proceed as for base for Mrs. America's pie (see page 78) with an 18–19-cm/7–7½-inch tin.

filling:

376-g/13¼-oz can crushed pineapple
½ packet pineapple jelly cubes
water
225 g/8 oz cottage cheese
78-g/3-oz packet Philadelphia cream cheese

to decorate:

orange and lemon jelly slices, halved grapes, or as desired

1 Drain the pineapple, keeping the juice.
2 Melt the jelly cubes in the pineapple juice made up to 150 ml/¼ pint with water, in a saucepan, stirring until the jelly is completely dissolved.
3 Mix the pineapple into the liquid jelly.
4 Rub both cheeses through a sieve into the pineapple, mix well, pour onto the biscuit base and leave to set in a refrigerator.
5 Turn out of the tin and decorate with jelly slices, halved grapes, or as desired.

Cranberry cheesecake

you will need for 6–7 servings:

METRIC/IMPERIAL

base:

Proceed as for base for Mrs. America's pie (see page 78) with a 20-cm/8-inch tin.

topping:

225 g/8 oz fresh cranberries
100 g/4 oz granulated sugar
3 tablespoons water
1 teaspoon arrowroot or cornflour

225 g/8 oz Philadelphia or other smooth cream cheese
1 teaspoon lemon juice
¼ teaspoon vanilla essence
75 g/3 oz castor sugar
2 eggs, separated
3 tablespoons boiling water
2 teaspoons gelatine

filling:

110 g/4 oz cottage cheese

1 Stew the cranberries with the granulated sugar and water, stirring, until they burst and are tender, 8–10 minutes.
2 Make the arrowroot or cornflour into a smooth paste with a little cold water, add to the cranberries and continue boiling for 2 minutes.
3 Rub the cottage cheese through a sieve into a basin and beat in the cream cheese, lemon juice, essence, castor sugar and egg yolks.
4 Pour the boiling water over the gelatine in a cup and stir occasionally until completely dissolved and clear. Pour into the cheese mixture whilst stirring vigorously.
5 Fold in the stiffly beaten egg whites, spread over the biscuit base and leave to set in a refrigerator.
6 Remove from the tin and spread the cranberries all over the top.

Note:
A 382-g/13½-oz jar of cranberry sauce may be used in place of the fresh cranberries, unthickened .

Orange shortbread cheesecake

you will need for 6 servings:

METRIC/IMPERIAL

base:

150 g/5 oz shortbread biscuits	50 g/2 oz castor sugar
	65 g/2½ oz butter or margarine, melted

Proceed as for base for Mrs. America's pie (see page 78) with a 20-cm/8-inch tin.

filling:

1 packet orange jelly cubes	6 tablespoons milk
300 ml/½ pint water	*to decorate:*
1 orange	quartered slices of orange or orange jelly slices
450 g/1 lb cottage cheese	
1 packet Dream Topping	

1 Put the jelly cubes into a saucepan with the water and heat, stirring, until the jelly is completely dissolved. Pour into a basin.
2 Stir in the grated rind and juice of the orange. Rub the cheese through a sieve into the liquid and mix thoroughly.
3 Leave until just beginning to set around the edges, then whisk in the Dream Topping whisked with the milk as directed on the packet. Pour over the biscuit base and leave to set in a refrigerator or cold place.
4 Remove from the tin and decorate with quartered slices of orange or orange jelly slices.

Avocado orange cheesecake

you will need for 6–7 servings:

METRIC/IMPERIAL

base:

125 g/4½ oz Nice and/or digestive biscuits	25 g/1 oz castor sugar
	65 g/2½ oz butter or margarine, melted

filling:

1 large or 2 small avocado pears	castor sugar
100 g/4 oz cream cheese	2 tablespoons boiling water
4 teaspoons lemon juice	2 teaspoons gelatine
150 ml/¼ pint soured cream	1 egg white
½ orange	*to decorate:*
	150 ml/¼ pint whipped cream, if liked

1 Put the biscuits, a few at a time, into a bag and with a rolling pin crush into crumbs. Place in a basin and stir in the sugar and melted butter.
2 Place an 18-cm/7-inch flan ring on a serving dish and press the crumb mixture onto the base. Leave to harden.
3 Peel and mash three-quarters of the avocado flesh and beat into the cheese. Brush the surface of the remaining avocado with a little of the lemon juice.
4 Stir the lemon juice, soured cream, and grated orange rind and juice into the cheese and beat until blended and smooth. Sweeten with sugar to taste.
5 Pour the boiling water over the gelatine in a cup and stir occasionally until completely dissolved and

smooth. Beat into the avocado mixture whilst stirring vigorously. Fold in the stiffly beaten egg white.
6 Raise the flan ring a little to stand well above the biscuit base, pour in the avocado mixture and leave to set in a refrigerator.
7 Pull off the ring and decorate the cheesecake with the reserved avocado cut into slices and brushed with lemon juice, and pipe whipped cream in the centre and around the base.

Canadian lemon pie

you will need for 4–5 servings:

METRIC/IMPERIAL

base:

Proceed as for Mrs. America's pie (see page 78) with a 20-cm/8-inch tin.

filling:

2 lemons	*to decorate:*
water	150 ml/¼ pint double cream, mimosa balls, glacé cherries or as desired
3 eggs, separated	
175 g/6 oz castor sugar	
⅛ teaspoon salt	
2 teaspoons gelatine	

1 Grate the lemon rinds and squeeze the juice. Make up to 175 ml/6 fl oz with water.
2 In a bowl over gently simmering water stir the egg yolks, lemon liquid, sugar, and salt until the mixture thickens a little, about 10 minutes.
3 Remove from the heat, stir in the gelatine until completely dissolved and pour into a basin.
4 Leave until just beginning to set around the edges then whisk with a wire whisk and whisk in the stiffly beaten egg whites. Pour onto the biscuit base and leave to set in a refrigerator.
5 Turn out and decorate with piped rosettes of whipped cream with a mimosa ball or halved glacé cherry in each.

Prune cheesecake

you will need for 6 servings:

METRIC/IMPERIAL

pie case:

225 g/8 oz digestive and Nice biscuits mixed	225 g/8 oz cottage cheese
50 g/2 oz soft brown sugar	115 g/4 oz curd cheese
100 g/3½ oz butter or margarine, melted	2 eggs, separated
	3 tablespoons lemon juice
filling:	4 tablespoons double cream
boiling water	¼ teaspoon vanilla essence
175 g/6 oz prunes	2 teaspoons gelatine
125 g/4½ oz castor sugar	*to decorate:*
	angelica 'leaves'

1 Put the biscuits, a few at a time, into a bag and with a rolling pin crush into crumbs. Place in a basin and stir in the sugar and melted butter.
2 Turn into a 20-cm/8-inch deep flan tin with a loose bottom and press over the base and up the sides to form a case. Leave to harden.

3 Pour boiling water over the prunes just to cover and leave for several hours or overnight.

4 Stew in the water with half the sugar until tender. Drain and cut in halves, discarding the stones. Keep 7 or 8 halves aside for decoration and chop the rest. Cover the base of the pie case with the chopped prunes.

5 Sieve the cottage cheese into a basin and beat in the curd cheese, egg yolks, lemon juice, cream, essence and the rest of the sugar.

6 Pour 2 tablespoons boiling water over the gelatine in a cup and stir occasionally until completely dissolved and clear. Stir vigorously into the cheese mixture.

7 Fold in the stiffly beaten egg whites and pour into the pie case. Leave to set in a refrigerator.

8 Turn out and decorate with the reserved prune halves and angelica 'leaves' for colour.

Ginger honey pie

you will need for 6–7 servings:

METRIC/IMPERIAL

pie case:
225 g/8 oz gingernuts
40 g/1½ oz castor sugar
100 g/3½ oz butter or margarine, melted
Proceed as for Prune cheesecake above.

filling:
350 g/12 oz cream or cottage cheese

150 ml/¼ pint soured cream or yogurt
3 tablespoons honey
1 medium orange
2 teaspoons gelatine
1 egg white

to decorate;
thin slices stem ginger and/or jellied orange slices

1 Put the cream cheese into a basin, or if cottage cheese rub through a sieve.

2 Beat in the soured cream or yogurt, honey, and grated rind of the orange.

3 Pour 3 tablespoons of boiling orange juice over the gelatine in a cup and stir occasionally until completely dissolved and clear. Beat into the cheese mixture whilst stirring vigorously.

4 Fold in the stiffly beaten egg white and pour into the biscuit case. Leave to set in a refrigerator.

5 Turn out and decorate with thin slices of stem ginger and/or jellied orange slices.

Chocolate nut cheesecake

you will need for 6 servings:

METRIC/IMPERIAL

base:
125 g/4½ oz chocolate (or plain) digestive biscuits

50 g/2 oz walnuts, chopped
65 g/2½ oz butter or margarine, melted

Proceed as for the base for Mrs. America's pie (see page 78) with a 20-cm/8-inch tin.

filling:
225 g/8 oz Philadelphia or other smooth cream cheese
125 g/4½ oz castor sugar
2 eggs, separated
1 teaspoon vanilla essence
200 g/7 oz unsweetened cooking chocolate

3 tablespoons boiling water
3 teaspoons gelatine
150 ml/¼ pint whipping or double cream

to decorate:
chocolate drops, walnuts, crystallized violets, or as desired

1 Cream the cheese and beat in the sugar, egg yolks, and vanilla essence.

2 Melt the chocolate in a bowl over hot water and stir into the cheese.

3 Pour the boiling water over the gelatine in a cup and stir occasionally until perfectly smooth and clear.

4 Beat into the cheese mixture whilst stirring vigorously. Fold in the stiffly beaten egg whites and the whipped cream, pour onto the biscuit base and leave to set in a refrigerator.

5 Remove from the tin and decorate with chocolate drops and walnut halves, or crystallized violets and angelica 'leaves', or as desired.

Zanzibar cheesecake

you will need for 6–7 servings:

METRIC/IMPERIAL

base:
175 g/6 oz Marie biscuits
40 g/1½ oz castor sugar
100 g/3½ oz butter or margarine, melted

Proceed as for base for Mrs. America's pie (see page 78).

filling:
4 egg yolks
115 g/4 oz castor sugar
¼ teaspoon ground cloves
3 tablespoons boiling water
2 teaspoons gelatine
2 tablespoons rum or brandy

450 ml/¾ pint whipping or double cream

to decorate:
chocolate drops or curls

1 Beat the egg yolks until light and creamy. Whisk in the sugar and cloves.

2 Pour the boiling water over the gelatine in a cup and stir occasionally until completely dissolved and clear. Whisk into the egg mixture with the rum.

3 Whip the cream lightly and stir into the egg mixture. Pour onto the biscuit base and leave to set in a refrigerator.

4 Remove from the tin and decorate with chocolate drops or chocolate curls.

Old English curd cheesecake

you will need for 7–8 servings:

METRIC/IMPERIAL

50 g/2 oz castor sugar
25 g/1 oz butter or
  margarine
1 tablespoon grated
  lemon rind
350 g/12 oz curd
  cheese
2 eggs, beaten
1 tablespoon soured
  or fresh cream, or
  top milk

40 g/1½ oz cut mixed
  peel
25 g/1 oz currants
20-cm/8-inch baked
  flan case of sweet
  flan or shortcrust
  pastry (see page 52)

1 Cream the sugar, butter, and lemon rind together until light.
2 Rub the cheese through a sieve and beat in the eggs and cream.
3 Stir into the creamed mixture with the fruit, turn into the flan case and smooth level.
4 Bake in a moderate oven (180°C, 350°F, Gas Mark 4) for 30–35 minutes until set.
5 Leave in the switched off oven with the door ajar until nearly cold, then turn out of the tin.

Ice Creams, Sorbets, Chilled Desserts

Ice creams and frozen desserts have long been favourites, the former especially with the young of course, whereas the latter can grace a table for sophisticated diners at any time.

Sorbets were more popular in the days of our ancestors when the palate and digestion were given a rest, or cleanser, between two rich or heavy courses. But now they are regaining some of their popularity as a light meal-ender, since we no longer have to suffer the overeating of the past.

There is often a little confusion over the difference, if any, between a water ice and a sorbet. Both are made from a basis of a sugar syrup, but sorbets should contain more egg white, and are therefore softer. They are usually served in tall glasses as they cannot be moulded.

The making of ice cream has become much less tedious since the advent of freezers, and refrigerators with three star markings, because in most cases these make it unnecessary to 'beat down' the ice cream during freezing. However, it will often give an added smoothness if this is done once.

For freezing in an ordinary refrigerator, it is essential to turn the setting down to maximum coldness for at least 1 hour before the ice cream is put into the ice compartment, because the quicker the ice cream can be frozen the smoother the texture will be. To prevent ice crystals from forming, when the mixture starts to freeze around the edges, in about 40–45 minutes, remove it and beat it well with a fork or wire whisk. It is best if this can be repeated a second time, but it is not absolutely necessary.

Ice creams can be made from a variety of ingredients from the most expensive whipped double cream and fresh fruit purée or other flavouring, down to the most economical made from evaporated milk and custard made from custard powder. But with judicious flavouring, these can also be delicious.

Points to remember on ice cream making are:

1 Freezing reduces the effect of sweetening, so the basic mixture should be well sweetened, but not over sweetened which might prevent the mixture from freezing properly.
2 The flavour should also taste quite pronounced at room temperature for it decreases during freezing. But freezing does not effect colouring, so add sparingly.
3 Cover the container with a lid or foil, or if to be beaten down, as soon as this has been done.
4 It is better to leave an ice cream to soften in a refrigerator for a longer time than to hurry the process by leaving it at room temperature, when the outside will melt whilst the centre remains hard.
  As a general rule rich cream ices soften more quickly and more evenly than the plainer custard types. Allow approximately 1 hour in a refrigerator for a cream type ice for 4–5 servings, but the length of time will vary according to the receptacle used for freezing, so keep on experimenting.
  If for party serving, use a proper ice cream scoop if possible, or a soup ladle or spoon dipped in tepid water. Place the scoops of ice cream in sundae dishes and return to the freezer, then remove to a refrigerator for the final 30 minutes before serving.
5 Water ices and sorbets should be removed only 10–15 minutes before serving as they melt much more quickly.
6 Ice creams do not last for more than 1–2 months in a freezer before losing their flavour.
7 There are also electric and hand operated churn or pail-type freezing machines which undoubtedly make the best ice cream. But to my mind such a gadget takes kitchen space and rather defeats the idea of quickly made ice cream.

Rich vanilla ice cream

you will need for 6 servings:

METRIC/IMPERIAL

300 ml/½ pint single cream or milk	2 eggs, beaten
100 g/3½ oz vanilla sugar or castor sugar and a vanilla pod	pinch of salt
	300 ml/½ pint whipping or double cream

1 Heat the single cream or milk with the vanilla pod if used and then allow to infuse for 15 minutes before removal.
2 Beat the eggs, vanilla or castor sugar, and salt together in a basin. Gradually pour the hot cream or milk onto them whilst stirring. Rinse out the pan.
3 Return to the pan and cook over gentle heat, stirring until the custard thickens a little, but do not allow to boil. Pour into a basin and stir occasionally until cold.
4 Whip the double or whipping cream softly, and gently fold in the custard. Pour into a generous 1-litre/2-pint polythene container or 1-kg/2-lb loaf tin and freeze.

Note:
This is nicer if beaten down once but this is not essential. Cover after beating, or from the beginning if not to be beaten.

Variations:
Coffee   Pour 1 tablespoon boiling water onto 2 teaspoons instant coffee powder and 1½ teaspoons Camp coffee essence. Stir into the custard before folding into the cream.

Chocolate   Melt 100 g/3½ oz plain chocolate with 1 tablespoon water and add as above.

Banana   Add 3–4 bananas, puréed.

Economical vanilla ice cream

you will need for 4–5 servings:

METRIC/IMPERIAL

small can evaporated milk	300 ml/½ pint milk
15 g/½ oz (2 tablespoons) custard powder	1 tablespoon sugar
	1 teaspoon vanilla essence

1 Cover the can of milk with water in a saucepan, bring to the boil and boil for 15–20 minutes. When cold, place in a refrigerator and leave for several hours or overnight.
2 Make the custard powder into a smooth paste with a little of the milk, add the rest, bring to the boil and boil for 2–3 minutes, stirring. Remove from the heat, stir in the sugar and vanilla essence. Leave until cold, stirring occasionally.
3 Turn the evaporated milk into a basin, and whisk until trebled in volume and the consistency of lightly whipped cream.
4 Beat a little into the cold custard until smooth, then gradually fold into the remaining beaten milk.
5 Turn into a 900-ml/1½-pint polythene container, cover and freeze.

Note:
Beat down if liked, but it is not absolutely necessary.

Strawberry or fruit ice cream

you will need for 6 servings:

METRIC/IMPERIAL

450 g/1 lb strawberries (400 ml/¾ pint purée)	400 ml/¾ pint whipping or double cream
75 g/3 oz castor sugar	

1 Hull the strawberries and purée in a liquidiser with the sugar. Or rub through a sieve and then stir in the sugar.
2 Whip the cream softly and stir in the strawberry purée.
3 Turn into a generous 1-litre/2-pint polythene container, or 1-kg/2-lb loaf tin, or individual moulds, cover and freeze.

Note:
This ice cream does not have to be beaten down if frozen in a freezer or a three star refrigerator. If frozen in an ordinary refrigerator, beat down once only, after ¾–1 hour.

Variations:
Allow 0·5 kg/1¼ lb raspberries, loganberries, blackberries; for gooseberries, rhubarb, blackcurrants, plums, etc., stew first with less water and more sugar than for stewed fruit (see page 43–4). After liquidising, rub through a sieve.

Economical raspberry or fruit ice cream

you will need for 4–5 servings:

METRIC/IMPERIAL

1 small can (or ½ large one) evaporated milk	75 g/3 oz castor sugar
225 g/8 oz fresh, frozen or canned raspberries	

1 Chill the evaporated milk for at least 1–2 hours.
2 Rub the raspberries through a sieve (or if fresh gooseberries, blackcurrants, plums, etc. stew them first, see page 43–4). There should be 250–300 ml/8 fl oz-½ pint purée. Proceed from stage 3 for Economical vanilla ice cream (see above).

Blackberry ice cream

you will need for 4 servings:

METRIC/IMPERIAL

350 g/12 oz blackberries	custard, or 1 packet Dream Topping whipped with 6 tablespoons (100 ml/4 fl oz) milk
1 tablespoon water	
75 g/3 oz castor sugar	
150 ml/¼ pint whipping, or double cream, or thick	1 egg white

1 Stew the blackberries with the water until mushy.
2 Rub through a sieve, or blend in a liquidiser and then rub through a sieve. Stir in the sugar until dissolved. Leave until cold.
3 Whip the cream lightly and stir into the blackberry purée. Fold in the stiffly beaten egg white.

4 Turn into a 450-g/1-lb loaf tin or 900-ml/1½-pint polythene container, cover and freeze.

Chocolate ripple ice cream

you will need for 4 servings:

METRIC/IMPERIAL

1 packet Dream Topping	1 egg
1 tablespoom sugar	2 tablespoons bottled or home-made chocolate sauce
6 tablespoons (100 ml/4 fl oz) milk	

1 Put the Dream Topping powder and sugar into a basin and whip in the milk until thick and creamy.

2 Whisk in the egg and 1 teaspoon of the sauce.

3 Spoon into a 900-ml/1½-pint polythene container or 450-g/1-lb loaf tin, rippling the rest of the sauce through it. Cover and freeze without beating down.

Carol's Canadian lemon ice cream

you will need for 4–5 servings:

METRIC/IMPERIAL

1 large lemon (or more if you like a strong flavour)	175 g/6 oz castor sugar 250 ml/8 fl oz whipping or double cream
1 egg	250 ml/8 fl oz milk

1 Grate the rind of the lemon finely and mix with the juice.

2 Beat the egg and sugar together with a wooden spoon until light and creamy.

3 Whip the cream fairly stiffly and whisk into the creamed mixture with the lemon and milk.

4 Turn into a 900-ml/1½-pint container or 450-g/1-lb loaf tin, cover and freeze.

Rhubarb and ginger ice cream

you will need for 5–6 servings:

METRIC/IMPERIAL

0·5 kg/1¼ lb rhubarb	1 teaspoon (approx) ground ginger
1 tablespoon water	
2 teaspoons lemon juice	chopped stem ginger (optional)
150 g/5 oz granulated sugar	
150 ml/¼ pint whipping or double cream	

1 Trim the rhubarb, cut into small pieces and stew with the water, lemon juice, and sugar until mushy. Put into a liquidiser and blend until smooth or rub through a sieve. Leave until cold. Taste and add more sugar if necessary.

2 Whip the cream softly and fold into the rhubarb purée. Add ground and stem ginger to taste.

3 Turn into a generous 1-litre/2-pint polythene container or 1-kg/2-lb loaf tin, cover and freeze.

Note:
Beat down if liked, but it is not absolutely necessary in a freezer or three star refrigerator.

Avocado and gooseberry ice cream

you will need for 4–5 servings:

METRIC/IMPERIAL

350 g/12 oz gooseberries	filling
	1 large or 2 small avocados
75 g/3 oz granulated sugar	50 g/2 oz castor sugar
6 tablespoons water OR	150 ml/¼ pint whipping or double cream
397-g/14-oz can gooseberry pie	

1 Stew the gooseberries with the granulated sugar and water until mushy. Put the stewed gooseberries or pie filling into a liquidiser and blend, then rub through a sieve.

2 Peel the avocado, cut in half and discard the stone. Put into the liquidiser with the gooseberry purée and castor sugar and blend until smooth, or rub through a sieve into the gooseberry purée and mix thoroughly.

3 Whip the cream softly and fold into the avocado mixture.

4 Turn into a 900-ml/1½-pint polythene container or a 450-g/1-lb loaf tin cover and freeze.

Note:
It is not necessary to beat down this ice cream.

Ginger-up ice cream

you will need for 6 servings:

METRIC/IMPERIAL

1 large can evaporated milk	to decorate: slice of stem ginger (optional)
3 tablespoons boiling water	
2 teaspoons gelatine	
2 127-g/4½-oz jars Ginger-up sauce	

1 Chill the evaporated milk for several hours in a refrigerator.

2 Pour the boiling water over the gelatine in a cup and stir occasionally until completely dissolved and clear.

3 Whip the milk until thick and trebled in volume, then whip in the gelatine.

4 Fold in the ginger-up sauce and turn into a generous 1-litre/2-pint polythene container or 1-kg/2-lb loaf tin, cover and freeze.

5 Scoop into sundae dishes and decorate with slices of stem ginger if liked.

Note:
This mixture does not need beating down.

Praline caramel ice cream

you will need for 6 servings:

METRIC/IMPERIAL

large can evaporated milk	50 g/2 oz flaked almonds, toasted
250 g/9 oz granulated sugar	4 egg yolks
water	pinch of salt

1 Leave the can of milk in a refrigerator for several hours to chill thoroughly.
2 To make the caramel, in a small saucepan just cover half the sugar with water, bring to the boil, stirring until the sugar has dissolved, then allow to boil gently without stirring until it turns a good dark brown.
3 Remove from the heat and cool for a minute or two, then pour in 150 ml/¼ pint boiling water (which will fizz up). Make up to 250 ml/8 fl oz with water if necessary.
4 To make the praline, with the remaining sugar, repeat as above for the caramel until it turns a light golden brown, tip in the almonds and stir until the caramel darkens a little.
5 Turn out immediately onto an oiled tin, spreading out as much as possible.
6 Leave to cool and harden, then between sheets of greaseproof paper smash into crumbs (not too finely) with a heavy instrument.
7 Put the egg yolks and caramel syrup into a bowl over hot water and stir until the mixture thickens like custard. Remove from the heat, stir in the salt and allow to get cold.
8 Whip the evaporated milk until thick and fold in the caramel and praline.
9 Turn into a generous 1-litre/2-pint polythene container or 1-kg/2-lb loaf tin and freeze.

Note:
This ice cream should be beaten down (see page 82) even in a freezer or three star refrigerator.

Brown bread ice cream

you will need for 6 servings:
METRIC/IMPERIAL

300 ml/½ pint double cream	1-1½ tablespoons rum or sherry
150 ml/¼ pint single cream	75 g/3 oz icing sugar
2 eggs, separated	115 g/4 oz stale brown breadcrumbs

1 Whip the double cream fairly stiffly and gradually whisk in the single cream.
2 Beat the egg yolks and rum or sherry together and lightly stir into the cream with the sieved icing sugar and breadcrumbs.
3 Whip the egg whites stiffly and fold in.
4 Turn into a generous 1-litre/2-pint polythene container or 1-kg/2-lb loaf tin and freeze. Serve with Butterscotch, Caramel, or Chestnut sauce (see pages 90, 91).

Note:
This ice cream should not be beaten down.

Variation:
Crispy brown bread ice cream

75 g/3 oz stale brown breadcrumbs	150 ml/¼ pint single cream
40 g/1½ oz butter or margarine	2 eggs, separated
75 g/3 oz castor sugar	1-1½ tablespoons rum or sherry
300 ml/½ pint double cream	40 g/1½ oz icing sugar

1 Fry the breadcrumbs gently in the butter until crispy, add the sugar and continue frying until the sugar begins to caramelize and the crumbs are a deep golden brown, then quickly spread out on a chopping board.
2 When cold, cover with a piece of greaseproof paper and roll into crumbs with a rolling pin. Proceed from stage 1 above.

Raspberry, strawberry, or blackberry bombe

you will need for 6 servings:
METRIC/IMPERIAL

300 ml/½ pint double cream	300 ml/½ pint fruit purée (see page 83)
75 g/3 oz meringues, roughly broken	

1 Whip the cream fairly stiffly and stir in the meringue pieces.
2 Fold the fruit purée into the mixture without stirring too much, to leave a marbled effect.
3 Turn into a special bombe mould or a generous 1-litre/2-pint pudding bowl, cover and freeze. Do not beat down.
4 Take out of the freezer 30 minutes before serving, dip quickly into hot water and turn out. Replace in a refrigerator until served.

Lemon water ice

you will need for 4–5 servings:
METRIC/IMPERIAL

3 large or 4 small lemons	175 g/6 oz granulated sugar
450 ml/¾ pint water	1 small egg white

1 Thinly pare the lemon rinds. Squeeze the juice which should measure 150 ml/¼ pint.
2 Bring the water and sugar to the boil, stirring until the sugar has dissolved. Add the lemon rinds and boil gently for 6–7 minutes without stirring. Strain into a basin and leave until cold.
3 Stir in the juice from the lemons and pour into a 900-ml/1½-pint polythene container or 450-g/1-lb loaf tin. Freeze until half frozen and mushy, ¾-1 hour.
4 Turn out into a chilled basin and beat up with a fork or wire whisk. Fold in the stiffly beaten egg white and mix thoroughly.
5 Return to the receptacle, cover and freeze. It will take 2–3 hours.
6 For serving, see page 82.

Variations:
Lemon sorbet

Make as above but add a second egg white. Spoon into tall glasses to serve.

Lemon granita

An Italian type ice. The consistency is of iced granules or crystals with liquid. Make as above but omit the egg white and freeze in the ice compartment of a refrigerator without stirring. Serve quickly after removal in large glasses.

Orange water ice

you will need for 4–6 servings:

METRIC/IMPERIAL

4 large (or 6 small to medium) oranges	300 ml/½ pint water
½ lemon	1 small egg white
150 g/5 oz granulated sugar	

1 Finely grate the rind of 1 orange and the lemon. Mix with the juice of all the oranges and the lemon. The juice should measure 325–350 ml/11–12 fl oz.
2 Bring the sugar and water to the boil, stirring until the sugar has dissolved, then allow to boil gently for 6–7 minutes.
3 Remove from the heat, pour in the fruit juice with the rind and leave until cold. Proceed from stage 3 for Lemon water ice (see page 85).

To prepare orange shells

Cut a good slice off the top of an orange, less than a quarter of the way down, and reserve it. Then, holding the orange in one hand, with a dessertspoon carefully cut down and round between the flesh and the skin to remove all the flesh, leaving the shell clean. Cut a very thin slice off the bottom to enable the orange to stand upright firmly. Repeat with the other oranges.
Place the shells in the freezer to harden. When the ice has had the egg white beaten in, spoon into the orange shells. Scoop out any flesh from the lids and replace on the filled oranges.

Fruit water ice

Use 300 ml/½ pint unsweetened fruit purée in place of the fruit juice and freeze as above.

Baked Alaska

you will need for 4–5 servings:

METRIC/IMPERIAL

18–20-cm/7–8-inch round sponge cake	175 g/6 oz castor sugar family block or
225–350 g/8–12 oz fresh or canned fruit	home-made ice cream
3 large or 4 small egg whites	

1 Place the sponge cake on a flat heatproof dish. If fresh fruit is used, crush lightly and sprinkle with a little sugar. If canned fruit, sprinkle a little of the syrup over the cake.
2 Whip the egg whites stiffly with up to half the castor sugar, then fold in the rest.
3 Place the ice cream (which MUST be frozen hard) in the centre of the cake and pile the fruit on top.
4 Cover everything, including the cake, with the meringue, leaving NO hole.
5 Place at once in a hot oven (230°C, 450°F, Gas Mark

8) for 3–4 minutes until the top is lightly browned. Serve immediately.

Note:
If an 18-cm/7-inch cake is used, the fruit can be piled into a dome shape before being covered with the meringue, or use more fruit for the same treatment for the larger cake.

Ogen Alaska

you will need for 4 servings:

METRIC/IMPERIAL

2 ogen or charentais melons	halved blanched almonds
2 egg whites	
100 g/4 oz castor sugar	
family block or home-made ice cream	

1 Cut the melons in halves horizontally and scoop out all the seeds. Cut a thin slice off the base of each half to allow them to stand upright firmly.
2 Whip the egg whites stiffly with up to half the sugar and fold in the rest.
3 Put a good portion of ice cream into the centre cavities and cover with the meringue, so that it touches the melon all round, and there are NO holes.
4 Stick in a few almonds and place at once in a hot oven (230°C, 450°F, Gas Mark 8) for 3–4 minutes until the tops are lightly browned. Serve immediately.

Mandarin pom-poms

you will need for 4 servings:

METRIC/IMPERIAL

298-g/10½-oz can mandarin segments	2 egg whites
4 thick slices Swiss roll	100 g/4 oz castor sugar home-made or family block ice cream

1 Drain the mandarin segments.
2 Place the slices of Swiss roll on the bottom of a grill pan and arrange a few of the mandarin segments on each.
3 Whip the egg whites stiffly with up to half the sugar and fold in the rest.
4 Place a slice, trimming it as round as possible, of HARD ice cream on top of each and cover completely with the meringue, leaving NO hole.
5 Slip under a low grill until the meringue is tinged with brown. Carefully remove each slice to a serving plate and arrange more mandarin segments around them.

Knickerbocker glory

you will need for 4 servings:

METRIC/IMPERIAL

½ packet strawberry jelly
225 g/8 oz fresh or frozen strawberries
150 ml/¼ pint double cream
castor sugar
300 ml/½ pint vanilla ice cream

4 tablespoons Cointreau (optional)
300 ml/½ pint strawberry ice cream OR a large mixed block

to decorate:
chopped nuts

1 Make up the jelly as directed on the packet and leave to set.
2 Hull the strawberries, keep 4 aside for decoration and cut the rest into halves or quarters. Whip the cream lightly.
3 Chop the jelly and put a quarter into the bottom of each glass, cover with a layer of strawberries and sprinkle with sugar. Place a quarter of the vanilla ice on top of each, then a second layer of strawberries and sugar, pour over the Cointreau if used, then cover with a layer of strawberry ice.
4 Top each with a swirl of cream, place a reserved strawberry in the centre and sprinkle with chopped nuts.

Kentish apple ice

you will need for 4 servings:

METRIC/IMPERIAL

225–350 g/8–12 oz sharp dessert apples, as red as possible
family block or home-made vanilla ice cream

to decorate:
chopped walnuts and 4 halves

1 Wash and grate the apples coarsely, skin included.
2 Mix with the softened ice cream and turn into sundae glasses.
3 Place a walnut half in the centre of each and scatter chopped nuts around it.

Coffee ice cruncher

you will need for 4 servings:

METRIC/IMPERIAL

65 g/2½ oz butter or margarine
100 g/4 oz soft brown sugar
75 g/3 oz cornflakes
home-made (half quantity see page 83) or family block coffee ice cream

to decorate:
150 ml/¼ pint double cream
Praline (see Praline caramel ice cream (page 84–5))

1 Make the praline and crush, or use any bought nut brittle and crush in the same way.
2 Melt the butter and sugar together over gentle heat until well blended. Remove from the heat and stir in the lightly crushed cornflakes.
3 Pack into a decorative shallow dish and leave to harden, or overnight.

4 Place scoops or slices of the ice cream in the centre, pipe whipped cream all round the edge and scatter with the praline.

Crème Suisse

you will need for 6 servings:

METRIC/IMPERIAL

4 eggs, separated
75 g/3 oz castor sugar
6 Petit Suisse cheeses (or 175 g/6 oz cream cheese)

150 ml/¼ pint double cream
4 tablespoons Grand Marnier

1 Beat the egg yolks with the sugar until creamy. Gradually whisk in the cheese, whipped cream, and Grand Marnier.
2 Whip the egg whites stiffly, fold into the cheese mixture and turn into a 900-ml/1½-pint polythene container and place in a freezer, or the ice compartment of a refrigerator (but without lowering the temperature) and leave for several hours or overnight.
3 To serve, divide into 6 sundae glasses and pour over Fruit sauce (see page 92). It is also good served with fresh peaches, strawberries, etc.

Frozen strawberry slices

you will need for 6 servings:

METRIC/IMPERIAL

350 g/12 oz strawberries (or 225 g/8 oz if for storage only)
225 g/8 oz digestive and Nice biscuits, mixed
1½ tablespoons clear honey

¼ teaspoon vanilla essence
3 tablespoons double cream

to decorate:
150 ml/¼ pint whipping or double cream

1 Line an 18–19-cm/7–7½-inch shallow square tin, or 2 ice trays from a refrigerator, with grease-proof paper to come 5–7·5cm/2–3 inches above the sides at two ends (for easy removal).
2 Keep 6 good strawberries aside and squash the rest thoroughly.
3 Put the biscuits, a few at a time, into a bag and with a rolling pin crush into crumbs.
4 Mix together the strawberries, biscuit crumbs, honey, vanilla essence and the cream.
5 Turn into the lined tin, levelling the top, and place in a freezer or the ice compartment of a refrigerator and leave for at least 1 hour.
6 When required, turn out and cut into 6 slices. Decorate with piped or swirled whipped cream and place a reserved strawberry in the centre of each. If to be stored, wrap in film or foil as usual.

Haroun el-rashid (stuffed pineapple)

you will need for 6 servings:

METRIC/IMPERIAL

1 medium-sized pineapple
2 tablespoons Kirsch
350 g/12 oz fresh or frozen raspberries
75 g/3 oz castor sugar

1 block or large tub pistachio or tutti-frutti ice cream
25–40 g/1–1½ oz shelled pistachio nuts, chopped

1 Cut the pineapple in half lengthways. Scoop out the flesh leaving a wall sufficiently thick to retain its shape. Cut out the core and slice the flesh thinly. Marinate in the Kirsch for at least 1 hour, turning the slices over occasionally.
2 Rub the raspberries through a sieve, pour off any excess juice to leave the purée fairly thick. Stir in the sugar until dissolved.
3 To serve, fill the pineapple halves with the ice cream, arrange the pineapple slices all around the edge, pour the raspberry purée over the centre and sprinkle with the chopped pistachio nuts.

Pêches Melba

you will need for 6 servings:

METRIC/IMPERIAL

3 large peaches
300 ml/½ pint water
75 g/3 oz granulated sugar
225 g/8 oz fresh or frozen raspberries
75 g/3 oz castor sugar

home-made (see page 83) vanilla ice cream or a family block

to decorate:
150 ml/¼ pint double cream

1 Drop the peaches into boiling water for 20–30 seconds, remove with a straining spoon and plunge into cold water, then skin.
2 Bring the water and granulated sugar to the boil in a saucepan, stirring until the sugar is dissolved. Lower the peaches into the syrup, cover and simmer very gently until the peaches are tender, 6–8 minutes, turning them over once. Remove and cut into halves, removing the stones.
3 Rub the raspberries through a sieve, stir in the castor sugar and stir until dissolved.
4 To serve, place scoops of ice cream in sundae glasses, put a peach half on each, pour over the raspberry purée and pipe rosettes of whipped cream on top to decorate.

Frozen Christmas fruit pudding

you will need for 6–7 servings:

METRIC/IMPERIAL

small can evaporated milk
2 large eggs, separated
50 g/2 oz soft brown sugar
¼ teaspoon mixed cake spice
⅛ teaspoon ground cinnamon
⅛ teaspoon ground ginger
3 tablespoons boiling water

3 teaspoons gelatine
225 g/8 oz mincemeat
50 g/2 oz glacé cherries (red and green if possible)
50 g/2 oz stem ginger or glacé pineapple, chopped
50 g/2 oz walnuts, chopped
1–2 tablespoons brandy or sherry (optional)

1 Treat the can of milk as for Economical ice cream (see page 83).
2 Beat the egg yolks, sugar, and spice together until creamy.
3 Pour the boiling water over the gelatine in a cup and stir occasionally until completely dissolved and clear.
4 Beat into the egg yolk mixture whilst stirring and add the fruit, nuts, and liquor if used.
5 Whip the evaporated milk until thick and at least trebled in volume, and stir in.
6 Fold in the stiffly beaten egg whites, turn into a generous 1-litre/2-pint pudding bowl, cover with foil and freeze.
7 To serve, dip the bowl for a few seconds into hot water and turn out onto a dish. Serve with Sabayon, Sherry, Orange syrup, or Orange almond sauce (see pages 90, 91).

Note:
The pudding can be turned out and left in a refrigerator for up to 2 hours before serving.

Sauces

Sauces can make or mar any dish, so it is worth the little extra time and thought necessary to make one to complement a particular dish.

Egg custard

you will need for 300 ml/½ pint or 4 servings:

METRIC/IMPERIAL

2 small eggs
1–2 tablespoons castor sugar

300 ml/½ pint milk
vanilla pod or slice of lemon rind

1 Beat the eggs in a basin with the sugar.
2 Warm the milk with the vanilla pod or lemon rind and pour onto the eggs while stirring.
3 Wash the milk pan and strain the custard into it or into a bowl and cook over hot water. Cook gently, stirring, until the custard thickens, being careful not to allow it to boil or it will turn into scrambled eggs.

Note:
Custard thickens as it cools, and if for serving cold, stir occasionally, or place a piece of dampened greaseproof paper on top to prevent a skin from forming.

Variation:
Chocolate custard

2 tablespoons (15 g/½ oz) custard powder
3 tablespoons (20 g/¾ oz) cocoa powder

40 g/1½ oz sugar
300 ml/½ pint milk

1 Make the custard powder, cocoa, and sugar into a smooth paste with a little of the milk.
2 Stir in the rest of the milk and bring to the boil, stirring with a wire whisk. Boil for 2–3 minutes.

Crème pâtissière

METRIC/IMPERIAL

1 egg, separated
1 extra egg yolk
50 g/2 oz castor sugar
2 tablespoons (15 g/½ oz) plain flour

3 tablespoons cornflour
300 ml/½ pint milk
few drops vanilla essence

1 Beat the 2 egg yolks and sugar together with a wooden spoon until cream coloured. Stir in the sifted flours and 2–3 tablespoons of the milk.
2 Bring the rest of the milk to the boil and pour onto the yolk mixture while stirring.
3 Return to the pan and stir over gentle heat just to boiling point (be careful or it will turn to scrambled eggs).
4 Pour about one-third into a bowl and fold in the stiffly beaten egg white. Return to the pan and cook over a low heat for 2–3 minutes, stirring gently. Remove and add vanilla to taste.

Variation:
Extra thick crème (for R. Lasserre's pancakes, etc.)

1 egg, separated
25 g/1 oz castor sugar
generous 15 g/½ oz flour and cornflour, mixed

6 tablespoons milk
few drops vanilla essence

Proceed as above, but the cream should not require cooking again after the egg white has been added.

Chantille cream

METRIC/IMPERIAL

150 ml/¼ pint double cream

25 g/1 oz icing sugar
1 egg white

1 Whip the cream and stir in the sugar.
2 Beat the egg white stiffly and stir enough into the cream to give the desired consistency for the dish.

Mock cream

1 Place a can (small or large as required) of evaporated milk in a pan, cover with water, bring to the boil and boil for 15–20 minutes.
2 Remove and when cold place in a refrigerator overnight.
3 Whip with an electric or rotary beater until thick and at least doubled in quantity.

Variation:

1 Take any quantity of evaporated milk and pour into the top of a double boiler or a bowl over water to come above the level of the milk.
2 Bring the water to the boil and allow to boil for 15–20 minutes.
3 Pour the milk into a bowl and when cold place in a refrigerator to chill.
4 Whip as above.

Note:
This milk should not be left for more than 7–8 hours before being whipped. And if mixed with fruit purée for a fool, etc., allow only 2–3 hours before serving or it may become liquid again.
If used for a fool, decrease the quantity of liquid given in a recipe before whipping, by 2–3 tablespoons, as the volume increases more than fresh cream when whipped.

Chocolate sauce I

you will need for 4–6 servings:

METRIC/IMPERIAL

100 g/4 oz plain chocolate
2 tablespoons golden syrup

small can evaporated milk

1 Put the broken up chocolate with the golden syrup and milk into a saucepan and over a low heat stir until the chocolate is melted and smooth.

Chocolate sauce II

you will need for 4–5 servings:

METRIC/IMPERIAL
100 g/3½ oz plain chocolate
1 teaspoon cocoa powder
50 g/2 oz vanilla sugar or castor sugar with vanilla essence

250 ml/8 fl oz water
25 g/1 oz butter

1 Break the chocolate into small pieces and put into a saucepan with the cocoa, sugar, and half the water. Stir over moderate heat until the chocolate is completely melted.
2 Add the rest of the water, bring to the boil and boil for 10–15 minutes until slightly thicker.
3 Remove from the heat and add vanilla essence to taste (if vanilla sugar is not used). Stir in the butter until melted. Heat through when required.

French chocolate sauce

you will need for 4–5 servings:

METRIC/IMPERIAL
200 g/7 oz unsweetened cooking chocolate
300 ml/½ pint water
1½ tablespoons cornflour

3 tablespoons sugar
pinch of salt
15 g/½ oz butter

1 Over a low heat melt the chocolate in a little of the water.
2 Make the cornflour into a smooth paste with a little more of the water and add to the chocolate with the remaining water, sugar, and salt. Bring to the boil, stirring, and boil for 1–2 minutes.
3 Remove from the heat and stir in the butter until melted.

Note:
These quantities are for a pouring sauce. Increase the amount of cornflour if a thicker sauce is required.

Syrup sauce

you will need for 4 servings:

METRIC/IMPERIAL
175 g/6 oz golden syrup
juice of ½ lemon
water

2 tablespoons (15 g/½ oz) arrowroot or cornflour

1 Make up the golden syrup and lemon juice to 300 ml/½ pint with water.
2 Mix the arrowroot or cornflour to a smooth paste with a little of the liquid, stir in the rest and bring to the boil, stirring. Boil for 3–4 minutes.

Variations:

Honey syrup I

Substitute honey for half the syrup.

Honey syrup II

3 tablespoons clear honey
3 tablespoons golden syrup

juice of ½ lemon
3 tablespoons water

1 Heat everything together until well blended.

Treacle

As Syrup sauce above, but substitute black treacle for half (or more) of the golden syrup and omit the lemon juice.

Orange syrup

Use the juice of 1 orange in place of some of the golden syrup (but keep the quantity to 300 ml/½ pint) and add the finely grated rind. Proceed as for Syrup sauce.

Jam sauce

you will need for 4 servings:

METRIC/IMPERIAL
5 tablespoons any jam
150 ml/¼ pint water
1–2 tablespoons sugar

liqueur, spirit, or flavouring as desired

1 Bring the jam, water, and sugar to the boil, stirring, and boil for 2 minutes.
2 Remove from the heat and add whichever flavouring is preferred.

Caramel sauce

you will need for 4 servings:

METRIC/IMPERIAL
100 g/4 oz soft dark brown sugar
25 g/1 oz butter

150 ml/¼ pint single cream or evaporated milk

1 Put the sugar, butter, and half the cream into a small thick-bottomed saucepan and stir over gentle heat until the sugar has dissolved. Bring to the boil and boil for 3–4 minutes.
2 Remove from the heat and when cool stir in the rest of the cream.

Butterscotch sauce

you will need for 4–5 servings:

METRIC/IMPERIAL
115 g/4 oz golden syrup
50 g/2 oz soft brown sugar

25 g/1 oz butter
150 ml/¼ pint double cream or evaporated milk

1 Put the golden syrup, sugar, and butter into a small thick-bottomed saucepan and bring to the boil, stirring until the sugar is dissolved. Boil for 6–7 minutes to a temperature of 125°–132°C/260°–270°F, or

until a little when dropped into a cup of cold water retains the shape of a thread instantly.

2 Remove from the heat and allow to cool, then stir in the cream gradually. Serve warm or cold.

Chestnut sauce

you will need for 5–6 servings:

METRIC/IMPERIAL

450-g/15¾-oz can sweetened chestnut purée	1 egg white rum or brandy (optional)
150 ml/¼ pint whipping or double cream	

1 Rub the chestnut purée through a sieve.
2 Whip the cream lightly and the egg white stiffly and fold both into the purée.
3 Flavour to taste if desired with rum or brandy.

Honey banana sauce

you will need for 4 servings:

METRIC/IMPERIAL

50 g/2 oz (2 tablespoons) clear honey	1 tablespoon custard powder
15 g/½ oz butter or margarine	175 ml/6 fl oz water
50 g/2 oz demerara sugar	¼ teaspoon lemon juice
	2 bananas

1 Put the honey, butter, and sugar into a thick-bottomed saucepan and stir until the sugar has dissolved, then simmer until the froth turns a rich brown (watch carefully at this point), about 5 minutes.
2 Remove from the heat and allow to cool for a few minutes.
3 Make the custard powder into a smooth paste with a little of the water, then add the rest. Pour into the saucepan with the lemon juice, bring to the boil, stirring, and boil for 1–2 minutes until thickened.
4 Remove from the heat and add the well mashed bananas.

Note:
The sauce will keep, covered, in a refrigerator for several days.

Orange almond sauce

you will need for 4–5 servings:

METRIC/IMPERIAL

1 large orange water	1 teaspoon arrowroot or cornflour
50 g/2 oz granulated sugar	15 g/½ oz flaked almonds

1 Grate the orange rind coarsely, but only the zest. Squeeze the juice and make up to 300 ml/½ pint with water.
2 Pour into a small saucepan with the rind and sugar and bring to the boil, stirring until the sugar has dissolved. Cover and simmer for 20–25 minutes until the rind is tender.

3 Mix the arrowroot or cornflour to a smooth paste with a little water, stir into the sauce, bring again to the boil and boil for 2–3 minutes until clear.
4 Stir in the almonds before serving.

Variation:
Use 1 lemon, but grate the rind finely and simmer for 8–10 minutes.

Sherry sauce

you will need for 4 servings:

METRIC/IMPERIAL

4 tablespoons medium sherry	2 teaspoons castor sugar
2 egg yolks	3 tablespoons cream

1 Put the sherry, egg yolks, and sugar into the top of a double boiler, or a bowl over hot water, and whisk with an electric or rotary beater until the mixture froths up and thickens a little.
2 Remove from the heat and whisk in the cream, when the sauce will lose its frothiness and become creamy. Keep warm over *warm* but not hot water.

Sabayon sauce

you will need for 8 servings:

METRIC/IMPERIAL

3 egg yolks	150 ml/¼ pint whipping or double cream
75 g/3 oz castor sugar	
3 tablespoons Marsala, or 2 tablespoons brandy and sherry, or rum	

1 Beat the egg yolks and sugar together until light coloured and creamy.
2 Place the bowl over hot but not boiling water, stir in the liquor and beat until thick enough for the impression of the whisk when raised to remain for a second or two, 8–10 minutes.
3 Remove the bowl and continue beating until cool, 4–5 minutes.
4 Fold in the lightly whipped cream and chill.

Note:
The sauce may be made a day ahead.

Brandy butter

you will need for 4 servings:

METRIC/IMPERIAL

100 g/4 oz butter or margarine	1 tablespoon brandy
100 g/4 oz icing or castor sugar	1 tablespoon sherry

1 Beat the butter to a cream, then beat in the sugar (sieved if icing sugar) until light and fluffy.
2 Add the brandy and sherry very gradually (or the mixture will separate) while stirring well.

Variations:

Light brown brandy butter

75 g/3 oz butter or margarine
40 g/1½ oz soft brown sugar

75 g/3 oz icing sugar
1 tablespoon brandy
2 tablespoons sherry

Proceed as above.

Dark brown brandy butter

Use 125 g/4½ oz dark soft brown sugar and equal quantities of brandy and sherry.

Rum butter

75 g/3 oz butter or margarine
½ teaspoon grated nutmeg

150 g/5 oz soft brown sugar
1–2 tablespoons rum

Proceed as for Brandy butter.

Fruit sauce

you will need for 6 servings:

METRIC/IMPERIAL
2½ tablespoons rum
4 tablespoons water
75 g/3 oz seedless raisins

40 g/1½ oz cut mixed peel
40 g/1½ oz glacé cherries, chopped

1 Bring the rum and water just to simmering point, and pour onto the raisins and mixed peel. Leave to marinate overnight.
2 Stir in the chopped cherries before serving.

Tropical zing sauce for ice cream

you will need for 4 servings:

METRIC/IMPERIAL
227-g/8-oz can pineapple pieces or slices
grated rind and juice of 1 small orange

water
3 teaspoons arrowroot or cornflour
1 tablespoon sugar

1 Drain the pineapple, keeping the syrup, and cut the flesh into small pieces.
2 Make up the syrup and orange juice and rind to 250 ml/8 fl oz with water. Make the arrowroot or cornflour into a smooth paste with the sugar and a little of the liquid and add the rest.
3 Pour into a saucepan, bring to the boil, stirring, and boil for 2–3 minutes. Remove from the heat and stir in the pineapple.
4 When ready to serve, warm through and spoon over the ice cream.

Sauce Pavilion

you will need for 4–5 servings:

METRIC/IMPERIAL
4 teaspoons cornflour
300 ml/½ pint strong black coffee
175 g/6 oz granulated sugar

2 tablespoons water
Grand Marnier

1 Make the cornflour into a smooth paste with a little of the coffee, then add the rest.
2 In a thick-bottomed saucepan heat the sugar and water together, stirring until the sugar has dissolved, then allow to bubble without further stirring until it turns a pale brown.
3 Remove from the heat immediately, and carefully stir in the coffee mixture. Bring to the boil, stirring, and boil for 1–2 minutes.
4 Remove from the heat and stir in 2 tablespoons Grand Marnier. Pour into a sauce boat and just before serving, add a 'floater' of Grand Marnier without stirring it in. Serve warm, over coffee or chocolate ice cream in particular.

Sauce Riviera

you will need for 4 servings:

METRIC/IMPERIAL
3–4 oranges
115 g/4 oz lump or granulated sugar
scant 1 tablespoon whisky

scant 15 g/½ oz butter
1½ teaspoons Grand Marnier

1 Butter the bottom and sides of a small saucepan thoroughly.
2 Squeeze the juice from the oranges to make up to 175–200 ml/6–7 fl oz and strain into the pan. Add the sugar and bring to the boil, stirring until the sugar has dissolved. Skim, and allow to bubble until the liquid begins to turn syrupy (107°C, 225°F), 15–20 minutes. Watch towards the end as the froth is apt to overflow.
3 When the syrup has reached this point, pour in 1½ teaspoons whisky and set alight immediately. Remove from the heat and stir in half the butter and the Grand Marnier.
4 Just before serving, reheat and stir in the rest of the whisky and butter.

Note:
This sauce can be made several days ahead.

Rum and raisin sauce

you will need for 8–10 servings:

METRIC/IMPERIAL
225 g/8 oz granulated sugar
150 ml/¼ pint water

225 g/8 oz seedless raisins
6 tablespoons rum

1 Put the sugar and water into a saucepan and over medium heat stir until the sugar has completely dissolved.
2 Add the raisins, bring to the boil, stirring, and simmer, uncovered, for 15 minutes.
3 Remove, cool, and stir in the rum.

Note:
This sauce will keep indefinitely in an airtight bottle in a cool place.

Index